THIRTEEN

NATIONAL PARKS
WITH ROOM TO ROAM

by
Ruthe and Walt Wolverton
Illustrations by Gary Mohrmann

Mills & Sanderson, Publishers
Bedford, MA

Library of Congress Cataloging-in-Publication Data

Wolverton, Ruthe.
    Thirteen national parks with room to roam / Ruthe and Walt Wolverton : illustrations by Gary Mohrmann.
        p. cm.
    Includes index.
    ISBN 0-938179-22-5 ; $9.95
    1. National parks and reserves--United States--Guide-books.
2. United States--Description and travel--1981--Guide-books.
I. Wolverton, Walt.   II. Title.
E158.W86   1990
917.304'838--dc20   90-39073
                                                     CIP

Printed and Bound in the United States of America

*Cover photo of Great Basin National Park was taken
by Walt Wolverton in 1989.
Park illustrations by Gary Mohrmann
Maps by Walt Wolverton
Cover design by Lyrl Ahern
Printed/Manufactured by BookCrafters, Inc.*

*To Kimberly, Tiffany, Travis, Luke, and Matthew,
with the hope that you will share your grandparents'
love of our country's wonderful national parks.*

ABOUT THE AUTHORS

*After Ruthe and Walt Wolverton retired from challenging careers, they turned to writing. Their first book, in 1988, was **The National Seashores: The Complete Guide to America's Scenic Coastal Parks** (Woodbine House).*

Acknowledgements

For assistance in the preparation of this book, we are grateful to many National Park Service staff members, both at park headquarters in Washington, D.C. and at the national parks, seashores, lakeshores, and recreation areas we visited. We always received prompt responses to our requests for information and copies of government material. In all our contacts with Park Service staff, whether they were superintendents, rangers, office staff, maintenance or seasonal staff, we were impressed with their dedication to the Park Service's mission and their desire to share their knowledge of the parks with visitors.

We especially appreciate having the comments and suggestions of the following persons who were kind enough to read early drafts of the chapters in this book: Bob Rothe at Big Bend National Park, Michael Nicklas at Great Basin National Park, Larry Frederick at Canyonlands National Park, Paul Gordon at Bighorn Canyon National Recreation Area, Daniel Brown at Coulee Dam National Recreation Area, Bill Laitner at North Cascades National Park, Neal Bullington at Sleeping Bear Dunes National Lakeshore, Gregg Bruff at Pictured Rocks National Lakeshore, Diane Chalfont at Apostle Islands National Lakeshore, Jim Dougan at Voyageurs National Park, Bill Harris, Superintendent of Cape Lookout National Seashore, Paul Swartz, Superintendent of Cumberland Island National Seashore, Lorenza Fong at Biscayne National Park, and Barry McIntosh at National Park Service Headquarters.

We would also like to say a word about the great number of volunteers who assist the parks in numerous ways—staffing visitor centers, assisting in interpretive programs, hosting campgrounds, maintaining trails and grounds, researching and maintaining records, and performing other valuable support services. Dedicated citizens have been key players in the creation and the growth of the national park system from its inception. In recent years when park visitation has greatly expanded while park budgets have not, the park service volunteer has played an increasingly important role in fostering the park visitor's knowledge and enjoyment of the parks. A heartfelt thanks goes to the volunteers!

Finally, we would like to acknowledge that the bulk of the information in the chapters on Cape Lookout and Cumberland Island National Seashores originally appeared in our book, *The National Seashores: The Complete Guide to America's Scenic Coastal Parks,* published by Woodbine House, Rockville, Maryland, in 1988.

CONTENTS

Thirteen National Parks with Room to Roam

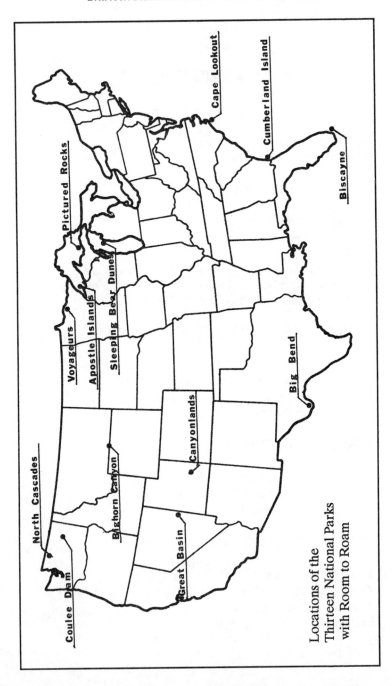

Locations of the
Thirteen National Parks
with Room to Roam

viii

Introduction

Are you looking for a place to spend your vacation where you won't have to line up to park your car or to view a magnificent sight, your budget won't be strained, and you can swim, snorkel, canoe, fish, hunt, horseback ride, hike, camp, drive a snowmobile, or cross-country ski?

Then one of the national parks described in this book may well be the answer to the question you've been pondering: Where shall we go this year?

If you are a footloose and fancy free individual, a family with school-age children, or retirees ready to explore new areas of the country, and you don't like crowded conditions, we recommend these parks. You will have a lot of fun, discover glorious scenery, and meet kindred spirits, and do all this at modest cost. Moreover, you will acquire a new understanding and appreciation of your national heritage.

Some national parks, like Yellowstone, Grand Canyon, Yosemite, Acadia, and Cape Cod National Seashore are well-known. The magnificence of these sites draws millions of people every year. That means there are crowds. In good weather, lots of people spend hours in slow-moving traffic to reach their destination or wait in long lines to be assigned a camping site. But the National Park System includes hundreds of places that are not so familiar. Like the popular parks, they too offer unusual scenery and a range of recreational activities. Units of the park system have a variety of official designations such as national parks, national parks and preserves, national recreation areas, national monuments, national seashores, and national lakeshores, but for purposes of this discussion, all of them will be referred to as "national parks."

The following chapters describe thirteen national parks located in the "lower 48" states, and what they offer. Of the more than 350 units of the National Park System, these parks were selected because they have not yet been discovered by mobs of people. They are parks that have space for you and your family and friends, and they offer a variety of outdoor activities. Equally appealing national parks in Alaska, Hawaii, and the Virgin Islands are not included because the added travel expense would significantly increase the cost of your vacation.

No matter what season of the year you like to take your vacation, the time is right in one of these parks. If, in winter, you are looking for sunshine and warm weather, try Biscayne National Park or Big Bend National Park. If winter sports are your special interest, go to the National Lakeshores or Voyageurs National Park. Spring is the ideal time to visit Big Bend and Canyonlands National Parks and Cumberland Island and Cape Lookout National Seashores. Summer is the high season for Bighorn Canyon and Coulee Dam National Recreation Areas, Great Basin, North Cascades, and Voyageurs National Parks and the Lakeshores. Fall can be a delightful time to visit all of the parks.

Most of these parks are located away from urban areas. But you do not have to be a camper to enjoy a visit to them. Visitors who prefer to stay in overnight lodgings can find comfortable and, in most cases, moderately-priced accommodations in the vicinity of the parks. When lodgings are termed "moderate," prices for a room for two people range from the low $30s to the mid $40s before discounts. If noted as expensive, prices are higher.

To aid in planning and budgeting for a vacation at these national parks, information about travel routes, accommodations, and costs is given. Where specific dollar figures are given for fees and other costs, they are prices as of press time. Prices may vary with the passage of time.

If camping facilities are limited and campsites tend to fill up early on holiday weekends, you are forewarned. A special paragraph in each chapter provides information about off-road driving, hunting, pets, and facilities for persons with a physical handicap. Additional tips to help you prepare for your visit are listed at the end of each chapter.

The parks are grouped regionally—in the West, in the north central part of the country, and along the Atlantic coast. To save travel expense, you may decide to concentrate on the parks nearest to you. But if you are looking for adventure and want to explore new areas, try a new sport, view unfamiliar scenery, and savor the natural wonders of your country—read all the chapters before you set the date of your vacation, pack your bags, and fill up the gas tank. You might take your best vacation ever!

BIG BEND NATIONAL PARK

The desert landscape rolls away in vast reaches like a continuous, boundless sea of sand. The vegetation is sparse and loses detail as your eye seeks relief from the monotony of endless space by focusing on the distant mountain backdrops.

Silence is almost complete. You hear only an occasional bird call or the gentle sough of a vagrant breeze. Even your footsteps are muffled in this desert air that absorbs sounds like a sponge sops up water.

Your shadow falls like an ink blot around your feet, for the sun is directly overhead. Even here in the desert there is a heat-of-the-day and although you may not feel uncomfortably hot, in this very dry air your body is losing fluid rapidly. The desert-wise drink water copiously to keep healthy, whether or not they feel thirsty.

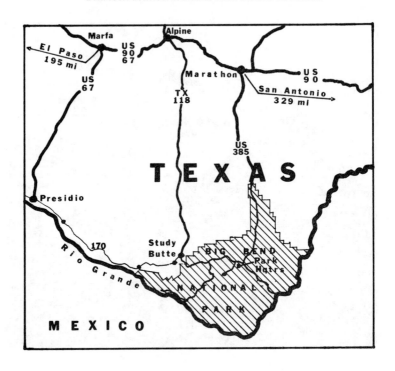

This is the Big Bend Country of Texas. This is the land of song and story, the fabled land west of the Pecos River and north of the Rio Grande. As you watch the whirling dust devils march slowly across a distant track in the desert your mind conjures up visions of cattle, of cowboys, and of their indispensable cow ponies working in a demanding climate to produce a marketable product of beef for the stock yards; of border brigandry that reduced men, women, and children caught in the lawlessness of the land to a life of fear; of the Spanish Conquistadors in their insatiable search for gold and silver and slaves; of the Native American nomads forced by their more warlike cousins into this northern end of the vast, searing Chihuahuan Desert.

The actual boundaries of Big Bend Country are imprecise. The borders of Big Bend National Park are well defined. The National Park includes only part of what is considered Big Bend Country, but it does include just about all of the flora, fauna, climate, and landforms—and the essence—of Big Bend Country.

Both Big Bend Country and Big Bend National Park derive their name from the Rio Grande. From El Paso, in the far southwestern corner of Texas, the Rio Grande flows in a southeasterly direction some 200 miles to Presidio, Texas. Beyond Presidio the wavering course of the river takes on a somewhat more easterly bent until it reaches a geographical feature known as Tight Squeeze in the Mariscal Canyon. And a tight squeeze it is. Here the river narrows to a relatively few feet and, perhaps more importantly, changes its course abruptly to flow northeastward for about 85 miles until it resumes its southeastward course to the Gulf of Mexico.

This change in course, from southeast to northeast then back to southeast, is the Big Bend in the Rio Grande and the name came to describe the pocket of land to the north as Big Bend Country and now gives its name to the National Park—Big Bend National Park.

Big Bend National Park has been set aside in perpetuity for all Americans to come to enjoy and savor the beauty, the historical significance, the mind boggling geology, the utter grandeur of a unique piece of our American landscape. Geologists tell us that this land is today the result of cataclysmic events in the building of our land surface. Apparently this land area, many eons ago, was formed as the bed of an ancient sea. Vast layers of sediment were laid down along with great quantities of the shells of mollusks and other sea creatures of that time.

At some later date this sea bed was elevated, probably by earth-shaping forces rather than by sea level changes, and what had been sea bed was thrust up high above the surrounding terrain. Later the forces of erosion began cutting down this elevated land and the carving of channels and canyons and the creation of flood plains began anew. At some point this process of earth sculpting was complicated by a return of vulcanism to the area. The evidence is replete in Big Bend National Park. For many of the scenic wonders here derive from volcanic activity.

But it is the Rio Grande that sets the stage for this magnificent park. Curving around the entire southern limits of Big Bend National Park, El Rio Bravo del Norte (as it is known in Mexico) creates an intermittent oasis of verdancy in the Chihuahuan Desert as it flows by patient stages on its way to the sea. As it enters the park just below Lajitas, it rushes through Santa Elena Canyon, a gash between the Sierra Ponce (in Mexico) and the Mesa de Anguila (in the U.S.).

Again at Tight Squeeze, nearly fifty miles down river from Santa Elena Canyon, El Rio Bravo del Norte flows through Mariscal Canyon where vertical sides seem to defy the laws of gravity. Here steep canyon walls have a newly-cut appearance compared with the broad river floodplain downstream—a green oasis stretching for miles along the river. The geological diversity and the likely events over the eons that resulted in such stark contrasts make geological research in Big Bend National Park intriguing.

Just beyond Rio Grande Village, about midway along the park's eastern border with El Rio Bravo del Norte, the river plunges into Boquillas Canyon, the third great canyon in Big Bend Park. Here between sheer canyon walls the river maintains its modest behavior before becoming a raging adversary to boatmen in its quickening rush to the sea.

There is mountainous terrain in several areas of Big Bend National Park. Isolated mesas rise out of the desert; portions of mountain ranges abut or extend into the park; eroded peaks lie scattered about, reduced now to little more than rumpled hills. All these, however, are but backdrops to Big Bend Park's massive centerpiece—the Chisos Mountains.

The Chisos rise up to 6,000 feet above the lower levels (along the Rio Grande) of Big Bend Park. At this elevation above the desert the mountains create a climate, an aura, a land unto themselves. Rising in the central portion of the park, the Chisos are a massive island remnant in the erosion process that created the desert that surrounds it. The Chisos Mountains are the southernmost mountain mass in the continental United States and the only mountain range entirely contained within a unit of the National Park System.

Here in the mountains the dryness and heat of the desert is replaced by increased rainfall and lower temperatures. Plant life is more varied, more verdant. Trees grow in copses and in small forests. The air is cooler and the landscape is greener. It is truly an oasis in the midst of the desert below.

In the heart of the mountains lies a beautiful valley today referred to as The Basin. Like past travelers through Big Bend, twentieth century visitors are drawn to the Basin, seeking a quiet, scenic refuge from the desert's heat.

Flora and Fauna of Big Bend National Park

Big Bend National Park supports an amazing diversity of flora and fauna. Over 1,000 plant species grow in the park. A total of 66 species of reptiles and amphibians, and 78 species of mammals have been identified in this ecosystem of river, desert, and mountains. It is particularly a birdwatcher's paradise with over 400 species observed as inhabitants or migrants.

Several of these species are endemic—they are found nowhere else in the United States. The Del Carmen white-tailed deer, the Colima warbler, the Mexican drooping juniper, and the Chisos agave (century plant) are examples of species unique to Big Bend in the United States.

Some of the individuals of the mammal species are probably wanderers. The occasional Mexican black bears sighted are likely to be visitors from across the Rio Grande that eventually return to the vaster wilds of the Chihuahuan Desert south of the border in Mexico. The wandering habits of the mountain lion or panther (about two dozen panthers are believed to be in the park at any one time) are being studied by researchers through radio collaring techniques. They may find that panthers are also prone to visiting abroad.

Yet this is not "visiting abroad" for them. For their habitat, the ecosystem of which they are a part, is the Chihuahuan Desert. And the Chihuahuan stretches from the lower third of the state of New Mexico deep down into the country of Mexico. It is some 800 miles long from north to south, and averages about 200 miles wide from east to west. It lies mostly in Mexico flanked on the east and west by the mighty Sierra Madre Oriental and Occidental mountain ranges.

Mexico is considering establishing a companion park to Big Bend National Park in the spectacular Sierra del Carmen country on its side of El Rio Bravo del Norte. Big Bend National Park is already designated by UNESCO as a Biosphere Reserve. What a grand enhancement it would be to Big Bend Country, to have our neighbors set aside for preservation and enjoyment another area of the majestic Chihuahuan Desert.

The People of Big Bend

Driving south on U.S. 385 amidst the vast expanse of grayness that is the Chihuahuan Desert, we wondered: Why did people choose to come here? Over the next several days we found out. And we began to empathize with those who came before us and to admire their courage and resourcefulness.

Thousands of years ago Big Bend Country was covered with grasses and woodlands. Ancient animals roamed from stream to stream and the bounty of the hunt for large game attracted the area's earliest human inhabitants.

Gradually the climate changed. Warmer, drier air caused the desert to creep up the slopes and prehistoric man lived a nomadic existence. Using stone weapons, hunters brought down bison and mammoth; later, people subsisted on the fruits and smaller animals of the desert and the mountains and the fish in the river. As more time passed, early Big Benders formed communities, fashioned tools from mountain ores, and traveled through the mountain passes and crossed the river when it was time to move on. [Archaeologists have designated the years 9000 B.C. to 1535 A.D. the Prehistoric era. Over such a long period man modified his lifestyle to adapt to changing climactic conditions. The Historic era, 1535 to the present, begins with the coming of the Spanish.]

The Spanish, lead by Alvar Nunez Cabera de Vaca, arrived in the mid 1500s looking for gold and other treasures. Finding none, and dissatisfied with what the land did offer, they left, their only trophies being the Indians they pressed into working in the profitable mines of Mexico and the conversion of many natives to the Christian faith.

The Spanish left their mark at Big Bend. By the time they left, Indians had become accomplished riders of Spanish horses. The Mescalero Apaches (eaters of the heart of the "mescal"—century plant) were fierce warriors. They expanded their range and, in this region, they became known as the Chisos Apaches. By the late eighteenth century, however, they, in turn, were overcome by their northern neighbors, the Comanches, who traversed Big Bend Country on their way to raid Mexico's stock of horses and cattle.

The war between Mexico and the United States ended in 1848, and the Rio Grande was fixed as the border between the two countries. Mexicans continued to cross the border freely (as they do today) to work together with the Americans. They mined copper, zinc, lead, and quicksilver; they made candles from the southwest's unique candelilla plant; and they talked over common problems at gatherings in the small villages centered around sources of water. Sometimes, hostilities erupted and U.S. Army troops were sent to repel Mexican bandits.

Then, as now and throughout the history of Big Bend, the availability of water determined the location and type of activity undertaken. Farmers grew their crops in the floodplains of the Rio Grande. Ranchers grazed their cattle, sheep, horses, and goats in the desert and lower elevations of the mountains, basing their operations near the few springs they could find or the windmills they were able to construct. But, in time, overgrazing denuded the grasslands. Erosion took its toll and the desert expanded.

However, the early seeds of a new chapter in the story of Big Bend were already being sown. In the first quarter of this century, a number of Texans came to the conclusion that their state, the largest in the nation, deserved to have a national park within its borders. After considerable discussion, they set their sights on the Big Bend area. Initially the state acquired the three canyons, Santa Elena, Mariscal, and Boquillas, designating the land as Texas Canyons State Park. The park became Big Bend State Park after the Chisos Mountains were added.

But this was a period when the United States was in the throes of a Great Depression. The federal government wasn't prepared to acquire state park lands, but a federal agency established to turn the energies of its unemployed young men to productive pursuits, the Civilian Conservation Corps (CCC), sent a contingent to Big Bend. Today, over fifty years later, the road the CCC built to the Chisos Basin, and some of the stone cottages they constructed on the hillside are still being used.

In 1944 the people of the state of Texas generously presented 1,100 square miles of Big Bend Country to the citizens of the United States, creating one of the nation's biggest and most diverse national parks. With the recent donation of the Harte Ranch, the park now consists of 1,252 square miles.

And now a new group of hardy souls frequent Big Bend country—park visitors. Since Big Bend became a national park, the Park Service has been working to restore the natural balance of resources in Big Bend with minimal interference by man. It is still rough country and some limitations on access to parts of the park are necessary to free the natural restorative powers of the land, and to protect the habitat of birds, plants, and animals, the as yet uncatalogued archaeological sites, and even the visitor himself.

Why Go to Big Bend National Park?

"Where rainbows wait for rain and the big river is kept in a stone box... where water runs uphill and mountains float in the air, except at night when they go away to play with other mountains..."
— A cowboy's description of Big Bend Country

It's a real effort to go to Big Bend National Park. Plans should be made well in advance. Different seasons offer different attractions. Places to stay are limited and some are at a considerable distance from park headquarters at Panther Junction, the central point from which distances within the park are measured. Even within the park, many miles separate the places you may want to go, and, if time is limited, choices have to be made.

At first glance, to the unaccustomed eye, Big Bend Country appears to be a wasteland. But Big Bend has rightly been called a "park of discovery." Linger a while, heighten your senses—keep a sharp eye out, sniff the air, listen with a keen ear—and as you traverse the river country, the desert and mountain roads and trails, you will notice the details. Then you will sense the magical appeal that is there today.

You will have your own memorable experiences at Big Bend, but here are some of ours:

▶ the Sierra Del Carmen white-tailed deer at dusk, quietly eyeing us as we shared the same Basin Loop trail;

▶ the sudden appearance of a coyote along the roadside, staring at us as if he wondered what we were doing there;

▶ the startling sight of a "pink snake" crossing the road on one of the scenic drives;

▶ capturing on camera the trio of road-runners racing along a Rio Grande Village byway;

▶ vultures gracefully gliding over Emory Peak;

▶ the sound of silence on the Window View Trail at twilight;

▶ the coterie of javalenas that found their way into fenced-in lodge grounds where newly planted cacti offered a delicacy to end their evening meal;

▶ the salmon pink, soft yellow, and dusky gray of the steep canyons, inspiring awe that no modern skyscraper can match;

▶ the enervating heat during a mid-day hike and the rejuvenation of spirits after a swig of water and a few moments' rest;

▶ our initial curiosity and subsequent appreciation of the names of numerous mountain peaks and rock formations such as Casa Grande, Mule Ears, and Panther Peak;

▶ the deliberately cautious step of the horse as he plodded down the steep, rocky path to "The Window" ("The Window" is an opening between two western mountain peaks through which grand distant views may be seen from near and far points in the Chisos Basin.)

▶ the vivid red, pink, and yellow blossoms on numerous varieties of cacti and the yucca plants as tall as full-grown trees;

▶ the waxy feel of the candelilla plant, the sharp prick of the tip of the blade of the tall, asparagus-like lechugilla stalk, the vast forest of sotol, and the twenty foot high stalk of the green/gray century plant silhouetted against a brilliant yellow-orange sunset;

▶ the soft touch of the feathery mesquite, the pungent odor of the creosote bush, and the roughness of the bark of the alligator juniper.

How to get to Big Bend National Park

You must drive to Big Bend National Park. There is no public transportation to or through the park. Allow lots of time to get there and plan to stay several days. Call the Texas Tourism office for a Texas state map to help you plan your trip.

There are two entrances. To enter from the north, at Persimmon Gap, drive south on U.S. 385 from Marathon, Texas, 42 miles away. To enter from the west, at Maverick, use State Rte. 118 from Alpine, Texas. If coming from Presidio on the Texas/Mexico border, take Ranch Road 170 to State Rte. 118 and thence through Maverick.

The main park roads are paved and in good condition. However, if one aspires to explore back country, a four-wheel-drive vehicle is needed in some areas. Recreational vehicles longer than 24 feet and automobiles towing trailers over twenty feet long should avoid driving on the road to Chisos Basin and parts of the road to Castolon because of the steep grades and sharp curves. Gasoline is available only at Rio Grande Village, Castolon, and a service station at Panther Junction.

If time and/or distance prohibits driving from your home, you may choose to fly or take the train to a Texas city and rent a car. The nearest commercial airport is Midland/Odessa, 230 miles northeast of park headquarters. Other major airports are at El Paso, 328 miles northwest and San Antonio, 405 miles east. Amtrak has passenger service to Sanderson, 123 miles northeast, Alpine, 100 miles northwest, and El Paso.

The entrance fee at Big Bend National Park is $5 per vehicle, $2 for each motorcycle rider, bicyclist, and pedestrian. The fee is good for one week. A special Big Bend pass, allowing park entrance for a year, may be purchased for $15. There is no charge for U.S. residents twelve and under, and holders of Golden Age, Golden Access, and Golden Eagle passes. See page 216 for information on "Golden" passes.

Where to Stay

Non-campers. There is only one place for non-campers to stay within the park. The Chisos Mountains Lodge, a concession-operated facility located in the Chisos Basin, has a limited number of motel units and stone cottages. It is essential to make reservations months in advance, even longer for a holiday period. No cooking facilities are provided. The lodge dining room and coffee shop offer meals at modest prices. Take-out lunches for daytime expeditions can be ordered. Accommodations for persons with physical disabilities can be arranged.

With Casa Grande, the imposing natural stone monument, and Emory Peak, the Chisos Mountain's highest point, as backdrops, the setting of the lodge complex is dramatic, yet peaceful. The motel units are comfortable and attractively furnished, reflecting the mood of the park. As you relax on private porches or patios, you enjoy close views of wildlife browsing among a mixture of desert plants and native mountain junipers and piñon pines. Short walks and longer hikes along mountain trails emanate from the Basin trailhead.

The Lodge operates a gift and bookshop year-round. There is also a store offering basic groceries, a public telephone booth, and a post office. There are no phones or television sets in the overnight units. Various units accommodate from one to six people with prices ranging from the low $40s to low $70s per night.

Lodging outside the park is available in motels in Study Butte, 26 miles west of Panther Junction, and Lajitas, 43 miles west. A list of places offering overnight accommodations in those communities can be obtained from park headquarters.

Campers: Recreational Vehicles. A concession-operated campground at Rio Grande Village offers 25 sites with electric, water, and sewer connections. Also available at the camp store are showers, laundry facilities, and a variety of groceries and other supplies, including gas, oil, and propane gas. The nightly fee for these sites is $10.50 per two-person vehicle, plus $1.00 for each additional person. Some recreational vehicles can be accommodated at other campgrounds, though there are no hookups. Rio Grande Village is especially popular during winter months as travelers from the north seek a warm spot to vacation in.

Tent Camping. Class A campgrounds, offering flush toilets, running water, picnic tables, grills, some overhead shelters, dump stations, and a water hose, are located both at Rio Grande Village and at Chisos Basin. There are 100 sites at Rio Grande Village and 63 sites at the Basin. The fee is $5 per night. Rio Grande Village campground is favored by many during cooler weather. The elevation above sea level is 1,850 feet. The campground fills up quickly during Easter/spring break periods and at Thanksgiving and Christmas. Elevation at the Chisos Basin campground is 5,400 feet and sites there are preferred during hot summer days.

If the Class A campground at Rio Grande Village is full, campers may stay at its overflow Class B campground where sites are available for $3 per night. These sites have drinking water and pit toilets only. Thirty-five Class B sites are also available at Cottonwood Campground, located between Castolon and Santa Elena. In addition to the facilities provided at Rio Grande Village Class B campground, Cottonwood Campground sites have picnic tables and grills.

Primitive Camping. Numerous sites have been designated for backpackers in various sections of the park. Hiking in is the only way to get to them. No facilities exist. Regulations regarding this type of camping should be obtained from a park ranger, who can also provide the required free permit.

All developed campsites are available on a first come, first served basis. To avoid disappointment after a lengthy drive, stop at the visitor center at Persimmon Gap, which is the north entrance, to inquire about campsite availability. If all sites are taken, the rangers can refer you to campgrounds outside the park. During especially busy periods like Thanksgiving, Christmas, and spring break, call the park from a nearby town before you go there and ask for advice on the best time to arrive.

What to Do at Big Bend National Park

Although Big Bend is a year-round park, the seasons vary in appeal. Winter is relatively warm and pleasant by the river. Spring is the time to go to Big Bend if you are eager to see desert wildflowers bloom, birds migrating, or you enjoy hiking in moderate temperatures. The temperature may vary, however, from the 70s and 80s in the Chisos Mountains area to the 90s and 100s in the desert and at Rio Grande Village. However, if you are looking for "room to roam," avoid Thanksgiving, Christmas, and spring break periods because the park is heavily patronized during those times.

Summer is very hot at Big Bend. It's the rainy season and sudden storms can fill the streams and washes quickly. But the waters dissipate rapidly and following the storm, dormant wildflowers bloom. The Chisos Basin and Mountains, truly then a "temperate island," is the place to be. Fall is a popular time for river rafting and observing the fall migration of birds. Temperatures are comparable to those in the spring, and the park is much quieter.

Hiking. Whatever level of walking or hiking ability you possess, there is a trail for you. There are self-guiding, easy walking trails from one-quarter mile to four and one-half miles in length, with interpretive signs or pamphlets to explain the significance of the trail. There are trails of medium difficulty where the wearing of hiking boots is recommended. Then there are the strenuous trails for experienced, conditioned hikers only.

Park Visitor Centers sell the *Hiker's Guide to Trails of Big Bend National Park,* and topographical maps. No matter what sort of hike you take, it is wise to wear sun-shielding hats, layered clothing, and, especially important, to carry water. The dry climate with almost constant sunshine quickly causes dehydration.

Depending on your personal interests, you can choose hikes for magnificent scenery, e.g. the Boquillas Canyon Trail, the Lost Mine Trail, and the Chisos Mountain's Window View Trail; for nature study, e.g. the Rio Grande Village Nature Trail, the Chihuahuan Desert Nature Trail and the Window Trail, a favorite with birdwatchers; or for visits to historic sites, e.g. the Castolon Historic Compound, the Hot Springs Historic Walk, and Laguna Meadow.

Horseback riding. The Chisos Remuda, a concession located in the Chisos Basin, conducts scenic trips on horseback. They range from two-and-one-half hour trips down to The Window, suitable for the inexperienced horseman, to all-day trips to the South Rim of the Chisos Mountains. Minimum age for riders is six years. Maximum weight for an individual is 210 pounds. For current rates, contact Chisos Remuda.

Fishing. No license is required for fishing in the Rio Grande. Blue catfish and long nosed gar are the most commonly caught fish. Fishing regulations are available at park visitor centers.

Swimming. Swimming in the Rio Grande is not prohibited, but it is not encouraged. Visitors are warned that it is dangerous because of strong undercurrents and drop-offs.

Raft trips. Rafting on the Rio Grande can be a very exciting experience. But it is not for the timid. The river varies from placidity to roaring waters.

There are three possible ways to take a raft trip: 1) use your own equipment; 2) rent the equipment from suppliers in Study Butte or Lajitas; or 3) join one of the trips of varying lengths conducted by the professional rafters in Study Butte or Lajitas. A free permit is required for rafting within the park.

Half-day trips on the Rio Grande are conducted upriver from the park. Prices of the professionally-run trips vary with the company and the distance. They start at $35 per person for a half-day trip. If you have the time and your vacation budget permits a one-time splurge, taking a raft trip through the canyons of the Rio Grande when river conditions are favorable will be a highlight of your trip to Big Bend.

For further information about rafting on your own or with a professional guide, contact park headquarters.

"Birding." Big Bend's environmental range—its canyons, vast desert, woodlands, and high mountain peaks—attracts an unusual variety of birdlife, more than any other U.S. national park—434 species at last count. Among them, the endangered peregrine falcon, a rare sight in nesting season when trails near its high canyon perches are closed to human traffic. The Chisos Mountains' own Colima warbler, unique to this area of the United States, arrives in mid-April from its winter home in Mexico and departs in mid-September. Commonly seen is the cactus wren which builds its nest in the most unusual places! Perhaps the most famous and easily recognized bird of Big Bend is the greater road-runner, El Paisano (Mexican for "fellow countryman"). Roadside signs bearing his image alert the driver to upcoming interpretive signs, and the park's official newspaper is named for this delightfully comic bird of the desert. Other southwestern desert birds permanently living in the park include the scaled quail, white-winged dove, and the ladder-backed woodpecker.

Birdwatchers will want to buy a check list of birds of Big Bend, available at the visitor centers. For the really dedicated bird-watcher, the park's bookshop at the Panther Junction Visitor Center sells the more detailed *A Field Guide to the Birds of Big Bend.*

Visits to Historic Sites. Archaeological and historic research is an important, ongoing activity at Big Bend National Park. One researcher estimates that there are potentially over 5,000 archaeological sites that could reveal important evidence of past life at Big Bend. The park has only scratched the surface. However, visitors do have the opportunity to conjure up images of Big Bend Country 64 million years ago with its then lush vegetation and its extinct forest dwelling animals, if they stop at the Fossil Bone exhibit on U.S. 385 and climb the path to the overlook at Tornillo Flat.

Moving along to historic times—several structures identified with man's activities in recent history have been preserved. Six places within Big Bend National Park are listed on the National Register of Historic Places. They are:

► the Castolon Historic District, a floodplain farming center and, for a short time, the base of the military's efforts to deal with border conflicts;

▶ Rancho Estelle, another floodplain farming center along the Rio Grande;

▶ the Homer Wilson Ranch, an example of structures associated with early ranching days at Big Bend;

▶ the Luna Jacal, a one-room house typically constructed from the native material available in its day;

▶ Hot Springs, where decades ago, an ailing man came to restore his failing health and remained to develop a resort community around "the fountain Ponce de Leon failed to find";

▶ Mariscal Mine, site of early twentieth century mining.

You can visit these and other historic sites, but high-clearance vehicles are needed to get to some of them.

NOTE: *Off-road driving is not permitted in the park. Hunting is not permitted. If firearms are brought into the park, they must be unloaded, broken down, and concealed. Pets are not permitted on trails, in public buildings, on the river, or off established roads. They cannot be left unattended in campgrounds or vehicles, and they must be on a leash. There are no kennels nearby. Some facilities, including the visitor center at Panther Junction, and most restrooms are accessible to persons with a physical handicap. As funds permit, additional facilities will be made wheelchair accessible.*

If You Have the Time.

▶ Have lunch in one of the little Mexican villages a stone's throw across the Rio Grande. Take a flatbottom rowboat trip to Boquillas or to Santa Elena and, at Boquillas, ride a burro from the riverside up the hill to the village. One senses the modest prices charged for transportation, meals, and items for sale are a significant factor in the economy of these third world communities. Routes to the points of embarkation are clearly marked on park maps. Passports are not necessary.

▶ Have a meal in Study Butte, a small town on the park's fringe appearing to subsist on tourist dollars.

▶ Visit Terlingua, the ghost town.

▶ Have lunch and shop at Lajitas, the "Palm Springs of Texas," an unusual resort and housing development built to recreate the spirit of the Old West while providing the amenities of luxury living.

Tips for Adding to Your Enjoyment of Big Bend National Park

1. Plan early for your trip to Big Bend, especially if you want to stay at Chisos Mountains Lodge.

2. Send for the park brochure and decide what you want to do while there. Ask for a schedule of ranger-conducted programs so that if you are interested in a particular activity, e.g. learning more about the geology of Big Bend, bird identification walks, photography, sketching, or seeing historic places, you can plan to be there on the day a particular program is scheduled.

3. Ask for the catalog of books, maps, videos, and color slides sold by the Big Bend Natural History Association so that you can order items you would like to examine before your trip.

4. If you intend to camp at the park, stop at the Persimmon Gap Visitor Center or at park headquarters at Panther Junction to check for available sites and, if primitive camping, to get a permit and the regulations.

5. Bring a first aid kit with you. The nearest paramedic assistance is at Terlingua, 26 miles from Panther Junction.

And finally—Take the time to savor the quiet among the cottonwood trees at the river's edge, the soft greenery of the floodplain, the awesome canyon vistas, the starkness, the haunting fragrances and vibrant colors of desert plants, the cheerful songs of the colorful mountain birds, the natural encounters with curious animals, and the brilliant sunsets in the western sky. You will be counting the days until you can return.

Sources of Information

Superintendent
Big Bend National Park
Texas 79834
Phone: 915-477-2251

Chisos Mountains Lodge
National Park Concessions, Inc.
Basin Station
Big Bend National Park
Texas 79834
Phone: 915- 477-2291

Chisos Remuda
Basin Rural Station
Big Bend National Park
Texas 79834
Phone: 915-477-2374

Texas Tourism
Phone: 800-888-8TEX

GREAT BASIN
NATIONAL PARK

The epitaph on the marker is simple and direct:

"Born 1300 B.C. Died 1700 A.D. "

You make the calculation mentally, 1,300 plus 1,700 equals 3,000. Three thousand years of living followed by nearly three hundred years after death—still standing, a monument to an almost indomitable will to live, to grow, to stand before the fierce natural elements of this broken-rock mountainside. The gnarled, twisted remains of this bristlecone pine tree, its inner grain exposed and polished to a gray sheen by centuries of wind-driven ice and snow, stands in mute testimony to the harshness of its environment.

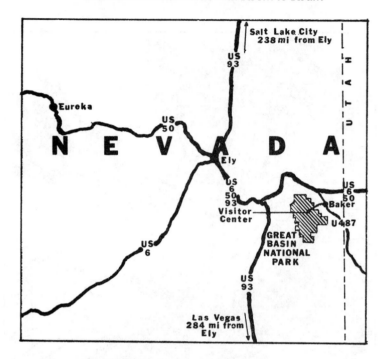

This tree is but one of many, both alive and dead, in a magnificent grove of bristlecone pines on the high north face of Wheeler Peak in Great Basin National Park. There are other stands in the park of these oldest of all living trees, but the Wheeler Peak grove is the most readily accessible. Some of these trees are from 3,000 to 4,000 years old. Many appear to be barely alive, for they consist mostly of dead wood, and have few areas of foliage. However, biologists think that the longevity of the bristlecones is at least partly explained by this circumstance. They believe that the trees tailor the amount of their current growth to that which can be supported by the changing water supply of their timberline environment.

At this elevation of about 10,600 feet above sea level the pace of all lifeforms is slowed. The reduced oxygen levels (thin air) slows your steps and demands more rest stops; stinging snow squalls may numb your face and senses; the clawing wind alerts you to the dread antagonist of mountain hiker and seaman alike—hypothermia. But then the sun comes out. Now the crystal-clear air fills your lungs, and the glorious scenery in light and shadow fills your eyes. You put the last squall behind you and trust it was the last one of the day!

The Great Basin is a vast land. It covers almost all of the state of Nevada, the western third of Utah, and small adjacent portions of Oregon, Idaho, and California. The Wasatch Mountains on the east, Sierra Nevada on the west, Columbia Plateau on the north, and Mohave Desert on the south, form the borders of the Great Basin. It is a "great basin" in that no surface water flows out of it—all its drainage system of rivers and lakes is self-contained and rainfall is either absorbed by the ground or evaporates back into the atmosphere.

Although it is classified overall as a desert, Great Basin is not a homogenous land. It is made up of smaller, separate basins, divided by over 200 individual mountain ranges, each oriented in a north-south direction.

Great Basin National Park, some ten miles wide at its widest east-west dimension and about seventeen miles from north to south, was established as a "representative segment of the Great Basin" in 1986. It is the newest national park on the mainland. The park straddles the southern end of the Snake Range of mountains in east central Nevada just inside its border with Utah. It includes only a small slice of the basins to the east and west of the Snake Range, but it does include most of the Great Basin features—and its mystique.

Wheeler Peak, the topographic centerpiece of the park, caps the rugged Snake Range. The second highest point in Nevada (by a matter of a few feet), Wheeler Peak dominates the scenery. It supports alpine lakes and meadows, stands of pines, junipers, aspen, spruce, and mountain mahogany on its flanks, as well as the grove of thousands-of-years-old bristlecone pines.

Lehman Caves on the lower eastern flank of Wheeler Peak are the park's subterranean centerpiece. Here, an ancient rock formation called the Pole Canyon limestone (actually a low grade marble) under the stresses of uplift and compression in the geologic past, developed mazes of vertical and horizontal cracks. At first, seep water from the ground surface above saturated it; then, probably due to further uplift of the strata, seep water drained out from its lower levels.

In the first stage, surface water became a weak solution of carbonic acid, dissolving the sides of cracks, turning them into fissures, then channels, and, after many eons, into tunnels. At this point the limestone contained a labyrinth of water-filled chambers—galleries, tunnels, and passageways.

The water table then lowered, and the water in the chambers was replaced by air. Water still percolated down from the surface, but now instead of individual streams joining the flowing water in the large passages, they trickled down and dripped into the open air of the passageways. Now the process of erosion was reversed. Instead of removing limestone from the passages, surface water now deposited lime as it dripped from the roof of the air-filled chambers, forming icicle-like projections from above (stalactites) and mound-like piles below (stalagmites). This condition prevailed for eons, until today the caves offer a profuse display of the myriad forms, shapes, and sizes of icicles of rock-hard calcium carbonate projecting downward from the roof and upward from the floor in fantastic chambers far beneath the earth's surface.

Life forms in the basin are diverse. Habitats range from upper Sonoran sagebrush communities to Arctic Alpine tundra life. Desert dwelling birds and mammals give way to forest birds and mammals at higher elevations. Antelope, deer, and mountain lions roam the lower reaches, while golden eagles use telephone poles in the desert and conifer trees in the mountains for perches.

Great Basin is a land of contrasts. Elevations range from a low of 3,000 feet above sea level to heights in the mountains over 13,000 feet. At lower levels the climate is dry and hot, while up in the mountains it is cool, even in summer, and rainfall increases. Thunder storms, scattered but torrential, are the only source of summertime precipitation. Winter precipitation usually falls as snow, particularly in the mountains, where snow can be encountered any month of the year. Wheeler Peak, in Great Basin National Park, at 13,063 feet above sea level, supports a permanent ice field on its northern flank that recent study has determined to be a true glacier.

The People of the Great Basin

There is much still to be learned about the people who inhabited or passed through the Great Basin in ancient times. But archaeologists have found evidence—animal bones, arrow points, and stone tools—that indicates people hunted in the Great Basin at least 11,000 years ago. Other findings show that Shoshone, Pueblo, and Paiute Indians lived here about 1,000 years ago. Early Native Americans grew corn and squash, hunted deer, pronghorn antelope, and mountain sheep, and ate nuts from the pinyon pines. (Pine nuts, as they are called today, are still a delicacy.) What is known currently about the lives of Indians who lived in Great Basin in the past, and how today's Native Americans are faring in Great Basin country, is the subject of one of the ranger programs presented at the park.

Several men—John C. Fremont, Absalom Lehman, George Montague Wheeler, and C. T. Rhodes—have been significant in the progression of white man's occupation and development of the mountains and valleys of the Great Basin.

Fremont was the man who first reported the area as a great basin. Following his expedition in 1843 and 1844 he said that the basin seemed to be "filled with rivers and lakes which have no communication with the sea."

Lehman, an adventurous soul who prospected for gold in California, successfully ran a wool business in Australia, and finally settled in eastern Nevada to become a prosperous rancher, is credited with being the first person to explore what is now called the Lehman Caves. Although the Indians had been aware of the caves, Lehman made them famous by exploring them and guiding visitors through the subterranean passages by candlelight.

Long after Lehman's death, in the early 1920s, C. T. Rhodes bought the property around the cave from Lehman's heirs, and built a resort that included nine cabins, a lodge, a dance hall, and a swimming tank. One of the cabins has been preserved and is a historic site located near the park's visitor center. This structure, the site of Lehman's apricot orchard, and a ditch he built to transport water to his farm, also near the visitor center, are listed on the National Register of Historic Places.

Wheeler, an Army lieutenant, led a survey party into the Great Basin in 1869 to report on its resources. He and his party spent several years mapping, making scientific observations which involved climbing the highest peak of the area, and reporting on the economic activity, primarily gold mining, ranching, and farming. His reports became the *Wheeler Survey,* and a geologist of his party named the highest point Wheeler Peak, a name that superceded previous names given to the high, rocky, natural formation.

The Lehman Caves were declared a national monument in 1922. Subsequently, the area around the road to Wheeler Peak which was administered by the U.S. Forest Service, was designated Wheeler Peak Scenic Area.

Most of the land in the state of Nevada is federally-owned, but the state had no national park. Led by the Nevada governor and the state's Congressional delegation, support grew in the 1980s for the establishment of a Great Basin National Park. Finally, in October 1986, legislation was enacted combining the Lehman Caves National Monument, Wheeler Peak Scenic Area, and portions of the Humboldt National Forest in one national park.

Certain concessions were made. Today, park visitors may be surprised to see cattle grazing in the fields or standing in the roads or walking on the trails, but cattle and sheep grazing is permitted in the park at the same level allowed when the land was under Forest Service jurisdiction. Mining and private water rights were left intact; however, there is little if any mining within the park today.

Why Go to Great Basin National Park?

Unless you live in Nevada, Utah, or California, you probably haven't heard of Great Basin National Park, the newest jewel in the National Park System. It's far from major population centers, and word about the park, so recently established, hasn't yet spread much beyond the Great Basin. All the more reason to be among the first to go there and see the startling, contrasting vistas of rocky peaks, forest groves, alpine lakes, and sagebrush covered valleys, the sudden glimpses of wildlife, and the gradual change in color, shape, and smell of plants and trees as you wend your way up the winding roads and hiking trails.

You almost feel like an explorer yourself as you plan your trip to Great Basin. The park is remote and promises new experiences. The Lehman Caves have drawn visitors for over 100 years, but there is much more to enjoy—whether you are car-bound, a family camper, or an experienced mountain hiker. Baker, Nevada, is not

There are riches headed your way.

a tourist center, so ⟨ ⟩ you want to go, study the map, and plan your route and ⟨ ⟩ 'll stay well in advance.

The weather is so. ⟨ ⟩ eep in mind. Because of heavy snowfall, Wheeler Peak ⟨ ⟩ e is not usually passable in its uppermost reaches befor⟨ ⟩ e June; hence, most people visit the park in the summe. ⟨ ⟩ can be a delightful time to visit, however. The brilliant ⟨ ⟩ s, and oranges of the tall aspens and roadside bushes co⟨ ⟩ in the dark green junipers, firs, and pines, a magnificent si⟨ ⟩ . Go prepared for changeable weather at all seasons of the year. Temperatures lower as you go up the mountain, even in mid-summer, and there is always the possibility of a sudden snow shower or thunder storm.

How to Get to Great Basin National Park

The visitor center and park headquarters are five miles west of Baker, Nevada, a small community of a few hundred people on Nevada State Route 487 near the Nevada-Utah border. U.S. Highway 50, which traverses the state, east to west, is about ten miles to the north. Highway 50 has been dubbed "the loneliest road in America" by Life Magazine, and the people who live in towns along the highway, with tongue in cheek, have capitalized on the description, passing out to visitors "Highway 50 Survival Kits."

U.S. 93, a main north-south route in eastern Nevada, is 40 miles west of the park. Salt Lake City is 234 miles north, Las Vegas, 286 miles southeast. It's a long way between towns in this part of the country, and you can drive many miles before passing another car. This is cattle grazing land, and the vistas across the sagebrush to distant mountain ranges are wide. Keep watch for occasional sightings of wildlife—antelope bouncing along the fields, or golden eagles perched on telephone poles.

Send to the Nevada Commission on Tourism for an official state map and other useful information about traveling in the state including, if you need it, a pamphlet about campsites and recreational vehicle parks in Nevada. On request, park headquarters will also send you a sheet detailing access roads to the park from various locations.

If you prefer to reduce total travel time, consider flying to Salt Lake City or Las Vegas and renting a car. There is a small connecting plane that flies from Salt Lake City to Ely, Nevada, about an hour's drive from the park. Amtrak has stops at Salt Lake City, Las Vegas, and Elko, Nevada, about 250 miles north.

There is no entrance fee to Great Basin National Park.

Where to Stay

Non-Campers. This is a new national park and, to date, it has been especially appealing to campers who have been the majority of summer visitors. Motels and other overnight lodging facilities in the area are very limited. In time, this will undoubtedly change as more of the traveling public learn about the park. The most complete range of services for non-campers is at the Border Inn on Highway 50 on the Nevada-Utah border. (Literally on the border. The motel units are in Utah and the restaurant in the complex is in Nevada.) The restaurant includes a bar, slot machines, video games, and a pool table—typical of waysides in Nevada. There is also a gift shop, but no major newspapers are sold in town!

Write to park headquarters for information about overnight accommodations in the vicinity of the park and a list of motels in Ely, a commercial center for this part of eastern Nevada. Other sources of information about tourist facilities are the Baker Chamber of Commerce and the White Pine Chamber of Commerce in Ely.

Campers, Recreational Vehicles and Tents. The park maintains three developed campgrounds. All sites provide water, pit toilets, barbecues, picnic tables, and tent pads.

The Lower Lehman Creek Campground is one and one-half miles up the Wheeler Peak Scenic Drive from the visitor center at an elevation of 7,500 feet above sea level. Some of the sites here and at Upper Lehman Creek Campground accommodate small recreational vehicles and trailers. (There is a dump station near park headquarters.) Campsites are beautifully situated in a forest of mountain mahogany and white fir, close to the creek. Lower Lehman Creek Campground is open year-round.

One-half mile farther up the Scenic Drive is the Upper Lehman Creek Campground, elevation 7,800 feet. It is open May 1 to October 1. It, too, is surrounded by mountain mahogany and fir, and some sites are along the stream.

The Wheeler Peak Campground is at the end of the Wheeler Peak Scenic Drive, elevation 9,951 feet. It is open only in summer and early fall. Campsites are located in a spruce and aspen forest grove. It is a popular spot for hikers to camp, since many trails leading to alpine lakes, the bristlecone forest, the glacier, and Wheeler Peak originate at the campground.

The fee for camping at the two Lehman Creek campgrounds, where drinking water is available, is $5 per night. Water at all other campsites must be boiled at least five minutes before drinking or using in food preparation.

Three campsites are available for primitive camping—Baker Creek on the Baker Creek dirt road, and Snake Creek and Shoshone Campgrounds off the Snake Creek dirt road. They are open only during the summer months and no fees are charged. Permits are not required to use these sites, but campers are requested to stop at the visitor center for the latest information on conditions at the campgrounds.

There are several privately-owned recreational vehicle and trailer sites in or near Baker. Send to park headquarters for information.

Evening campfire programs to which all visitors are invited are conducted by park rangers in the summer at Upper Lehman Creek and Wheeler Peak Campgrounds.

What to Do at Great Basin National Park

Start with a trip to the visitor center to see the slide show about the park and a film on the Lehman Caves. There are also exhibits and publications related to the park. Be sure to find out about ranger-conducted programs—nature walks, evening campfire programs, and "patio talks" which are given at the visitor center in the summer at 10:15 a.m. and 2:15 p.m. A concession-operated restaurant and gift shop in the same building is open spring through fall. The visitor center is open every day from 7:30 a.m. to 6 p.m. in summer, 8 a.m. to 5 p.m. in winter. It is closed on Thanksgiving, Christmas, and New Years Day.

Many activities take place near the visitor center. The Lehman Caves tour begins here. A short walk leads to the Rhodes Cabin and a nature trail. There is a picnic area in a grove of trees nearby.

Bear in mind that Great Basin National Park is only a few years old, and when it became a park, facilities and roads already on site were acquired and became the basis for park operations.

The park is in the process of long-range planning. Park officials and the interested public are trying to determine ways to protect park natural and cultural resources and also provide new programs and facilities of benefit to park visitors. Sometime in the future, the park visitor center may be moved to a new location, and access roads to important park destinations may be modified or relocated. So send to park headquarters for a current park brochure before you go.

Tour Lehman Caves. Rangers lead a tour through the Lehman Caves every day, hourly Monday through Friday, every half-hour on Saturday and Sunday. This venture into the amazing underground world takes you into a series of "rooms" formed by water-charged carbon dioxide dripping through surface marble, a process begun millions of years ago.

Your guide explains how this all happened and points out stalactites dripping from the ceiling, stalagmites formed on the floor, "draperies" on the walls, huge, fluted columns, and other peculiar shapes. Over the years, names like the Gothic Palace, the Music Room, the Grand Palace, and Sunken Gardens have been given to the various chambers connected by corridors and winding tunnels. The tour takes one and one-half hours. Wear a sweater or jacket. The temperatures in the caves average fifty degrees. The tour is limited to thirty persons at a time. On holidays that number is reached quickly, so get your tickets in advance. Fees for cave tours are $3 for adults, $2 for children six to fifteen, free for children five and under. Holders of Golden Age Passports are charged $1.50.

Candlelight tours of the caves are conducted daily at 6 p.m. These tours are shorter than daytime tours.

Spelunking Tours. The more adventurous park visitor may want to go on a spelunking tour. The ranger-guided tour of Little Muddy Cave is for novice cavers and is aimed at teaching safe spelunking practices. Each tour is limited to six persons at least fourteen years old. Advance sign-up is necessary. The tour starts one-quarter mile from the visitor center where participants first meet for an orientation which includes crawling through a test structure ten inches high and twenties inches wide. The trip takes you through a level, maze-like course and is not for the claustrophobic person. Spelunking tours leave on Saturday and Sunday at 1:30 p.m., Memorial Day through Labor Day.

Experienced spelunkers may tour other caves on their own, but first they must check at the visitor center for advice and permits.

Take Scenic Drives. When weather permits and the road is open, a drive up the twelve-mile Wheeler Peak Scenic Drive is a must for all park visitors. The views of the valleys and the distant Wasatch mountains are spectacular. Occasional parking areas allow you to stop, take photographs, go on short walks, and watch deer scrambling up the hillside. One walk leads from a historical marker explaining that, in the late 1880s, 300 laborers gouged a ditch in the rocky hills, built a wooden flume, and bored a 600 foot tunnel to bring water eighteen miles from Lehman Creek to the Osceola gold mining camp, enabling miners to extract five million dollars worth of gold.

Several other scenic roads exist in the park, but most require high-clearance vehicles to navigate them. Some are graded gravel roads; others, ungraded dirt roads. At times, gravel and dirt roads are suitable for two-wheel-drive cars. If you are not driving a four-wheel-drive vehicle, check at the visitor center for road conditions before starting out. (There are no facilities near the park for renting four-wheel-drive vehicles.)

Hike Scenic Trails. For the person who enjoys hiking in natural settings far from the madding crowd, Great Basin National Park is ideal. Trails range in length from the one-quarter mile nature walk near the visitor center to the steep, rugged 3,000 foot climb to Wheeler Peak, a ten mile round trip.

A trail guide to the nature walk, explaining the plant life and geology of the area, is available at the visitor center. If you plan to hike other trails, e.g. to the bristlecone forest on the side of Wheeler Peak, the alpine lakes, or to Lexington Arch, a 75 foot high limestone arch at the south end of the park, get a sheet describing all the trails from park headquarters. Also very useful to have is a copy of *Trails to Explore in Great Basin,* a paperback book published by the Great Basin Natural History Association. It is more than a trail guide. It includes interesting historical and geological information and is beautifully illustrated.

When you hike at higher elevations, be sure to take a container of water with you and wear hiking boots. Most trails have sections covered with uneven, rocky surfaces.

Horseback Riding. Horseback riding is permitted in the park. There is a horse loading parking area a short distance from the Wheeler Peak Campground. At present, no nearby facilities exist for renting horses or taking guided pack trips through the park.

Fishing. Persons with a Nevada fishing license may fish in the lakes of the park. Licenses are sold at a store in Baker. However, fishing is not a primary park activity, since the quantity of fish is limited. At some time in the past, the lakes were stocked with non-native fish. In an effort to encourage recovery of native fish species, stocking is no longer done.

NOTE: *There is no off-road driving in the park, mountain bikes included. All vehicles must stay on designated roads. Hunting is not allowed in the park. There are limited facilities for the physically handicapped visitor, including one campsite at Upper Lehman Creek Campground. The picnic area near the visitor center accommodates handicapped persons, and it is possible for persons in wheelchairs to visit the first room of the Lehman Caves. Pets may be brought to the park if they are kept on a leash at all times. Where they may be taken is limited, however. They are not permitted in the visitor center, on trails, at ranger-led activities, or in the backcountry.*

If You Have the Time

▶ If your travel route takes you through Ely, visit the Nevada Northern Railway Museum, a complete historic railroad exhibit. Tours are conducted in summer and rides on steam engines are offered on summer weekends. For information, write Nevada Northern Railway Museum.

▶ Visit the Ward Charcoal Ovens on Highway 50, seventeen miles south of Ely. These are giant beehive-shaped brick ovens built in the 1870s to produce charcoal for local smelters.

Tips for Adding to Your Enjoyment of Great Basin National Park

1. Send early to park headquarters for a park brochure and information of special interest to you, e.g. lodging and recreational

vehicle accommodations near the park or in Ely, and make reservations as soon as possible.

2. Send to the Nevada Commission on Tourism for a Nevada state map and other travel information.

3. If you plan to hike, prepare for changeable weather. Take warm, layered clothing, rain gear, hiking boots, and water canteens. (Hypothermia is possible during all seasons, and thunderstorms come up quickly.)

4. If you are not accustomed to hiking in the thin air of high elevations, start out slowly and be prepared to rest frequently.

5. Take your camera and binoculars.

6. If you would like to do some background reading about the Great Basin, the caves, hiking trails, or the flora and fauna of the area before you go to the park, send to the Great Basin Natural History Association for a publications catalog and order form.

And finally—Go to Great Basin National Park with an inquisitive mind. Find out why these steep rock-faced mountains exist, why there is a glacier so close to the desert, why 3,000-year-old bristlecone pines still grow among the rocks, what created the galleries and passages of the caves, why there are no fish in Stella Lake, what the Clark's nutcracker does with the nuts of the pinyon pines. This could be the most enjoyable field trip you ever took!

Sources of Information

Superintendent
Great Basin National Park
Baker, NV 89311
Phone: 702-234-7331

Nevada Commission on Tourism
Capitol Complex
Carson City, NV 89710
Phone: 1-800-237-0774 (out of state)
or 702-885-3636

Great Basin Chamber of Commerce
Baker, NV 89311
Phone: 702-687-4322

White Pine Chamber of Commerce
636 Aultman Street
Ely, NV 89301
Phone: 702-289-8877

Great Basin Natural History
Association
Baker, NV 89311
Phone: 702-234-7270

Nevada Northern Railway
Museum
Box 40
East Ely, NV 89315
Phone: 702-289-2085

"Beauty, spiced with wonder, is the greatest lure to travel."

—Confucius

CANYONLANDS NATIONAL PARK

Hiking up the all-but-dry stream bed in the bottom of the canyon we were experiencing many impressions—the deep silence surrounding the crunch of heavy hiking shoes in the sand and gravel; the stark contrast of shades and colors in the towering canyon walls; the instant cooling when we reached the shade of an overhanging cliff; the endless twists and turns of the canyon itself. But the overriding feeling was of anticipation that perhaps our quest would be fulfilled just around the next bend!

We were in Horseshoe Canyon, a part of The Maze District of Canyonlands National Park in southeastern Utah. Trudging our way (the only way to get there) to view one of the country's finest examples of prehistoric rock art, we were beginning to feel lonely.

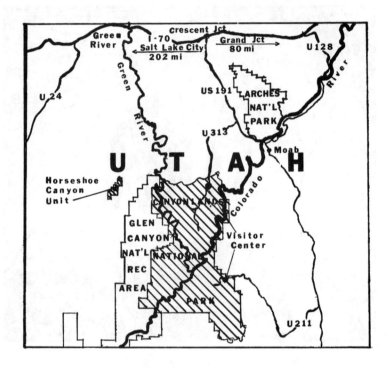

It had been a couple of hours since we had heard or seen anyone else. Earlier we had encountered a park ranger who had given us directions about what to see and where to see it, but that was two or three hours ago. Now we were conversing in low tones, with a nagging apprehension rising in our minds as we rounded bend after bend in this desolate gash in the earth. We mentally retraced the long trip back to our car, including the final precipitous climb over deep, loose sand and greasy slickrock ledges for several hundred vertical feet out of the canyon.

A sudden, raucous voice blaring unintelligible syllables stopped us dead in our tracks. Startled and unnerved we looked at each other in consternation. Then as we spoke slowly in normal tones, back came that strident, magnified echo again, for that's what it was, our voices bouncing back from an overhanging wall across the canyon, unbelievably magnified and repeated! After trying a few more phrases and being properly rewarded with stentorian echoes, we felt much better. The canyon was friendly! It was talking to us!

And sure enough, when we rounded the next bend, there was the Great Gallery of Horseshoe Canyon. High on the wall of the canyon, prehistoric Americans had painted a huge mural of surprising artistry. The human figures, life-size in the foreground, diminishing in the background, were a marvelous triumph of the art of perspective, a panorama of such size and sophistication that, like a magnificent tapestry, becomes more beautiful with each moment of contemplation.

A short while before, we had stopped to eat lunch (and rest) in a recess in the canyon wall called The Alcove. Interesting as that niche was with its fewer, smaller rock paintings (and turn-of-the-century cowboy graffiti) it did not prepare us for the grandeur of the rock art in The Great Gallery.

The culture, the people, the artists who produced this highly sophisticated art are shrouded in mystery. Experts in art and archaeology are still groping for answers. Present scientific thought dates the paintings anywhere from eight thousand to many hundreds of years old. The miracle remains, no matter the time interval, that the individual figures, the family groupings, the pet dogs at their feet, still conjure up the visions and emotions that the artists surely must have intended.

There are other known rock paintings and carvings in the park; however, the wildness and remoteness of much of the park may conceal yet unknown murals in this heart of the geological formation known as the Colorado Plateau.

This is a vast area of deep, flat layers of sedimentary rock tortured by eons of erosion into countless vari-colored canyons, buttes, mesas, arches, and spires. Two great river canyons dominate the park and effectively slice the park into three separate, isolated areas. Flowing across the park from northeast to southwest, the Colorado River coils its way through its deep Meander Canyon to the south central part of the park, where it is joined by the Green River flowing south from the northwest corner of the park through Labyrinth Canyon and Stillwater Canyon. These are all deep, sheer-walled canyons and the river courses are sinuous, with several long oxbows, and moderate currents and pitch. Below the confluence, the Colorado, augmented by its Green River tributary, enters Cataract Canyon. In this canyon is a fourteen mile stretch of wild rapids, one of the country's most treacherous runs of white water, rivaling any in the Grand Canyon.

The two rivers divide Canyonlands into three physically independent regions or districts: Island in the Sky, the northern section of the park lying between the two rivers; The Maze, west of the Green River and the lower portion of the Colorado; and Needles, on the east side of the Colorado. Each region is vast and different in many ways, but all are similar climatically and geologically. All are part of the high desert of the Great Basin.

Island in the Sky is aptly named. A high, broad, level mesa sandwiched between the Green and Colorado rivers, it serves as Canyonlands' observation tower, providing panoramic views of the whole park. It has by far the best vehicular access to the park. It also has a sensational four-wheel-drive vehicle trail—the White Rim Trail, a hundred-mile long trail extending around all but a small section of the circumference of Island in the Sky. The trail takes its name from the geological formation it follows, a nearly continuous, whitish sandstone stratum exposed in the canyon wall and forming a bench some 1,200 feet below the top of Island in the Sky, and 1,000 feet above the rivers.

The Maze, lying west of the Green and Colorado Rivers, is one of the wildest, most remote, and inaccessible areas in the United States. Here is a confusing hodgepodge of canyons that truly is a maze of blind, intersecting, and circuitous paths. This is a land of fantastic shaped towers, buttes, and mesas. The Land of Standing Rocks, Ernies Country, the Doll House, and The Fins (to cite a few of the many intriguing names) identify special features in this jumble of geological wonders.

Needles, the park district east of the Colorado River, is the land of startling rock sculptures with such descriptive names as Devils Kitchen, Angel Arch, Elephant Hill, Caterpillar Arch, Gothic Arch, and Paul Bunyans Potty. The Needles themselves are a fantasy of rock pinnacles of orange and white sedimentary layers. They remind you of the colorful bastions of castles in childhood magazines.

Vegetation throughout Canyonlands is more varied than appears at first glance. The four major plant groups or associations of the park have distinct, well-defined boundaries formed by abrupt change in the makeup and moisture of the subsoil:

Cottonwood-Tamarisk-Willow Community. Found on river banks and in sandy washes. Only the cottonwood and willow are native. Tamarisk is an exotic that threatens native species.

Northern Desert Shrub Community. Found in valleys, on slopes, and on benches with sandy soil; examples are blackbrush, sagebrush, and greasewood.

Pinyon-Juniper Woodland. Mixed in with the Desert Shrub community in sandy, rocky, or bedrock sites.

Hanging Garden Community. Found on steep rock walls where dripping springs nurture a dense growth of water-loving plants.

A very special plant community occurs throughout the park. It exists only at soil level. Called cryptogamic, this unusual community of lichens, mosses, and algae forms a carpet-like ground cover that resists the effects of erosion and enhances the efforts of other plant communities to become established. Cryptogamic plants are extremely important in the life processes of the park biota. They also are highly susceptible to damage by even light foot traffic. Park literature and posted signs implore visitors to avoid disruption of cryptogamic plants and the soil that nourishes them.

Animal life in Canyonlands includes several species on the Federal endangered species list: bald eagle, peregrine falcon, humpback chub, and Colorado squawfish.

Other species of wildlife occurring in the park are various raptors, rodents, snakes, small mammals, coyote, beaver, porcupine, kit fox, gray fox, badger, mountain lion, bobcat, and mule deer. Numbers of any one of these species may be rather small; the fact that they continue to populate this harsh environment attests to their ability to adapt to trying conditions.

The People of Canyonlands

A visitor inevitably becomes intrigued with archaeology and the findings of students of prehistoric cultures when he goes to Canyonlands National Park. Evidence abounds that for thousands of years people have lived, worked, and found nourishment in the canyons, along the rivers and hidden springs, and on the mesas of this rugged country. Due to the dry, desert environment, many of their cultural remains have been preserved.

A hike away from the park's popularly traveled roads leads to fascinating sights: overhanging cliffs and alcoves with obvious signs of occupation by prehistoric Indians and nineteenth and early twentieth century cowhands, rock granaries in which Indian-grown corn and other foodstuffs were stored, and distinctive art forms—pictographs and petroglyphs—fashioned by ancient peoples.

Archaeologists are still working to unravel the mysteries of past life in Canyonlands, and future research may modify some of their current beliefs. There is general agreement that the earliest Americans, called Paleo-Indians, frequented the area 8,000 to 10,000 years ago, searching for the food that big game animals could provide. They stayed on after the mammoths and other big game animals disappeared, living in open caves and crudely-built shelters, hunting deer, elk, and mountain sheep, and gathering edible wild plants for food.

More is known about the next identifiable people of canyon country—a northern branch of the Anasazi, native southwestern Americans, ancestors of today's Pueblo Indians. By the time B.C. turned into A.D., the Anasazi were growing corn, building primitive houses, and forming social groups in Canyonlands. In the next few hundred years they prospered. Their agriculture included beans and squash; pottery-making was added to basket-weaving; and bows and arrows replaced the atlatl, the spear throwing hunting weapon of the Paleo-Indians.

The Anasazi made their contribution to Canyonlands' rock art and the stylistic difference from ancient rock art is apparent. Some researchers speculate the art of this era was created or influenced by the Fremont, Indians living north and west of the park area.

About 700 to 800 years ago, in the thirteenth and fourteenth centuries A.D., both the Anasazi and the Fremont disappeared from canyon country. There are various theories about the reason for their departure—exhaustion of resources, change of climate, and social disintegration. As yet, no one is sure about what force led them to abandon their homeland.

Not until the Spanish arrived in the 1700s is there evidence of the people who followed the Anasazi. It is known that Ute, Paiute, and Navajo roamed the area then. Soon others, surveyors, geographers, scientists, outlaws, and ranchers were spending time in canyon country.

Major John Wesley Powell explored the rivers and canyons of southeast Utah in 1869 and 1871. His account of his impressions shows that he experienced the same awe felt by visitors today.

"The sun is yet two hours high, so I climb the cliffs and walk back among the strangely carved rocks of the Green River bad lands. These are sandstones and shales, gray and buff, red and brown, blue and black strata in many alternations, lying nearly horizontal, and almost without soil and vegetation. They are very friable, and the rain and streams have carved them into quaint shapes. Barren desolation is stretched before me; and yet there is beauty in the scene. The fantastic carvings, imitating architectural forms and suggesting rude but weird statuary, with the bright and varied colors of the rocks, conspire to make a scene such as the dweller in verdure-clad hills can scarcely appreciate."

Excerpted from *The Exploration of the Colorado River and Its Canyons,* by John Wesley Powell. Introduction by Wallace Stegner, Penguin Books, 1987. First published under the title *Canyons of the Colorado,* 1895.

Livestock ranching in canyonlands began about one hundred years ago. Within park boundaries are remnants of cattle-running days—a camp at Cave Springs in Needles, camping implements, rock inscriptions, pastures, cattle trails, and names given by cowboys to various natural forms. One of the park's most popular trails, available to high clearance vehicles, is the Shafer Trail in Island in the Sky. Ranchers built this trail over an old Indian trail to move cattle from high country to winter range on the canyon's White Rim.

1964: Canyonlands Preserved

Excitement about the potential for establishing a national park among "the most fantastic colored jumble of natural wonders" had been building since 1908 when President Theodore Roosevelt established by presidential proclamation the Natural Bridges Monument in southeastern Utah. (Quote attributed to Bates Wilson who became the park's first superintendent.) Surveys followed but world wars diverted attention from the proposal.

In the early 1960s Bates Wilson, custodian of Arches National Monument at the time, a man who had been exploring and extolling the virtues of this unique area for years, succeeded in enlisting the support of then Secretary of the Interior Stewart Udall. In 1964, after three years of updated surveys and controversy, President

Lyndon Johnson signed legislation creating Canyonlands National Park. In 1971, Horseshoe Canyon was added to the park specifically to preserve rare archaeological resources.

The park now includes 527 square miles of "Red Rock Country." Because of the primitive nature of the land, recommendations have been made to designate 75 percent of it as a national wilderness area.

The park is bounded on all sides by federal lands. The Bureau of Land Management administers land to the north, south, and east. Glen Canyon National Recreation Area, administered by the National Park Service, adjoins the west side of the park.

Especially significant in Canyonlands National Park is the abundance of archaeological sites. Particularly treasured are the artistic works of first-known Americans. Three sites have been placed on the National Register of Historic Places: the Horseshoe Canyon Pictograph Panels, Salt Creek Archaeological District in Needles, and the Harvest Scene Pictographs in The Maze.

Why Go to Canyonlands National Park?

Canyonlands National Park is only a part of the Colorado Plateau, a land of breathtaking vistas, desert wilderness, and colorful rock formations. But it is a piece of that unique landscape that has been set aside by law for preservation and the enjoyment of all.

The range of recreational opportunities is wide. Park visitors who enjoy driving on well-maintained roads with views of majestic scenery, visitors who like to take modest hikes to off-road overlooks and special points of interest, and people who relish the physical challenge of long hikes in rugged terrain, horseback riding in wild and remote areas, or thrilling several day float trips—all can indulge their particular form of pleasure at Canyonlands National Park.

Great variation in climate typifies Canyonlands. Temperatures range from 110 degrees in summer to twenty degrees below zero in winter. The dry, high desert country has an average precipitation of five to seven inches, most of it coming from late summer thunderstorms and winter snowfall. The best times to visit are spring and fall when the air is clear, sunshine is abundant, and temperatures are moderate.

Over half of the park's visitors come from California, Colorado, Utah, and foreign countries. Easterners and mid-westerners have yet to discover the beauty and remoteness of this wild, ancient land.

How to Get to Canyonlands National Park

Much of the park is readily accessible, though to reach each of the park's three districts, different approaches are required. More than one day is needed to visit all sections. Each district is different from the others in appeal and the kind of recreational opportunities offered.

Canyonlands National Park is south of Interstate 70. To drive to Island in the Sky, take U.S. 191 from I-70 toward Moab. From 191, Utah 313, a paved road, leads directly to the park's Visitor Center in Island in the Sky, a distance of 35 miles from Moab.

The Maze can be reached by taking Utah 24 south from Interstate 70 and driving east on unpaved roads to various parts of The Maze. Road conditions can vary. Four-wheel-drive vehicles are best used on these roads, although, at times, some roads leading to Horseshoe Canyon are suitable for two-wheel-drive automobiles. Allow plenty of time because it is slow going. Before making a trip to The Maze and to Horseshoe Canyon, a detached unit of the park, check with park rangers about road conditions. It will also be helpful to have a detailed road map.

To visit Needles district, drive south from Moab on U.S. 191 and take Utah 211, a paved road, 34 miles west to Needles Visitor Center. Rangers at the Visitor Center will provide information and guidance for your trip through Needles.

Entrance fees are charged March through October at Island in the Sky and Needles: $3 for a passenger vehicle, $1 per person for bicyclists, mountain bikers, and hikers. Holders of Golden Passes are exempt. See page 216 for information on Golden Passes.

Visitors coming from distances far from the park may choose to fly to Salt Lake City, 245 miles from Moab, or Grand Junction, Colorado, 115 miles from Moab, and rent a car. Amtrak's nearest stop is at Thompson, Utah, 40 miles northwest of Moab.

Where to Stay.

Non-Campers. Park headquarters is in Moab and that town is a central point from which to start your visit. Island in the Sky is 35 miles away. Moab, a community of 4,000 people, is geared to servicing park visitors. There is a variety of motels and restaurants. Most small towns near the national parks discussed in this book have very modest eating facilities, but Moab's wide range includes two gourmet restaurants, one high on a hillside in the former home of a uranium "king," and one in a historic ranch house listed on the *National Register of Historic Places.* For information about hotels and restaurants in Moab, write to the Grand County Travel Council.

Needles District is 75 miles from Moab and 53 miles from Monticello. For information about lodging in Monticello, contact the office of the San Juan County Travel Council.

The Maze District is a considerable distance from Moab, about 139 miles. If that is your destination, it would be better to stay in Green River. Green River is 76 miles from Horseshoe Canyon and 86 miles from Hans Flat which is located within Glen Canyon National Recreation Area but serves as the entrance to The Maze. Information about lodging in Green River can be obtained from the office of the Grand County Travel Council.

Campers. Camping is permitted in all three Districts. Designated campsites are available on a first come, first served basis. However, the 20 sites along the popular White Rim four-wheel-drive route in Island in the Sky require advance reservation. To reserve a White Rim campsite, write to White Rim Reservations at park headquarters. Contact the Island in the Sky Ranger Station, 801-259-6577, for further information.

There are 12 sites at Willow Flat Campground, Island in the Sky District, 26 at Squaw Flat Campground in Needles District, suitable for campers driving two-wheel-drive vehicles. No special facilities exist for recreational vehicles. Three campgrounds in Needles accommodate group camping, for which reservations should be made by writing to park headquarters in advance. Other campsites in all three districts are available only to four-wheel-drive vehicles. There is a $6 per night fee for campsites at Squaw Flat Campground. There are no fees for other campsites.

Backcountry camping is permitted in most parts of the park. Free permits are required for such camping, as well as for horseback riding, rock climbing, and white water raft trips. For information about regulations that apply, contact park headquarters.

Water is available during the summer at Squaw Flat Campground in Needles. Campsites in Island in the Sky and The Maze have none.

What to Do at Canyonlands National Park.

Some of the recreational activities enjoyed in the park have been mentioned previously, but here is a summary:

Take Scenic Drives. Island in the Sky is replete with magnificent scenery. A guide to the forty-mile round trip drive, starting at the visitor center, shows many places to stop and take short walks to some of Canyonlands' pageantry. Two picnic areas are provided along the route.

Highlights include:

▸ Mesa Arch Trail, a half-mile loop through a pinyon-juniper woodland to a picturesque arch at the mesa's edge through which the majestic La Sal mountains can be seen in the distance;

▸ the White Rim Overlook Trail (not to be confused with the four-wheel-drive White Rim Trail) leading to views of White Rim country;

▸ the Grand View Trail overlooking the rock wilderness carved by the Green and Colorado Rivers;

▸ the Crater View Trail, leading to a site overlooking Upheaval Dome where the erosive geologic forces that shaped canyon country are exposed for all to see.

A drive on the paved road of Needles offers views of fascinating red rock formations. It includes several stops from which short walks can be taken to historic sites such as an Indian granary. A two-wheel-drive dirt side road leads to a cowboy camp under a massive rock overhang.

Self-guiding pamphlets are available for many of the trails. They point out the natural features and describe the vegetation along the path, as well as the significance of the sites. Because of the dry, desert air, the park recommends that people carry water on all walks, at all times of the year.

Four-Wheel-Driving. In all of The Maze District and many parts of Island in the Sky and Needles Districts, the terrain is so rugged and the area so remote, only a four-wheel-drive vehicle can take you there. All vehicles, including jeeps, dune buggies, and motorcycles, must be street legal with license plates, driven by licensed drivers, and driven only on designated roads. Three and four wheeled All Terrain Vehicles are not permitted anywhere in Canyonlands National Park.

Mountain bike riders must also stay on designated roads. The park has prepared a special brochure for mountain bikers. It lists roads suitable for mountain bikes with approximate mileages and times indicated and gives advice on ways to enjoy the ride.

If you do not have a four-wheel-drive vehicle and want to explore remote areas of the park, several commercial tour companies offer guided trips in jeeps on four-wheel-drive roads. Jeeps may also be rented in nearby communities. For information, check with park headquarters, the Grand County Travel Council, or the San Juan County Travel Council.

Hiking. Dedicated backpackers can hike many miles of challenging trails through canyons and dry stream washes and up and down slickrock.

River Trips. White water raft trips on the Colorado River are conducted by several commercial tour companies. They run from one-half day to seven days. Only trips of two or more days actually go through the waters of the park. Prices range from $24 per person to several hundred, depending on age and number of days. Rafts, kayaks, and canoes may also be rented in Moab.

Horseback Riding. There are no horseback riding concessions within the park but private companies outside the park have permits to conduct pack trips on park lands. Contact the park for information.

Rock Climbing. Experienced rock climbers may engage in this sport but permits are required. The park can provide information on guided expeditions of this sort.

Educational Programs. Persons camping within the park may enjoy evening campfire programs conducted by park rangers. Rangers also lead interpretive walks during the day. Schedules of these programs are available at visitor centers and ranger stations. A more intensive educational experience is available at seminars, backcountry trips, and workshops conducted by a nonprofit association, Canyonlands Field Institute.

NOTE: *Off-road driving is not permitted. Pets are not permitted on any hiking trail, river trip, or in any backcountry roadless area, or in Horseshoe Canyon. In other places, pets must be on a leash no more than six feet long and physically restrained. There is no hunting. Loaded firearms, bows and arrows, pellet/BB guns, and similar devices are prohibited within the park. Visitor centers, restrooms, park headquarters at Moab and the park office in Monticello, are accessible to persons with a physical handicap. Vault toilets in campgrounds are wheelchair accessible with some assistance.*

If You Have the Time

▶ Take a float, jeep, or horseback trip;
▶ Visit Arches National Park, five miles north of Moab, bordering U.S. 191;
▶ Visit Deadhorse Point State Park;
▶ Take a scenic drive along the Colorado River to Fisher Towers and to the foothills of the La Sal Mountains;
▶ Visit Lake Powell in Glen Canyon National Recreation Area.

Tips for Adding to Your Enjoyment of Canyonlands National Park.

1. Plan early. Write to park headquarters for a park brochure and information and regulations applying to your particular area of interest, e.g. camping, bicycling, rock climbing; if interested, request information on commercial rafting, jeep, and packhorse trips.

2. If you'd like to prepare more fully for your visit, write to Canyonlands Natural History Association at park headquarters for a current mail order catalog of books, videos, and maps of canyon country. For information on seminars and other educational programs, contact Canyonlands Field Institute.

3. Send to the Grand County Travel Council for a copy of *Moab Lodging and Restaurant Guides.*

4. Write to Grand County or San Juan County Travel Councils for information about lodging in Green River and Monticello and private and public campgrounds.

5. Write to the Utah Travel Council for a state map and other travel information.

6. Take with you a camera, binoculars, water container, hiking boots, and a first-aid kit for emergencies.

And finally—Leave the pressures of the workaday world behind and take time to gaze at the natural wonders of Canyonlands, to contemplate the full view of the earth's creative forces, and to marvel at the artistic skills of "the ancient ones." Your life surely will be enriched after experiencing Canyonlands.

Sources of Information

Superintendent
Canyonlands National Park
125 West 200 South
Moab, UT 84532-2995
Phone: 801-259-7164

Grand County Travel Council
805 N. Main St., (Hwy. 191)
Moab, UT 84532
Phone: 800-635-MOAB
or 801-259-8825

San Juan County Travel Council
Box 490-C88
Monticello, UT 84535
Phone: 801-587-3235

Utah Travel Council
Council Hall-State Capitol
Salt Lake City, UT 84114
Phone: 801-538-1030

Canyonlands Field Institute
Box 68
Moab, UT 84532
Phone: 801-259-7750

Superintendent
Arches National Park
Box 907
Moab, UT 84532
Phone: 801-259-8161

Glen Canyon National Recreation Area
Box 1507
Page, AZ 86040
Phone: 602-645-2471

BIGHORN CANYON
NATIONAL
RECREATION AREA

It was August, yet the air was cold. He had been awake all night, but the chill of the air had not reached him until now. The first glow of light in the east preceding the dawn renewed his awareness of his surroundings, dulled by a night-long vigil of spiritual concentration. The light in the east intensified and began to surround his vantage point on the high mountain ledge. As his senses sharpened with the vibrance of the dawn, a falcon came winging past him, swung back to examine him, then hovered above as if to share with him the wild freedom of the heights. The falcon turned and flew off down the mountainside, but not

before the Crow Indian boy had recognized and understood the significance of the moment. This was the sign, the spiritual fulfillment, the personal completion of his days of fasting and self-imposed isolation in the pursuit of his Vision Quest. The falcon would be his talisman, leading him through a life of devotion to his people, comforting him in adversity, aiding him in his victories.

Like the rest of his tribe this Crow youth embarking on manhood in the early 1800s would probably need all the help he could get from his guardian spirit. Bighorn country, the core of the Crows' living space, was surrounded by several warlike Indian tribes, had the extremes of mountain and desert climate, and provided food sources that were sometimes meager.

The Crow Indians, more than most of their Indian neighbors, were at ease with their lot in Bighorn country, perils and all. To them the land was of great beauty; the creatures of the field, stream, and air were their friends; the trials and hardships they experienced were molders of courage, honor, and dignity. They were at one with the land, giving to as well as receiving from nature.

History books credit early white explorers with naming this area of Montana and Wyoming, as well as its mighty river and dominating mountain range, Bighorn. Crow tradition, however, tells another story. An Indian boy and his stepfather were hunting bighorn sheep in the mountains above what is known today as Bighorn Canyon. The stepfather was a cruel man and jealous of his stepson's popularity in their tribe. While the boy was peering over the cliffs down into the canyon, the stepfather pushed him over the rim, watched his body disappear in a clump of juniper on a ledge far below, then returned to the tribe mourning the boy's fall and death as accidental.

The juniper brush, however, had broken the boy's fall and he was not seriously hurt. But he was marooned on the ledge, unable to climb up or down. After being trapped for several days, the boy was joined by a band of bighorn sheep lead by a great ram called Big Metal (for his horns and hoofs of metal). Big Metal's band had come to save the boy and to be his helpers. They bestowed upon him their keen vision, fleetness of foot, acute hearing, and great balance, as well as the human attributes of deep insight, quick senses, intuition, and wisdom. And the great ram gave the boy his name, Big Metal. He also warned that the river and the mountains above must thenceforth be called Bighorn if the Crows wished to prosper, for if the name Bighorn should fade away so would the Crows as a people.

The boy Big Metal then rode the back of the great ram out of the canyon, returned to his people, became their wise leader, and finally died an old man, revered by generations of the Crow people. Today, he is still revered, and Bighorn country is still Crow country.

Bighorn Canyon National Recreation Area is but a part of Bighorn country. The Recreation Area consists of the Bighorn River and land immediately adjacent from a few miles south of Lovell, Wyoming to Fort Smith, Montana. Yellowtail Dam, at Fort Smith, turns the river into a deep reservoir called Bighorn Lake all the way south to Lovell. Wide in the north and south ends, Bighorn Lake narrows in its middle reaches between the walls of Bighorn Canyon, where the former rapids and white water of the river lie hundreds of feet below waters now plied by pleasure boats and waterskiers.

Gliding today over the surface of the water in the narrower parts of the canyon and looking up at sheer walls hundreds of feet high on either side, it is hard to visualize the great depth of the water under your boat. It is harder still to visualize the practically impassable rapids that once roared far beneath you.

Like so much of the western part of the United States, most of today's Bighorn country is the remains of vast sea beds laid down eons ago. Over geologic time a succession of periods of compression, uplift, vulcanism and erosion created the Bighorn Mountains on the eastern side, the Pryor Mountains on the west, and Bighorn River and Canyon in between. Twenty separate layers of sandstone, limestone, shale, and siltstone varying from 75 to 2,600 feet thick have been identified in this 9,000 foot deep sandwich of sedimentary rock.

Each vista of the mountains where vertical faces expose the edges of the rock layers provides a veritable kaleidoscope of earth tones, ranging from the greens and grays of the shales to the striking reds and browns of sandstones and siltstones, punctuated by the white limestones.

Cruising by boat between the sheer rock walls of Bighorn Canyon is like entering another world. Where the sun is bright, the colors are vibrant. Where there is shadow, the pinnacles, caves, and turrets of erosion become fantastic shapes, part real, part imagination. Rounding each bend of the canyon is an adventure in anticipation followed by a breathtaking panorama of nature's sculpture.

The canyon air is often chill. There is the awesome sense of man's inconsequence in this setting of towering walls, of watery depths, and of timelessness. You feel a momentary qualm at man's temerity in his dealings with nature. It takes rounding another bend of the canyon to restore the intriguing sense of exploration, of challenge, of natural beauty. After all, the Crow survived this land, came to peace with it, and became one with it. So can we.

The People of Bighorn Country

In Bighorn Country, Native Americans continue to live, work, uphold their traditions, and influence today's political decisions.

Members of the Crow tribe have lived in Bighorn Country for nearly 300 years. Though other tribes sometimes hunted and fought here, the Crow controlled the land when white men arrived looking for furs, and later, for ranching. By adapting to changing environmental and social conditions and effective negotiation, the Crow have maintained an independent, productive, and proud lifestyle in their homeland.

The Crows were not the earliest inhabitants of Bighorn Country. Archeological evidence shows that small bands of hunters and gatherers were wandering about the area as early as 10,000 B.C. As changes occurred in the climate, patterns of living altered.

Five thousand years ago, people were moving seasonally from canyons to mountains to grasslands, to take advantage of available plants, animals, and weather conditions. Researchers have found tepee rings—circles of stones placed to hold down the hides that covered their conical tents. They also have identified buffalo jump sites. Jump sites were developed as a technique for harvesting buffalo. Buffalo were gathered in a grazing area, then forced down a path of rocks aligned in a pattern leading to a cliff edge—a drop of fifteen to 250 feet. Nearby such sites is evidence of encampments established to process bison meat, hide, and bones.

Life changed drastically for the Indians of the Northwest Plains when the Europeans showed up. They soon became expert horsemen and, already bold warriors, they eagerly traded furs for guns. With the realization that white men had a different set of values and were aggressively exploiting the land for their own purposes, attitudes of some Indians changed and conflicts developed between them and the explorers, settlers, and the military. The Crow were not hostile, however, and often cooperated with the U.S. Army in battles with tribes the Crow also had grievances against.

Despite the harshness of life and perilous conditions in Bighorn country, cattle ranching and sheep grazing persisted. Following the 1868 treaty between the U.S. government and the Crow, establishing the first Crow reservation, the lifestyle of the Crow changed once more. Great bison herds no longer roamed the plains. Many Indians became ranchers and farmers and when the law permitted individual ownership of parcels of reservation land, others leased their land to non-Indian cattlemen and farmers, a practice that is widespread today.

Yellowtail Dam and the National Recreation Area

Until the building of the Yellowtail Dam, the lack of a consistent, dependable water supply was a concern. In the early 1900s, a section of the Bighorn River was dammed and a canal was constructed to irrigate some of the arid land. In the 1960s, the time was ripe, both nationally and locally, to undertake a major federal operation that would solve the water problems of Bighorn country.

Built in 1965 as part of the larger Missouri River Basin project, Yellowtail Dam backs up the water of Bighorn River for 71 miles. The reservoir does many things: generates power, provides municipal and industrial water, irrigation, recreation, and sediment and flood control. The Dam, located between the walls of Bighorn Canyon at Fort Smith, Montana, spans 1,480 feet along its crest. Its concrete walls rise 525 feet from the floor of the canyon to the top. The dam was named for Robert Yellowtail, a famous Crow leader. The Afterbay Dam, an integral part of the water control project, was built to minimize downstream fluctuations in the Bighorn River.

Many official voices are heard in setting policies and programs of Bighorn Canyon National Recreation Area. Although the National Park Service administers the Recreation Area, other governmental bodies administer lands within or adjacent to the boundaries and they must be consulted. Among them are federal agencies: Water and Power Resources Service, Bureau of Land Management and U.S. Forest Service, various Wyoming and Montana state government units and three local counties. By law, all matters affecting traditional Crow tribal hunting lands are subject to negotiation with the Crow Tribal Council.

Why Go to Bighorn Canyon N.R.A.?

It's romantic. It's spectacular. It conjures up visions of the Old West. It's a place where you feel "away from it all," yet there are plenty of things to do. Bighorn Canyon National Recreation Area appeals to active recreationists: power boaters, waterskiers, swimmers, fishermen, hunters, and hikers. It also captivates people seeking scenic beauty, views of rarely-seen wildlife, and a glimpse of Native American and pioneer history. A bonus opportunity is to see how an engineering feat of man has brought control to the waters of an ancient river, making the land consistently more productive.

Most of the park's visitors come from the surrounding region. In summer, it is a popular weekend destination for campers, boaters, and fishermen. Fishing is a year-round activity. Fall is a good time for hunting, hiking, and wildlife viewing as elk, deer, sheep, and bighorn rams move about at lower elevations. There is ice-fishing and ice-skating in winter.

The direct benefits from the creation of the Bighorn Canyon National Recreation Area as part of the building of the Yellowtail Dam accrue to the residents of Wyoming and Montana. However, under the federal policy of multiple-use of dam-building projects, the National Park Service was given responsibility "to provide for public outdoor recreation use and enjoyment... by the people of the United States and for preservation of the scenic, scientific, and historic features... of such lands and waters."

Cross-country travelers and persons from all parts of the nation looking for a different vacation experience therefore have their own invitation to explore this little-known piece of the Old West.

How to Get to Bighorn Canyon N.R.A.

Decide whether you want to start your visit at the southern end of the park at Lovell, Wyoming, or the northern end at Fort Smith, Montana. There is no direct road between the two districts. Original development proposals called for a road to extend the length of the recreation area, but objections by the Crow Tribal Council and others prevented implementation of the plan.

U.S. Route 14-A, an east-west highway, goes through Lovell in north central Wyoming. If coming from Billings, Montana, take U.S. Route 310 south from Interstate 90, just west of Billings. After stopping at the attractively-sited Bighorn Canyon Visitor Center on Route 14-A east of the center of Lovell, take State Route 37 north. This road is known as the trans-park highway. It follows the route of the Bad Pass Trail, used by early Native Americans to reach buffalo hunting grounds, and by white men to avoid crossing the Bighorn River. This section of the park contains many scenic overlooks, campgrounds, hiking trails, and two major centers of water-related activity.

Park headquarters, a visitor center, the Yellowtail and Afterbay Dams, campgrounds, and several launching sites for fishing boats are located at the north end in Fort Smith. To reach Fort Smith, go south on Route 313 from I-90 at Hardin.

To go from one section of the park to the other, the shortest route is through the Crow Indian Reservation. Ask park rangers for directions.

There are no entrance fees at Bighorn Canyon National Recreation Area.

Where to Stay

Non-Campers. There are a number of motels in Lovell, the "Rose City of Wyoming." Write to the Lovell Area Chamber of Commerce for information. Public accommodations at Fort Smith, which are very limited, primarily cater to fishermen. Check with park headquarters for information. There is a wider selection at Hardin, 42 miles northeast of Fort Smith. For information, write to Hardin Area Chamber of Commerce and Agriculture.

Campers—Recreational Vehicles. In the South District, Horseshoe Bend and Barry's Landing campgrounds accommodate recreational vehicles but only Horseshoe Bend has drinking water, flush toilets, and a dump station. Horseshoe Bend charges a $3 fee per night on weekends from Memorial Day to Labor Day. There are no fees for camping in other campgrounds. In the North District, the Afterbay campground has space for recreational vehicles. The campground has drinking water, vault toilets, and a dump station. Boat launch ramps are at all three campgrounds. There are no showers or hook-ups.

Campers—Tenting. Tenters may use all the campgrounds mentioned plus the Medicine Creek boat-in or hike-in site in the South District and Black Canyon boat-in site in the North District. There is no fee for tent camping and all campsites are available on a first come, first served basis. When you arrive at the park, check at the visitor centers for availability of campsites.

Backcountry camping is permitted upon obtaining a free permit and information on restrictions at a visitor center or ranger station.

Other campgrounds within the vicinity of the park are provided by the Town of Lovell, the U.S. Forest Service, and private operators. For information about these places, write to the Lovell Area Chamber of Commerce and the U.S. Forest Service.

What to Do at Bighorn Canyon N.R.A.

First, spend some time at the visitor center at Lovell or at Fort Smith. Built in 1976 at a time when the nation was very much aware of dwindling and costly energy resources, the Lovell Visitor Center is solar heated. Rangers will show you how the system works. An orientation film, "Bighorn Canyon Experience," shown on request, will immediately immerse you in the essence of the park. You will enjoy other films—about the wild horses roaming the Pryor Mountains, and about an ancient, mysterious "Medicine Wheel" sometimes compared to England's Stonehenge—and exhibits. The Lovell Visitor Center is open from 8 a.m. to 6 p.m. Memorial Day through Labor Day weekend, 8 a.m. to 5 p.m. at other times.

You may see exhibits, get information, and view a film, *Land of the Bighorn,* at the Fort Smith Visitor Center. It is open 9 a.m. to 6 p.m. Memorial Day through Labor Day weekend, 9 a.m. to 4:30 p.m. at other times.

Scenic Drives. One intriguing sight after another confronts you on the eleven-mile drive on the trans-park road north from the Lovell Visitor Center. Distant views of the Bighorn Mountains to the east and the Pryor Mountains on the west, capped with dark green Ponderosa and Lodgepole pines, loom high over the sandy soil and gray-green desert vegetation. Occasionally a mass of red sandstone juts up and breaks the monotony of unchanging color. Glimpses of wild horses roaming the Pryor Mountain Wild Horse Range through which the road travels, buffalo grazing on a private range, mountain goats treading securely on nearby rock outcroppings, and, if you are lucky, bighorn sheep, are exciting events.

For a full appreciation of the grandness of Bighorn country, take the side road to Devil Canyon Overlook and peer down at Bighorn Lake, 1,000 feet below, where it is joined by Porcupine Creek flowing in from the east. The lake disappears from view quickly as it squiggles like a corkscrew between the 2,200 foot high canyon walls. Looking up at an azure sky, flecked with snow-white wispy clouds, reassures you that this is not the River Styx flowing through an underground cavern. But you do wonder where and how a person exits from this narrow, watery path through the massive layers of white Madison limestone and red Amsden Formation rock walls.

The paved road ends just after the turn-off to Barry's Landing, but a dirt road called the Dryhead Road continues fifteen more miles through a remote area. High clearance vehicles are needed. For additional guidance on a scenic drive in the South District, borrow a 45 minute cassette tape from the Bighorn Visitor Center at Lovell. It is loaned free of charge.

In the North District at Fort Smith, the Ok-A-Beh Road winds eleven miles through high grass prairie land to the Ok-A-Beh (Crow word for cove) boat launching facility. Views of the Bighorn Mountains, the river valley, and the Yellowtail Dam are highlights of this drive and, if you travel in early morning or at dusk, you are sure to see wildlife. Black bear, coyote, deer, bobcats, and fox are among the Recreation Area's natives. Spring travelers will additionally be rewarded with the colorful sight of great varieties of wildflowers.

Boat Tour. A must for any park visitor is to take the trip on Bighorn Lake on the U.S. Coast Guard certified boat tour. The humbleness you inevitably feel from this close personal experience with the visible evidence of the awesome power of the natural forces that created Bighorn Canyon is unforgettable.

Normally the boat leaves from Horseshoe Bend, one of the two boat launching sites in the South District, from mid-June to mid-September. An interpreter is on board to explain geologic features dating back 400 million years, and to help you spot bighorn sheep. Check at the Lovell Visitor Center for information about departure times, fees, and reservations.

Water Sports. Many park visitors bring their own boats to Bighorn for fishing, water skiing, or just to float on the water and observe along the shore Great Blue Herons, bald eagles, songbirds, muskrat, or beaver. There are four boat launching ramps in the North District: Ok-A-Beh on the lake, Afterbay, Bighorn River north of Afterbay Bridge, and NPS River Ranch on the river. The South District has two boat launching ramps—one at Horseshoe Bend, the other at Barry's Landing. Concessioners provide services at Horseshoe Bend Marina and at Ok-A-Beh from Memorial Day through Labor Day. Boats may also be rented on an hourly basis at Horseshoe Bend. For regulations that apply to boating on Bighorn River, write to the Superintendent of the Recreation Area or check at visitor centers, ranger stations, or the marinas.

A small life-guarded area is provided at Horseshoe Bend in summer for campers and others who wish to swim.

Fishing. Bighorn Lake (south of Yellowtail Dam) and Bighorn River (north of the Dam) are prime destinations for avid fishermen. The river is considered a "World Class" blue ribbon trout fishery. The town of Fort Smith is especially geared to servicing fishermen. In addition to modest accommodations (but not inexpensive), boat rentals, guide services, and fish-cleaning stations are offered.

Walleye, brown trout, yellow perch, and catfish are frequent catches. Most fishing is on a catch and release basis. Fishermen must have a license from either Montana or Wyoming, according to the state they are fishing in. No license covers both states. Licenses and information about state fishing regulations and current fishing conditions may be obtained from Horseshoe Bend Marina and stores in Lovell and Fort Smith.

Hiking. A short walk on a self-guided path or a longer hike along the canyon rim or on former ranchlands offers the chance to explore the countryside in solitude and become acquainted with new flowers and plants or visit the few structures remaining from early twentieth century settlements. There are trails in both districts; among them, the .2 mile Beaver Pond Nature Trail which starts at the Fort Smith Visitor Center, the Om-Ne-A Trail, a three-mile trek along the canyon rim from Yellowtail Dam to the Ok-A-Beh boat ramp, and the 2.5 mile hike from the end of the paved trans-park road to the former cattle ranch owned by Caroline Lockhart, a well-known Western novelist. For hikers seeking a more rugged backcountry experience, permits and advice may be obtained at visitor centers and ranger stations. The fortunate backcountry hiker may get a glimpse of a golden eagle or prairie falcon. Hikers who create their own off-trail routes in Bighorn country are warned to be on the lookout for prairie rattlesnakes and blackwidow spiders.

Hunting. Hunting for waterfowl, upland game birds such as pheasant and turkey, whitetail and mule deer, and other game is allowed in specified sections of the Recreation Area in accordance with Montana and Wyoming game laws. By treaty agreement, only members of the Crow tribe are allowed to hunt or fish on Crow tribal lands and waters within the Recreation Area. For details, contact park headquarters. The Yellowtail Wildlife Habitat Unit, located a few miles west of Bighorn Lake is maintained by the Wyoming Game and Fish Department and is also open to hunters.

Visit Historic Sites. Very few structures remain from the early days of cattle ranching in this sparsely-settled country. One group of buildings that is being maintained by the Park Service, and you may visit, is the Mason-Lovell Ranch. This complex includes a bunkhouse, blacksmith shop, and ranch hands' cabin associated with an open range cattle operation in the late 1800s. Ask rangers at the Lovell Visitor Center for a brochure about the ranch; then drive east on Route 14-A across Bighorn Lake. A turn-off to the right, three miles from the lake, leads to the ranch site.

In the South District, you can visit the Lockhart ranch, mentioned earlier, by driving in a four-wheel-drive vehicle or hiking two and one-half miles on the Dryhead road at the end of the paved trans-park road. An approximate one-mile hike starting near the campground at Barry's Landing leads to the former settlement of Hillsboro. Some buildings associated with an early dude ranch and the community's post office remain.

The town of Fort Smith derives its name from one of the three forts constructed along the Bozeman Trail to protect would-be miners from hostile Indian attack as they took this shortcut to reach the mines of western Montana. The trail went through prime Indian hunting grounds and was bitterly resented by Sioux and Cheyenne. The site of the fort, which was abandoned following peace treaties in 1868 and no longer exists, is now on private land. When available, park rangers will take visitors there and explain the events that occurred and tell you stories relating to the soldiers' lives at the fort.

Tour Yellowtail Dam. The Bureau of Reclamation maintains a visitor center at the dam with exhibits relating to the construction of the dam. Free tours of the dam are conducted from Memorial Day through Labor Day. For information, contact the visitor center.

NOTE: *There is no off-road driving at Bighorn Canyon National Recreation Area. Motorcycles, motor scooters, mountain bikes, and four-wheel-drive vehicles must be driven only on park roads. All must* *have valid state license plates and be driven by persons carrying a valid state driver's license. Pets must be leashed or under physical restraint at all times. Firearms are not allowed except those used by persons actively hunting in areas open to hunting. Visitor centers and restrooms at Afterbay and Horseshoe Bend campgrounds are equipped for use by physically-handicapped persons.*

If You Have the Time

▶ Take a scenic drive on Route 14-A east up into Bighorn National Forest and visit the site of the Bighorn Medicine Wheel, a circle of stones seventy feet in diameter with stone spokes leading to a hub twelve feet in diameter, a structure presumably of ancient, religious significance.

▶ Visit Custer Battlefield National Monument, 44 miles northeast of Fort Smith. Stop at the visitor center and see the exhibits and films and tour the battlefield in the Little Bighorn River Valley where Lt. Col. George Armstrong Custer and all of the men under his immediate command lost their lives in the famous battle with northern Plains Indians led by Sioux Chief Sitting Bull.

▶ Drive through the Yellowtail Wildlife Habitat Unit east of Lovell just west of Bighorn Lake. Walk the nature trail, take a picnic, and watch for wildlife.

Tips for Adding to Your Enjoyment of Bighorn Canyon National Recreation Area

1. Write in advance to the Chambers of Commerce for information on motels in Lovell and Hardin.

2. Write to the Wyoming and Montana State Travel offices for state maps and other information about traveling in those states.

3. Write to Recreation Area headquarters for information about regulations of special interest to you, e.g., boating, fishing, hunting, and backcountry camping, and for information about accommodations in Fort Smith.

4. If you have a special interest in the geology, wildlife, plantlife, Indian culture or history of the area and would like to read more extensively before going to Bighorn Canyon National Recreation Area, send to the Bighorn Canyon Natural History Association for a list of publications that may be ordered.

5. Take your camera and binoculars.

6. If you plan to hike, take a first-aid kit with you for emergencies.

7. When you arrive, check at a visitor center for information about ranger-conducted programs and walks, and take part in some of them.

And finally—Free your imagination as you traverse the land and waters of Bighorn country and try to identify with the early Native Americans, the daring explorers, the bold pioneers, and the seekers of fortune who took on the daily challenge of surviving in this inhospitable, yet magnetic frontier land.

Sources of Information

Superintendent
Bighorn Canyon National
Recreation Area
Box 458
Fort Smith, MT 59035
Phone: 406-666-2412

Bighorn Canyon Natural History
Association
Box 458
Fort Smith, MT 59035
Phone: 406-666-2412

Lovell Area Chamber of Commerce
287 East Main
Lovell, WY 82431
Phone: 307-548-7552

Hardin Area Chamber of Commerce
and Agriculture, Inc.
200 North Center Avenue
Hardin, MT 59034
Phone: 406-665-1672

Travel Montana
1424 9th Avenue
Helena, MT 59620
Phone: 800-548-3390 (non-resident)
or 406-444-2654

Wyoming Travel Commission
I-25 at College Drive
Cheyenne, WY 82002
Phone: 307-777-7777

Superintendent
Custer Battlefield National
Monument
Box 39
Crow Agency, MT 59022
Phone: 406-638-2621

Bighorn National Forest
Medicine Wheel Ranger District
604 East Main Street
Lovell, WY 82431
Phone: 307-548-6541

Yellowtail Dam Visitor Center
Bureau of Reclamation
Fort Smith, MT 59035
Phone: 406-666-2443, Ext. 234

Manager
Yellowtail Wildlife Habitat
Management Unit
Wyoming Dept. of Game and Fish
Box 845
Lovell, WY 82431
Phone: 307-548-7310

COULEE DAM NATIONAL RECREATION AREA

Coulee Dam National Recreation Area is in the heart of a land of superlatives—both natural and man-made. The Recreation Area consists of 130 miles of the water and shorelines of Lake Franklin D. Roosevelt, a vast reservoir created by the construction of the Grand Coulee Dam on the Columbia River in eastern Washington.

Grand Coulee Dam, like the wide, nearby gulch from which it gets its name, is an unparalleled creation. It is one of the largest concrete structures built by man. Rising 550 feet above its bedrock anchored footings, the dam stretches nearly one mile (5,223 ft) across the Columbia River gorge. It backs up a reservoir of water

in the Columbia River 151 miles long covering an area of approximately 130 square miles. It provides irrigating waters that turn vast areas of desert into productive farmlands, and its generating capacity of 6,494,000 kw of electrical power makes it the second largest plant in the world.

These are man-made superlatives. But the story of Grand Coulee Dam and Coulee Dam National Recreation Area begins with the story of the land and how it was shaped by a natural process of geological events resulting from another superlative—a veritable cataclysm of nature.

Millions of years ago molten rock welled up through cracks in the granite bedrock, alternately flowing over the land, then cooling and solidifying into basalt. Distinct layers were formed. Over tens of thousands of years, they were fractured by shrinkage cracks as each layer cooled. Layer after layer of lava accumulated; a veritable sea of basalt formed up to 10,000 feet thick.

Following the eruptions, the entire lava field was uplifted and tilted like a gigantic saucer with its northeast rim about 2,000 feet higher than its southwest rim. The lava field also became deformed in several places by a series of folds. One of these folds, the Coulee Monocline in the north central part of the lava field, became a prime actor in the events that later shaped the ragged, wide Grand Coulee valley.

Next came a period when a windblown layer of silt, called loess, began to accumulate over much of the lava field, in places eventually reaching a thickness of 200 feet. Now the stage was set! Here was a region underlain by a thick, tilted saucer of fractured basalt, warped into ridges and folds, and overlaid with a topping of windblown silt. It must have been a peaceful landscape of undulating grassland with herds of grazing buffalo, antelope, and camels—a sea of tranquility before the catastrophic deluge!

Glaciation of the northern hemisphere had been going on for at least two million years. Glaciers waxed and waned with the ages and with changes in climate. In one glacial advance the Columbia River, forced to change course, carved a bed which became the forerunner of Grand Coulee.

About 18,000-20,000 years ago, a massive glacial lobe advanced along the Clark Fork River in Idaho, to the northeast of the basaltic saucer, and like a gigantic stopper, backed up the water from a huge drainage area in Idaho and Montana. Known as Glacial Lake Missoula, it is estimated to have contained 500 cubic miles of water—half the volume of today's Lake Michigan. At the ice dam end it built up to a depth of nearly 2,000 feet, more than twice the depth of Lake Superior. Traces of its ancient shoreline are visible today at Missoula, Montana, and indicate a depth at that point of about 950 feet.

Drainage into Glacial Lake Missoula increased as other glacier lobes melted, water level in the lake overtopped its ice dam, cut deeply into it, then destroyed it as a massive wall of water roared out across the land. The lake's 500 cubic miles of water may well have gushed down the Clark Fork River in as little time as a day or two, a drainage rate unmatched by any other known flood. Water velocities probably equalled ten times the combined flow of all of today's world rivers and 1,500 times the average flow rate of the Columbia River today.

This vast torrent of water could go but one way—downhill, and as it rushed southwestward over the tipped, saucerlike area of southeastern Washington, it planed, chiselled, gouged and channeled the land before it. Most of the loess was swept away. Channels of raging water drove deep into the underlying basalt, sweeping up its broken columns, reducing them to mere particles of gravel. Only the bedrock granite deep below could withstand the onslaught of this overwhelming flood.

Thus was created a landscape of deep canyons, maze-like channels, rugged buttes, immense rolling beds of gravel—and Grand Coulee. Deserted by the Columbia River many thousands of years ago, bulldozed by flood into a wide valley, and now utilized by man as storage for a vast irrigation system, Grand Coulee again flows with water from the Columbia River.

The Grand Coulee Dam is the prime component of the Columbia River Basin project. The Bureau of Reclamation, the Bonneville Power Administration, and the U.S. Army Corps of Engineers all have responsibilities relating to the operation of the dam. However, the National Park Service administers the Coulee Dam National Recreation Area, which was created to provide public recreation on the waters and shoreline of Lake Roosevelt that are not within the Colville and Spokane Indian Reservations.

The People of the Coulee Dam Area

For 9,000 years before the transformation wrought by the building of Grand Coulee Dam, men and women dared to face the vicissitudes of living in this land of abundant and clear but untamed water and terrain that ranged from forested mountains and moist valleys to treeless, arid plains. For most of the year, the first inhabitants moved around in small groups following big game or the fruits of the season, but during the summer months everyone settled along the banks of the river where salmon, sturgeon, trout, and other fish were plentiful. Socially, they got along with each other, a cultural fact-of-life which allowed them to devote their energies to providing sustenance rather than warfare.

When Europeans arrived on the vast North American continent, they were busy exploring and settling in more accessible regions for nearly three centuries, and they didn't get to this part of the Columbia River until the early 1800s. When they arrived, they observed the spectacle of hundreds of Indians from various tribes gathered at Kettle Falls for salmon fishing. It was here that the "roaring and noisy waters" of the Columbia dropped 33 feet in less than half a mile through the rocky formations. Fishermen could stand on the rocks and catch salmon with spears and large baskets as the prized fish battled their way upstream to spawning territory. An annual event, it was also a time for exchanging goods, a practice that Canadian fur traders quickly recognized and capitalized on.

In 1825, the Hudson's Bay Company built Fort Colvile near Kettle Falls, named after Andrew Colvile, a director of the company. This stockaded enclosure was one of the company's largest posts in the northwest, serving as district headquarters for the next forty years. During this time, there was constant and friendly contact between the fur traders and the Indians. The traders taught the natives agriculture; they exchanged new European products for the furs from the animals the Indians trapped; and they introduced the natives to new religious ideas and practices.

By the time Catholic missionaries arrived two decades later, many Indians, now familiar with Christian dogma, were ready to attend worship services and be baptized. The chapel for St. Paul's Mission was built, French-Canadian style, in 1847 on a bluff above the falls, replacing a temporary structure built two years earlier by the Indians. The mission building was used off and on until the 1880s; by then, it had deteriorated. A few years ago, the chapel was restored and it is now one of the historic sites that may be viewed by visitors to the National Recreation Area.

In the mid 1850s, the Indians began to experience the "down side" of white man's migration to their homeland: a smallpox epidemic, heavy drinking, and a lack of religious fervor among both whites and Indians following the opening of a saloon, and encroachment on their lands when farmers and merchants followed miners after gold was discovered in the Colville area. The Indians became restless and tensions developed. A military presence became necessary.

Fort Collville, a military post, was established in the Colville valley in 1859. (This fort is spelled with two l's.) Its mission was first, to protect white settlers, and second, to assist surveyors in efforts to establish a treaty-authorized boundary line between British and American territories. A period of stability ensued. Migration continued and communities of white farmers and ranchers began to form.

The Colville Indian Reservation was created in 1872 on lands set aside for the exclusive use of Indians. Soon after, the Spokane Indian Reservation was established. Military efforts then shifted to protecting Indian reservation lands from white intrusion. A new military post was established at the confluence of the Spokane and Columbia Rivers in 1880, and in 1882 it officially became Fort Spokane Military Reserve.

Military duty was not demanding at Fort Spokane. Indians were adjusting to the reservation and whites were concentrating their energies on building farms and commercial enterprises. After a few years the soldiers were moved to other posts and by the time the Spanish-American war erupted in 1898, the military abandoned Fort Spokane.

The federal government's "Indian Service" took over the fort. Over the next several years it was a boarding school for children from the Colville Indian Reservation, then a sanitarium for Indian children with respiratory ailments, and finally an Indian hospital. The fort was abandoned once again in 1929, and in 1960 the National Park Service assumed responsibility. The fort site is now one of the main facilities of the recreation area with a number of recreational activities available to visitors during the summer.

In the late nineteenth and early twentieth centuries farmers continued to eke out a living in the upper Columbia River area, but it became increasingly clear that to prosper, a dependable irrigation system was essential. A number of proposals were considered, and by 1918 they had narrowed down to two. One called for building a long canal system from a lake in Idaho; the other, the construction of a large dam on the Columbia River at Grand Coulee.

The Coulee Dam proposal won out in 1933, when the Washington State legislature appropriated money for preliminary studies and President Franklin D. Roosevelt designated $63 million of Public Works Administration (PWA) funds for dam construction.

The geographic feature known as Grand Coulee had fascinated people for centuries. One of the early explorers recorded his impression as follows:

Coulee Dam

"We made a short stay at a place called the Grand Coulé, one of the most romantic, picturesque, and marvellously-formed chasms west of the Rocky Mountains. If you glance at the map of Columbia, you will see, some distance above the great Forks, a barren plain extending from the south to the north branch of that magnificent stream; there, in the direction of nearly south and north, lies the Grand Coulé, some eighty or one hundred miles in length. No one traveling in these parts ought to resist paying a visit to the wonder of the west."

"The sight in many places is truly magnificent; while in one place the solemn gloom forbids the wanderer to advance, in another the prospect is lively and inviting, the ground being thickly studded with ranges of columns, pillars, battlements, colour. Here and there, endless vistas and subterraneous labyrinths add to the beauty of the scene; and what is still more singular in this arid and sandy region, cold springs are frequent; yet there is never any water in the chasm, unless after recent rains. Thunder and lightning are known to be more frequent here than in other parts and a rumbling in the earth is sometimes heard. According to Indian tradition, it is the abode of evil spirits. Altogether it is a charming assemblage of picturesque objects for the admirer of nature."

Alexander Ross, *The Fur Hunters of the Far West*, 1855, cited in
"Grand Coulee in History", by Edmond Meany,
Washington Quarterly, Vol. 15, 1924

Once construction of Grand Coulee Dam began, another wave of newcomers to the Coulee area began. Construction workers arrived, so many that two new cities, Mason City and the city of Coulee Dam, and several work camps were built to house them. At the peak of the project, 2,600 men were employed.

Changes wrought by the building of Grand Coulee Dam, with the many economic benefits it brought to the northwest, probably were as drastic in scope as those resulting from the arrival of the Europeans a century earlier. A significant price was paid. Casualties include the historic Kettle Falls Indian salmon fishing site, the Hudson's Bay's Fort Colvile, a number of archeological and historic sites, and ten small towns along the river, together with farms, orchards, and roads. All were inundated by the backwaters of the dam; only when there is a spring drawdown are some of these remains of past cultures visible.

Why Go to Coulee Dam National Recreation Area?

Undoubtedly what draws first-time visitors to Coulee Dam National Recreation Area is its neighboring attraction, Grand Coulee Dam. A chance to behold the gigantic structure, and to see the inner workings of one of the world's greatest producers of hydroelectric energy is an opportunity not to be missed if a person is anywhere in the vicinity of eastern Washington. But there is much to do at Coulee Dam National Recreation Area. The scenery and the water-based recreation at Lake Roosevelt makes it worthwhile to spend several days at the recreation area.

Summers generally have comfortable temperatures, making boating, swimming, and fishing prime activities. The park is fully geared for an influx of visitors at this time, and many special events are scheduled. Early fall has the added appeal of colorful vistas in the mountains and along the shore. The golden hue of larches stands out among the dark green Ponderosa pines and Douglas firs at the higher elevations, and, at the water's edge, an appreciative eye will light on the deep reds, roses, and dusty blues of shoreline vegetation.

How to Get to Coulee Dam National Recreation Area

The city of Coulee Dam, where park headquarters is located, is on State Route 155, just off State Route 174, which goes through the city of Grand Coulee. From Spokane, the nearest major city, take U.S. Route 2 west and, at Wilbur, take State Route 174 northwest. Spokane is 87 miles from Grand Coulee. To drive to Kettle Falls, at the northern end of the park, take State Route 25 from U.S. Route 2 at Davenport, 35 miles west of Spokane, or take U.S. 395 from Spokane.

If traveling east from Seattle, 228 miles from Grand Coulee, there are several optional routes, depending on whether you want to travel on an interstate highway or you prefer a scenic route through North Cascades National Park or through Snoqualmie National Forest. Check a Washington state map.

If you live a considerable distance from eastern Washington and you want to reduce travel time, you may want to fly or take the train for part of your trip. Major airlines, Amtrak, and car rental agencies serve both Spokane and Seattle.

There are no entrance fees at Coulee Dam National Recreation Area.

Where to Stay

Non-Campers. There are several moderate-priced motels in Coulee Dam and Grand Coulee, at the western end of the park. Some have rooms with windows overlooking the spillway face of the dam with good views of the summertime nightly laser light show. For information, contact Grand Coulee Dam Area Chamber of Commerce.

When you visit the northern end of the recreation area, the place to stay is Kettle Falls, which prides itself on being "the home of 1,256 friendly people and one grouch." (The "grouch" is officially designated at an annual community celebration in June). Kettle Falls was originally a settlement on the banks of the Columbia River, but when it was due to be inundated by the waters of Lake Roosevelt, the people moved upland a few miles and settled in the unincorporated town, Meyers Falls. Eventually, Meyers Falls was absorbed into the relocated community of Kettle Falls. For information about motels and other community facilities, contact the Kettle Falls Chamber of Commerce.

Campers, Recreational Vehicles and Tents. The lure of Lake Roosevelt's outstanding water-based recreation attracts thousands of outdoor enthusiasts in the summer season. A large portion of these visitors camp in one of the 600 developed campsites in the park's 31 campgrounds. There are no hook-ups, but most sites can accommodate recreational vehicles. Boat-in only campsites are the exception.

The main campgrounds in the southern end of the recreation area are Spring Canyon, the nearest campground to Grand Coulee Dam (78 sites), and Keller Ferry, fourteen miles farther up (55 sites). There is a designated swimming beach at Spring Canyon and, in summer, park rangers present evening campfire programs in the amphitheater.

There are eleven campgrounds along the lakeshore at the northern end of the park, many of them in remote, wooded areas. Among the largest are Kettle Falls campground, a few miles from the community of Kettle Falls (76 sites), and Evans campground, ten miles north (56 sites). There is a small marina at Kettle Falls Campground. The Kettle Falls Ranger Station, near the campground's entrance, also serves as an information center. Evans Campground is popular with Canadian visitors. It is also an excellent campground for families with young children. There is a fine playground.

The largest of the several campgrounds near Fort Spokane District is at the fort (62 sites). Located near the Spokane River, campsites are nestled under ponderosa pine trees. Attractions include a park visitor center, historical tours, swimming, hiking trails, boat launching facilities, and ranger-conducted programs. The park office is open 9:30 a.m. to 5:30 p.m. during summer, at various times during the rest of the year.

A fee of $6 per night is charged for campsites at developed campgrounds. Sites are available on a first come, first served basis. However, group campsites at Spring Canyon, Fort Spokane, and Kettle Falls Campgrounds may be reserved.

Most campgrounds fill up early on holiday weekends and sometimes on weekends in July and August. For information on availability of campsites, call park headquarters 509-633-9441, the Fort Spokane Visitor Center 509-725-2715, or the Kettle Falls Information Station 509-738-6266.

Live-Aboard Boaters. Vacationing in a houseboat, plying the waters of Lake Roosevelt, is becoming increasingly popular. Fully equipped houseboats accommodating up to twelve people may be rented on a weekend, mid-week, or weekly basis. Rates range from about $800 to $1,600, depending on season and number of days. Contact park concessioners, Roosevelt Recreational Enterprises and Lake Roosevelt Resorts and Marinas for information.

What to Do When Visiting Coulee Dam N.R.A.

Visit Grand Coulee Dam. Grand Coulee Dam is not within the recreation area, but if you have not seen the dam before, start your visit at the U.S. Bureau of Reclamation's Visitor Arrival Center. Watch the movie, "The Columbia, the Fountain of Life." To get an overall picture of the operation and benefits of the dam, look at the map of Columbia Basin Project facilities, the three dimensional model of Grand Coulee Dam, and other fascinating exhibits. Then pick up an explanatory brochure and take the self-guided auto tour of the main features of the dam: the pump-generator plant, the spillway, and two of the three main power plants.

You can park on top of the dam and go inside the plants for a close look at the whirling machinery. At stop number five, in the summer, take a guided tour which includes a ride on a glass-enclosed inclined elevator to a level 329 feet below. You will be enthralled with the sight of churning water producing hydroelectric energy.

At night, station yourself in the best viewing and listening area for enjoying the evening's free entertainment—the laser light show. Through the medium of multi-colored laser beams projected on the spillway of the dam, the story of the Columbia River is told. The program is narrated and includes sound effects and music. It is unforgettable! On Memorial Day weekend, there is also a spectacular fireworks display over the dam.

Take Scenic Drives. North and south paved roads run along both sides of Lake Roosevelt and along the Sanpoil and Kettle Rivers, offering lovely vistas of the waters of Lake Roosevelt. On the east side of the lake, the road passes through the Spokane Indian Reservation and the Huckleberry Mountain range. West of the lake, scenic drives run east and west through the Colville Indian Reservation and the Colville National Forest. Though there is little resident wildlife within the narrow land boundaries of the recreation area, white-tailed and mule deer, black bear, mountain lion and some smaller fur-bearing mammals inhabit the wooded areas surrounding the park. Watch carefully as you travel the uncrowded, winding drives through the mountain ranges and you may see some of these woodland creatures.

If you start on one side of Lake Roosevelt and want to go to the other, you can cross the lake on one of two free ferries. One departs from Keller Ferry, near the campground. The other, about halfway between Fort Spokane and Kettle Falls, is near the community of Gifford.

Boating. Many people take their own boats to Lake Roosevelt; others rent a houseboat, fishing boat, or water ski boat at one of the marinas on Lake Roosevelt. There is access to the lake from 18 free public boat ramps. When you boat on Lake Roosevelt, you will not only indulge in a favorite water sport; you will also get a close look at some of the dramatic features of the landscape shaped by volcanic and glacial action millions of years ago. Looking skyward from your boat at one of these sites, Whitestone Rock, a massive granite wall rising 700 feet above the lake, you will undoubtedly experience the same awe felt by travelers passing through Coulee country years ago.

Lake Roosevelt is 151 miles long, and several rivers and streams flow into it, making for a variety of boating conditions. Because of long distances between marinas, park officials urge boaters to carefully plan their boating ventures. Before boating on Lake Roosevelt, contact park headquarters and get detailed information.

Late summer and early fall are ideal times to canoe on Lake Roosevelt. Campgrounds along the 660 mile shoreline are accessible to all boats. If canoeists or other boaters intend to camp, unless they meet specified conditions, they must spend the night in one of the park's campgrounds. Water levels on the lake vary with the seasons, and other conditions, such as dangerous rapids and swells, are present in certain places. So check with park headquarters or a visitor center before starting a canoe trip.

If you are a novice and want to learn how to paddle a canoe, join one of the park rangers' free canoeing classes. If you already know how, you will enjoy an evening canoe trip on quiet Crescent Bay Lake, led by a park ranger.

Fishing. Troll, cast from shore or from a boat, or fly fish. Whichever sport you prefer, you can try your luck on Lake Roosevelt. Most commonly caught fish are walleye. About 35 different species of fish are found in recreation area waters, among them trout, salmon, bass, and sturgeon, the largest fish, sometimes up to thirteen feet long and weighing over 1,000 pounds. Fall and the months of May and June are the most popular times to fish.

A Washington state fishing license is required. Licenses and state fishing regulations are available at local hardware and sporting goods stores. If fishing in the area adjacent to the Spokane Indian Reservation, a Tribal License is needed. The National Park Service has prepared a pamphlet providing detailed information about the type and location of fish in Coulee Dam National Recreation Area. Send for a copy if you plan to fish.

Swimming. You can swim at beaches in six recreation area campgrounds: Spring Canyon and Keller Ferry near Coulee Dam, Fort Spokane and Porcupine Bay near Fort Spokane, and Kettle Falls and Evans near Kettle Falls. If you want to learn to snorkel, join one of the ranger-led snorkeling lessons.

Hunting. During the fall season, portions of the recreation area are open to hunting for white tail and mule deer, black bear, pheasant, and other game birds. A state license is required.

Hiking. The only federally-owned land in the recreation area is a narrow strip bordering Lake Roosevelt. Hence, trails on park property are short. They are located at campgrounds and historical sites: Bunchgrass Nature Trail at Spring Canyon Campground (.5 mile), Sentinel Trail at Fort Spokane (one mile), Mission Point Trail at St. Paul's Mission (.5 mile), and Beach Trail from Kettle Falls Ranger Station to the swimming beach (one mile). There are trailside signs and exhibits along the Sentinel and Mission Point Trails and a self-guiding booklet is available at the trailhead of the Bunchgrass Prairie Trail. More challenging trails are available eight miles south of Grand Coulee at Steamboat Rock State Park, on Banks Lake, and at Northrup Canyon, across the road.

Visit Historic Sites. To visit St. Paul's Mission and Fort Spokane, the park's two historic sites, is to take a step back in time. When you go to the Mission, examine the rustic structure, a replica constructed in the same manner as the original; picture Father De Vos, the church's first permanent missionary, conducting mass and relating Christian beliefs and parables in terms meaningful to his Indian worshippers; and walk along the edge of the bluff and envision the congregation of hundreds of Indians for salmon fishing at the Falls only 150 years ago.

If you can, time your visit to Fort Spokane on Sunday morning during the summer. That's when park rangers put on a "living history" performance, in which the routine of a soldier's life at the fort is demonstrated. You may also browse through the publications for sale at the visitor center in the 1892 guardhouse, see exhibits relating to the fort, and take a walking tour of the grounds. The Fort Spokane Military Reserve and the Kettle Falls Archeological District are listed on the National Register of Historic Places.

NOTE: *Off-road vehicles may only be driven in the area below the high water line during the periods of low water, and only established roadways may be used to reach that area. During hunting season, loaded firearms are not allowed within half a mile of developed recreation sites; at other times, all firearms must be broken down and encased. Pets may be taken to the recreation area, but regulations specify where they may and may not be taken. If you plan to take a pet with you, send for a copy of the regulations. More recently built facilities at the recreation area are accessible to persons with a physical handicap.*

If You Have the Time:

▶ Take your camera and drive to Crown Point Vista, an overlook of Grand Coulee Dam and the countryside, built and maintained by the Washington State Parks and Recreation Commission. To reach the site, located 626 feet above the Columbia River, take State Highway 174 two miles west of Grand Coulee and watch for signs to the Vista.

▶ Visit the Colville Confederated Tribes Museum and Gift Shop in Coulee Dam and see exhibits depicting Indian traditions and beautifully crafted cedar baskets and jewelry.

▶ Take a drive through the wooded hills and valleys and along the lakes of the Colville Indian Reservation. For information about the reservation and the recreation opportunities and special events non-Indians may enjoy on reservation land and waters, write to the Planning Department of the Colville Confederated Tribes. For information on hunting and fishing licenses on reservation property, address your inquiry to the Fish and Game Department.

▶ Take a free tour of the Kettle Falls Generating Station at Kettle Falls, operated by the Washington Water Power Company and see how wood waste is turned into energy. Tours are offered on weekdays, 8 a.m. to 3 p.m.

Tips for Adding to Your Enjoyment of Coulee Dam NRA

1. Write to park headquarters and request a park brochure and specific information on matters of special interest to you, e.g., boating, fishing, camping, canoeing, and hunting.

2. Write to the Coulee Dam and Kettle Falls Chambers of Commerce for information about motels and private campgrounds.

3. If you would like to learn more about the geology, vegetation, and people of coulee country, or want to study area maps and charts before going to Coulee Dam National Recreation Area, send for the publications catalog of the Pacific Northwest National Parks and Forest Association, available at recreation area headquarters.

4. Take your camera and binoculars with you.

5. When you arrive, check on times and subjects of ranger-conducted programs. Park headquarters is at 1008 Crest Drive in Coulee Dam. It is open on weekdays 8 a.m. to 4:30 p.m. year-round. Park visitor centers and ranger stations are open daily during the summer. On weekends, check the Visitor Arrival Center at Grand Coulee Dam for information about the recreation area.

And finally—Whether your visit is short or long, slow your pace, and relish the grandeur all around you. Enjoy some quiet time on woodland paths or along clear creeks and streams, and store up memories. Some day a picture, a word, or a happening will take you back to Coulee Dam National Recreation Area.

Sources of Information

Superintendent
Coulee Dam National Recreation
Area
Box 37
Coulee Dam, WA 99116
Phone: 509-633-9441

Coulee Dam Area Chamber of
Commerce
Box 760
Grand Coulee, WA 99133-0760
Phone: 509-633-3074

Kettle Falls Chamber of Commerce
Box 276
Kettle Falls, WA 99141
Phone: 509-738-6514

U.S. Bureau of Reclamation
Grand Coulee Project Office
Attention: Code 140
Box 620
Grand Coulee, WA 99133
Phone: 509-633-1360

Colville Confederated Tribes
Planning Department
Box 150
Nespelem, WA 99155
Phone: 509-634-4711

Public Affairs Office
Washington Dept. of Transportation
Transportation Building
Olympia, WA 98504-5201
Phone: 206-753-2150

Roosevelt Recreational Enterprises
Box 587
Grand Coulee, WA 99133-0587
Phone: 800-648-LAKE (WA only)
or 509-633-0201

Lake Roosevelt Resorts & Marinas
Box 340
Kettle Falls, WA 99141
Phone: 800-635-7585 (WA only)
or 509-738-6121

"... An area where the earth and its community of life are untrammeled by man, where man himself is a visitor who does not remain."

> —Definition of a national wilderness area,
> National Wilderness Act, 1964

NORTH CASCADES NATIONAL PARK COMPLEX

From the deck of the Lady of the Lake the shoreline across half a mile of the waters of Lake Chelan reminds one of a finely detailed landscape painting. Scattered vacation homes nestle under towering evergreens, rock-faced slopes rising behind them, and massive, rough-hewn mountains as a backdrop—each part of the picture is placed in a relationship of size, location, and pattern that satisfies the rules guiding an artist's composition.

This vast land of the North Cascades encompasses countless such vistas replete with soaring mountains, roaring falls, and cataracts fed by hundreds of glaciers, idyllic mountain meadows, and pure alpine lakes—called the American Alps for good reason.

The North Cascades National Park Complex consists of three separate and distinct units, North Cascades National Park, Ross Lake National Recreation Area, and Lake Chelan National Recreation Area. Each entity was created for a particular purpose, but all three are combined under one administration.

Preservation of existing natural resources is the prime responsibility of the national park. Recreational use and conservation of resources is the purpose of the recreation areas. Although the mandates differ mostly in emphasis, they do result in such seeming paradoxes as hunting being prohibited in the park, but allowed in the recreation areas. Most of the park has been designated a wilderness area; hence, guidelines for development of access and facilities are strict. As a result, the park is the realm of the rugged long-distance hiker and mountain climber, while the recreation areas appeal to those seeking less vigorous recreational experiences.

The North Cascades Complex totals a little over 1,000 square miles of forest and alpine environments, deep valleys, and sparkling lakes. It straddles the northern third of Washington State's Cascade Range, extending from the Canadian border to a few miles south of the community of Stehekin at the north end of Lake Chelan. It is surrounded by public lands—national forests and wilderness areas in Washington, and a provincial park, recreation area, and forest lands in Canada.

Almost three quarters of the North Cascades Complex lies within the national park. The park is divided into two sections, a North Unit and a South Unit, separated by the Ross Lake Recreation Area. Lake Chelan National Recreation Area, is at the southern end of the complex. It is located at the north end of Lake Chelan and includes the community of Stehekin.

Access to the national park is primarily by trails. Only one road penetrates the edge of the park, the unpaved Cascade River Road, which provides motor access to a great overlook and the trailhead for the Cascade Pass Trail. Amid the high jagged peaks, the endless number of cascades and waterfalls, the glacially gouged out valleys, and the blinding snowfields, lie scattered 318 glaciers, over half of the total in the lower 48 states.

Ross Lake National Recreation Area runs down the northeastern edge of the Complex, then slices west along the Skagit River valley. Three hydroelectric dams, Ross, Diablo, and Gorge, are within its borders. North Cascades Highway cuts through the east-west part of the Recreation Area, providing ready access, spectacular scenic vistas, and nearby lodging for the motorist. This is the prime area of the park complex for day use.

Lake Chelan National Recreation Area is accessible by boat, by plane, or by foot. There is no vehicular access. Contact between the recreation area and the outside world is primarily via the regularly scheduled ferryboats plying the 55 miles of Lake Chelan between Stehekin and the town of Chelan at the lake's southern end. Stehekin and, by extension, Chelan serve as gateways to Lake Chelan National Recreation Area.

North Cascade Mountain terrain was formed, geologically, a relatively short time ago. What you see today is the direct result of natural forces active 10,000 to 20,000 years ago. Unlike the Cascade Mountains south of central Washington State, the northern Cascades are not the result of recent vulcanism. The mountains here consist of material formed millions of years ago by a combination of sedimentary, metamorphic, and volcanic episodes that resulted in a gigantic uplift of a land consisting of hard, dense rock. At some later time the glaciation of the Northern Hemisphere began, and unimaginable overburdens of miles deep ice accumulated on the land. The weight of the ice was so great that its lower layers became plastic and flowed out from under the top layers like gelatin under your foot.

But this gelatin-like layer was abrasive, studded with broken rock, and under the irresistable pressure of its crushing overburden, bulldozed tablelands into channels, channels into valleys, valleys into deep gashes in the earth. Left standing above all this is the network of peaks, ridges, and cols we see today. Scoured out below are deep valleys and lake bottoms.

The depth of Lake Chelan has been measured to be 1,528 feet at its deepest point. At that depth the lake bottom is some 426 feet below sea level! The glacier that carved out this tremendous gash, as it flowed from north to south, reached a point near Chelan where it melted as fast as it advanced. Its melt waters discharged gravel in such vast quantities, in what is called a terminal moraine, that it formed a dam at its southern end that holds back the waters of the lake. (The natural level of the lake has been raised 21 feet by further damming to increase hydro-electric power output.)

The Flora and Fauna of the Cascades

Like other mountain ranges, the North Cascades strongly influence the surrounding climate. Prevailing west to east winds drive air masses loaded with moisture from the Pacific Ocean against and over the western side of the Cascades, causing much of the moisture to be released as precipitation on the west side of the mountains. As a consequence, western portions of the North Cascades National Park Complex have almost rain forest conditions, with about eighty inches of rain annually. On the eastern side, in the lee of the mountains, annual precipitation is about 34 inches, resulting in semi-arid conditions.

Consequently, the variety of flora within the Complex is striking. Of particular note are the forest trees, especially evergreens. In the wetter western region are the mountain hemlock, Alaska yellow cedar, subalpine fir, Pacific silver fir, western hemlock,

Douglas fir, and western red cedar; in the drier eastern region are the white bark pine, alpine larch, subalpine fir, lodgepole pine, and ponderosa pine.

The flora variety, wide range of habitat, and remoteness of the backcountry support an abundance of wildlife. Mule deer and black bear are frequently seen; the more secretive mountain lion, coyote, wolf, mountain goat, elk, and moose are there for the more dedicated naturalist to see. There is the tantalizing inherent possibility of the Park Service not ruling out the likelihood of a visit from a wide-ranging grizzly bear.

Smaller mammals of the squirrel and rabbit family range throughout the North Cascades Complex. Around 200 species of birds have been identified in the area, including song birds, raptors, and waterfowl. Beaver are occasionally seen along the rivers and streams. And the ubiquitous mosquito, black fly, and notorious no-see-um are abundant in the North Cascades; just to remind you that this is no big-screen movie, this is no TV documentary, this is no marvelous dream—this, is the real thing!

The People of the North Cascades

The rugged mountains and passes are so remote and challenging for foot travelers that for a long time it was thought early Americans avoided the North Cascades. However, recent archeological research has shown that man hunted and fished and fashioned stone tools in the North Cascades as long as 8,000 years ago. The Cascade Pass was used as a seasonal travel route by Indians for several centuries.

When white men reached the North Cascades in the early 1800s, Indians frequented the area, hunting mountain goats, deer, bear, elk, and marmot. Below the Newhalem Gorge, they fished for salmon.

Alexander Ross, a Canadian fur trader, is believed to have been the first white man to cross the Cascades, in 1814 using the route of the Indians. White trappers soon braved the forbidding land, searching for beaver, wolves, lynx, marten, and fox for the lucrative European market.

Gold fever brought fortune hunters to the Cascades in the last half of the nineteenth century. Some searched for ore deposits along the Skagit River banks. Others based their operations in the

Stehekin valley. The earliest hotels were built there to service the miners. The fever soon waned. Long periods of rough weather, difficulty in bringing equipment in and transporting ore out, and disappointment in the quality of the strikes were factors. The historically curious may see the remains of the Black Warrior mine in Horseshoe Basin by taking a 2.5 mile hike from the last stop of the shuttle bus the Park Service runs along the Stehekin Road.

A small amount of mining for other products—silver, copper, lead, tungsten, mercury, and iron—went on around the time of the two world wars. Except for the extraction of sand, gravel, and building stone, for the use of Stehekin residents, mining is no longer permitted.

Logging in the lower elevations of the North Cascades was a significant economic factor during this period. Visitors to North Cascades Park and the Recreation Areas today, however, enjoy the sight of magnificent stands of old 230 foot tall Western red cedar and even taller Douglas fir because very little logging was done within the area now encompassed by the park complex. The rough terrain and problems of transporting logs discouraged lumber harvesting in remote areas.

However, today, commercial foresting is an active, ongoing activity within sight of the national park. Driving up the Cascade River Road on your way to see the moving glacier at Johannesburg Mountain or to hike the Cascade Pass trail, a visitor may be startled at the sight of a patch of clear-cut forest land on a western hillside. A roadside sign brings you face to face with the reality of twentieth century life, informing you that the logs from this patch are enough to build 1,000 homes.

The next and last wave of settlers before the creation of the park complex were the dam builders. In 1918, Seattle City Light started to build three dams on the Skagit River to serve the hydroelectric energy needs of Seattle. By the late 1940s, the company had built the Gorge Creek, Diablo, and Ross Lake dams and a railroad to facilitate dam building and access to company towns, Newhalem and Diablo. Both reservoirs created by Diablo and Ross dams are now within the Ross Lake National Recreation Area and additionally serve as recreation resources.

The North Cascades Complex: A Unique Entity.

In the 1950s and early 1960s, two major concerns, one national and one regional, led national park supporters to focus on the future of the North Cascades. Americans throughout the nation had more leisure time; there was growing interest in outdoor recreation; and many vacationers were eager to explore the country beyond their home territory. It was recognized that for the benefit of present and future generations the federal government should build more facilities in its already strained national parks, and also acquire more land for public outdoor recreation in all its forms.

Most of the North Cascades had been in federal ownership for over one hundred years. There were five national forests and one national park, Mt. Rainier, a national park since 1899. Although the Forest Service was setting aside land for camping and hiking in national forests, and also designating large sections of forest land for wilderness preservation, many hiking, conservation, and civic organizations worried about the future. They watched roads being built on virgin land for timber cutting purposes and they deplored the visual effect of vast patches of hillside, sometimes as large as twenty acres, denuded of giant, old-growth trees.

Washington's legislators tried to get Congress interested in the North Cascades as a potential national park site. Here was a vast area of unusually scenic forests, lakes, and rivers in close proximity to five major cities—Tacoma, Seattle, Everett, Bellingham, and Vancouver—and less than a day's drive from Oregon and California.

But while there were many proponents of a national park in the Cascades, there were others who feared the creation of a national park would adversely affect the local economy and would interfere with traditional hunting practices. A team was appointed to make a detailed study of the North Cascades' wide range of resources and the controversies surrounding the administration and use of them, and finally, to make recommendations to the President to guide the management of the federal lands within the Cascades. The team included representatives of the two federal agencies that had long-standing interests in the area but different missions: the National Park Service in the Department of the Interior, and the Forest Service in the Department of Agriculture. Also included were representatives of other federal and state agencies with a special interest in the resources of the area.

The ensuing report, made in 1965, was a masterpiece of reconciliation of all concerns. It made detailed recommendations in areas of special concern to wilderness advocates, active outdoor recreationists, timbering interests, and local residents. Most of the recommendations eventually were incorporated in principle in the law passed in 1968 creating a new type of national park administrative unit—the North Cascades Complex:

1. A new national park was created to preserve "majestic mountain scenery, snowfields, glaciers, and alpine meadows" in all their glory. Ninety-two percent of the park is now officially designated as wilderness area. The National Wilderness Act (1964) defined a wilderness area as one "where the earth and its community of life are untrammeled by man, where man is a visitor who does not remain." The land must "generally appear to have been affected primarily by the forces of nature, with the imprint of man's work substantially unnoticeable."

2. Two national recreation areas were created to provide outdoor recreation opportunities in glorious mountain, lake, and river settings for outdoor enthusiasts who may not want to engage in strenuous backpacking and mountain climbing. Convenient access would be provided to one of them by the building of an east-west highway through the park complex.

3. The hydroelectric power needs of Seattle would not be jeopardized because the interests of Seattle City Light, builder of the existing dams, would be protected.

4. Most of the area suitable and planned for lumbering and hunting was excluded and remained within the Forest Service jurisdiction.

5. The continued existence and preservation of two small, secluded communities within the boundaries of the new park complex would be facilitated by prohibiting the Secretary of the Interior from approving road construction that would alter the existing methods of access to them.

The administration of the park complex and adjacent forest lands, with their varied constituencies, requires the active cooperation and recognition of the interests of all parties involved—the National Park Service, the Forest Service, Seattle City Light, and the communitiy of Stehekin. It seems to be working.

How to Get to North Cascades National Park

There are three ways to reach the park and recreation areas—from the east, from the west, and from the north. The one you take depends on your destination or if you are just driving through. The main route through the park is Washington State Route 20, designated as the North Cascades Scenic Highway. It traverses the Ross Lake National Recreation Area, and provides easy access to the mid section of the park complex.

If driving west to east, take Interstate Highway 5 north from Seattle or Tacoma, or south from Bellingham to Burlington, then east on State Rte. 20. It is 45 miles to Marblemount from there. Marblemount is just west of the Ross Lake National Recreation Area boundary.

If approaching the park from the east, e.g., from Coulee Dam, take State Rte. 174 west, then State Rte. 17 north until it joins U.S. 97. Go south on U.S. 97. Just outside Pateros, take State Rte. 153 north to pick up State Rte. 20 at Twisp.

If your destination is Stehekin in Lake Chelan National Rec- •reation Area, keep traveling south on U.S. 97 to Chelan. Boat and plane transportation to Stehekin is available at Chelan. For information, contact Lake Chelan Boat Company and Chelan Airways.

If going to Stehekin after driving through the park west to east on Rte. 20, after passing through the town of Twisp, take State Route 153 to U.S. 97 and continue south to Chelan.

The only vehicle access to Ross Lake is a forty mile drive south on an unimproved road from Hope in British Columbia.

Write to the Washington State Transportation Department for a Washington State map to guide you on your journey.

There is no entrance fee to any of the units of the North Cascades Complex.

Why Go to the North Cascades National Park, Ross Lake and Lake Chelan National Recreation Areas?

► To see moving glaciers, snow-covered mountain peaks, and snow-streaked glacial valleys—even in mid-summer;

► To gaze up beyond the timberline to see 9,000 and 10,000 feet high rocky pinnacles silhouetted against a bright azure sky;

▸ To raft on the waters of a flowing river so clear you see every grain of sand below you;

▸ To ride a gentle horse up a steep mountain trail to a remote alpine lake, catching glimpses of deer and mountain goats along the way;

▸ To move in solitude on a forest trail among giant stands of craggy western red cedar ten feet in diameter, and along an icy blue rock-strewn stream, even if confined to a wheelchair;

▸ To boat and fish in a deep emerald-green lake.

There are many good reasons to go to the North Cascades. The park is so big and so varied that rewarding experiences await all types of vacationers, from travelers who enjoy looking at magnificent scenery from the comfort of their cars, to mountain climbers and backpacking campers.

Although some visitors regularly come to marvel at the vivid color of fall foliage against the dark green evergreen backdrop, or to cross-country ski in winter, visiting the park and recreation areas is primarily a summertime activity. Highway 20, the trans-park road, is usually closed from late October to the first of May because of heavy snowfall or avalanche hazards.

To get the full flavor of the North Cascades, plan to spend several days. Move about to enjoy the pleasures awaiting in all three units of the park complex or, if you prefer, concentrate on your favorite outdoor sport. But if time does not permit lingering, just driving from the dry, orchard-strewn hills on the east side of the mountain to the lush western side is still a memorable "Oh Wow!" experience.

Where to Stay

Non-Campers. Overnight accommodations within the park and recreation areas are very limited. Housekeeping cabins are available at two resorts, Diablo Lake Resort and Ross Lake Resort, both within Ross Lake National Recreation Area. Ross Lake Resort is on a floating deck on Ross Lake and you can reach it only by boat or on foot. Boats can be rented at both places by advance arrangement. Write directly to the resorts for details. There are a limited number of motels, inns, and cabins at various price ranges in towns along Route 20.

If you plan to stay overnight in Stehekin at the head of Lake Chelan you have a choice of accommodations. North Cascades Lodge, a park concessioner, is a short walk from the boat landing. It offers modern rooms, housekeeping units, and a restaurant, plus bicycle, boat, and car rentals.

The Stehekin Valley Ranch, nine miles up the valley from the boat landing, is a rustic complex nestled within a grove of maple trees. Sleeping accommodations are in canvas-roofed wooden cabins (no heat, no plumbing, no electricity). The cabins overlook an alfalfa field where horses graze and deer browse, and, in the distance, snow-covered mountains rise above tall Douglas fir trees. Meals are served in a central dining room. There are indoor showers and laundry facilities. Outhouses are discreetly located among the trees. Staying at Stehekin Valley Ranch is like camping without toting camping equipment or doing your own cooking. The ranch arranges for guided raft trips on the beautiful, clear Stehekin River, and horseback trips up the mountain to Coon Lake. Transportation is provided to hiking trails and to and from the boat landing.

Other options at Stehekin are bed and breakfast accommodations and housekeeping cabins.

Prices for overnight accommodations in Stehekin are in the expensive range.

A Park Service shuttle bus provides transportation along the Stehekin road to trailheads, primitive campgrounds, and scenic areas, including the majestic Rainbow Falls. This service is offered May 15 - October 15. Fare is $2 for each of the two zones one way. All lodgings are operated seasonally and may have repeat visitors. It is important, therefore, to book reservations as early as possible. Contact park headquarters for a listing of all facilities within or near the park.

Campers: Recreational Vehicles and Tent Camping. The North Cascades is a camper's paradise. The park complex, adjacent national forests, state and county campgrounds, and communities along Highway 20 provide such a range of camping options, that whether you camp in a recreational vehicle, trailer, or tent or prefer backcountry camping, you are sure to find a spot to suit your needs.

Park campgrounds accessible to vehicles are at Goodell Creek, Newhalem Creek, and Colonial Creek along Highway 20. There are over 300 sites in total. Most sites accommodate trailers.

Newhalem Creek and Colonial Creek campgrounds have flush toilets and trailer dump stations but no hookups. Goodell Creek is open year-round; Colonial Creek, from May through November; Newhalem, mid-June through Labor Day.

Hozomeen Campground at the north end of Ross Lake has vehicular access only from Canada. The campground has 122 campsites, accommodating tents and trailers. There are pit toilets. No trailer hookups or dump stations.

During the summer, modest fees are charged for the use of campsites at Goodell Creek, Newhalem Creek, and Colonial Creek Campgrounds. There are no fees at Hozomeen Campground. Rangers conduct campfire programs nightly at Colonial Creek Campground and on certain nights at Newhalem and Hozomeen Campgrounds. Rangers also lead nature walks and conduct interpretive programs at the Golden West Visitor Center in Stehekin.

Camping: Backpacking. Backcountry camping is permitted throughout the park and recreation areas and special regulations apply. Free permits are required both for backcountry camping and mountain climbing. For information, write to park headquarters.

Special information about campsites, including those suitable for persons with physical handicaps, may be obtained at the following places: park headquarters in Sedro Woolley, the joint Forest Service/Park Service information offices at Chelan and at Glacier, the Ross Lake NRA office at Marblemount, the joint park and Seattle City Light information station at Newhalem, the Lake Chelan NRA Golden West Visitor Center in Stehekin, and Forest Service offices at Washington Pass, Early Winters, Darrington, and Winthrop.

What to Do at North Cascades

A first-time visitor should stop at the first Park Service or Forest Service visitor or information center on his chosen route to the park. They are listed above. Most centers have exhibits, publications for sale, free information sheets on particular aspects of the park, and the park's newspaper, The *North Cascades Challenger,* which provides up-to-date information on park resources and activities. Here is a summary of the many things to do at North Cascades National Park and the Recreation Areas.

Take Scenic Drives and a Scenic Boat Trip. By approaching the park on Highway 20, North Cascades Scenic Highway, you have already begun your scenic driving. Keep on this route, stopping at Gorge Creek Falls and Diablo Lake and Ross Lake Overlooks for ever-changing spectacular vistas.

At Marblemount, take the Cascade River Road through the eastern end of Mt. Baker-Snoqualmie National Forest and the southwestern end of the national park. This is a gravel road, 22.3 miles long, terminating at a parking area at the Cascade Pass trailhead. From this point there are good views of Cascade Peak, moving glaciers, and the Cascade valley. Interpretive signs explain the features. There are picnic tables and rest rooms. Pause and listen for the distant boom of a moving glacier and the soft sound of far-off waterfalls. Take your camera to record the sight. If the view whets your appetite, hike the 3.7 mile trail to Cascade Pass where you will see more mountain peaks and glaciers.

A must for anyone who can spend at least a full day within the Lake Chelan National Recreation Area is the boat trip on Lake Chelan. The Lady of the Lake departs departs from Chelan at 8:30 a.m. and arrives at Stehekin Landing four hours later. This trip on the fjord-like lake waters is so replete with magnificent scenery, time passes quickly. There is a window-lined inside cabin where snacks are sold, but most people line the decks, binoculars and cameras in hand, scanning the mountainsides. The ship's captain alerts passengers to upcoming sights of wildlife and other attractions.

The boat makes two scheduled stops—at Field's Point to pick up additional passengers, and at Lucerne, where passengers disembark to visit a religious retreat or to begin backcountry hiking. Sometimes the boat makes additional stops to deliver mail, groceries, and other supplies to lakeside residents for whom the boat serves as their link to the world beyond.

There is a one and one-half hour layover in Stehekin, allowing time for lunch, a visit to the Golden West Visitor Center, and a walk through the community to visit shops and historic sites. Some people choose to take the boat one way and return by seaplane, providing views of the lake and surrounding countryside from a different perspective. Round trip cost of the boat trip is $21 for adults, $10.50 for children age six to eleven. Air taxi rates are $70 round trip. Flying one way and boating the other direction can be arranged at a total cost of $54. A faster boat, The Lady Express, also leaves at 8:30 a.m. but arrives at Stehekin at 10:30 a.m. The cost is considerably higher and reservations are recommended. For information, contact Lake Chelan Boat Company and Chelan Airways.

Hiking. Whether you enjoy a several-day backcountry trek in the alpine wilderness, a half-day hike along a clear mountain stream tumbling over the rocks, or a short walk into the woods from your car or campsite, there is ample opportunity for you to do what you like. The park maintains over 300 miles of trails, including a small piece of The Pacific Crest National Scenic Trail.

Among the information sheets describing trails are *Selected Long Hikes, Trails Accessed From North Cascades Highway, Diablo to Colonial Day Hikes, Day Hiking in Stehekin, and The Happy Creek Forest Walk.* The Happy Creek Walk is a boardwalk trail into an old-growth forest that is accessible to people in wheelchairs. Ask park representatives for the sheet of greatest interest to you.

Boating. Boating on North Cascades lakes and rivers is popular. Many people take their own boats to the park. There are launch ramps at Colonial Creek Campground and Diablo Lake Resort for Diablo Lake, at Hozomeen Campground for Ross Lake, and in the town of Diablo, for Gorge Lake. Many people enjoy river-running in rafts and kayaks in the upper Skagit River. There is a launch ramp for this purpose at Goodell Creek Campground. For information about rental of watercraft and about guided float trips, write to park headquarters.

Fishing. Both novice and experienced anglers fish in the lakes and streams of the park. Rainbow, Dolly Varden (Dolly Varden is one type of trout.), and brook trout are prime catches. Lake Chelan's bounty includes kokonee and chinook salmon, rainbow and cutthroat trout, and freshwater cod. A Washington State fishing license is required. To obtain a license and a copy of state fishing regulations, write to the Washington Wildlife Department. Licenses are also sold at local stores.

Hunting. Hunting, primarily for deer, is allowed in season in both Recreation Areas. It is strictly forbidden within the national park. It is important, therefore, for hunters to know park and recreation area boundaries. A Washington State hunting license is required. To obtain a license and a copy of regulations that apply, write to the Washington State Wildlife Department.

Horseback Riding. Riding a horse on woodland trails is another way to enjoy the remote areas of park and recreation areas. Whether you are a novice or an experienced rider, a guided trip can be arranged. For information on companies offering trips of a few hours or several-day pack trips, contact park headquarters.

Mountain Climbing. Climbing the rugged, rocky, snow-covered slopes of the North Cascades is a challenge to be faced only by the most experienced climbers. It is a hazardous endeavor. Climbers must be prepared for deep snow and ice on glacially-scoured mountainsides and the changeable weather of high elevations. Climbers are required to get a free permit and to register their intended route with a park ranger. Permits and climbing guidebooks are available at the Marblemount Ranger Station and the Golden West Visitor Center.

Visit Historic Sites. Forty-nine sites and structures associated with explorers, settlers, and early commercial ventures within the boundaries of the North Cascades Complex are listed on the National Register of Historic Places. Most of these accessible to non-backpacking visitors are in Stehekin: the Buckner Homestead and orchard, the Golden West Lodge (one of the original tourist facilities, now adapted for use as a park visitor center), the one-room log schoolhouse (only recently replaced as a center of elementary school education by a new building), several cabins built by the earliest Stehekin residents, and the Black Warrior Mine. Rangers conduct a guided walk to the Buckner home, outbuildings, and apple orchard during afternoon hours in the summer.

Other historic properties include seasonal backcountry shelters, three fire lookouts, and Devil's Corner, a suspended walkway along the Skagit River. If you would like to visit any of the historic places, check at a visitor center or ranger station for accessibility and directions.

NOTE: *All vehicles, including trail bikes, must be driven only on established roads. There is no off-road driving. Pets on a leash are permitted in the recreation areas and along the Pacific Crest Trail, except in posted areas. Within the national park, pets are allowed on access roads and in parking areas where they also must be on a leash. Firearms are allowed under certain conditions. Check with park* rangers for details. *Most park information offices, several trails, overlooks, campsites, and the Diablo Lake Resort are accessible to physically handicapped persons. For a detailed list, write to park headquarters.*

If You Have the Time.

▶ Take the tour of the Diablo Lake and Ross Dam hydroelectric facilities, sponsored by Seattle City Light. The tour includes a cruise on Diablo Lake and a ride in the historic Incline Railway. There is a fee for the tour. Contact Seattle City Light for information and reservations.

▶ Spend some time in Chelan, a tourist-oriented city at the southern end of Lake Chelan. Visit the waterfront park and the Lake Chelan Museum and drive along the lakeside.

▶ Stop in Newhalem and see gleaming Old Engine Number 6, the historic Seattle City Light locomotive used to haul supplies to build the dams.

▶ Browse through the craft shops in Stehekin and stop and chat with local residents about what it is like to live year-round in a remote, scenic community with no vehicular access from the outside world. (Seventy people do!).

Tips for Adding to Your Enjoyment of the North Cascades.

1. Send early to park headquarters for a park brochure, information of special interest to you, e.g. regulations on backcountry hiking, boating, mountain climbing, and a list of lodging possibilities within the park complex and in nearby communities.

2. If you plan to stay in Chelan, write to Lake Chelan Chamber of Commerce for motel information.

3. Take binoculars, camera, and a first-aid kit with you. Commercial services and medical facilities are far apart.

4. If you would like to read more about the North Cascades before you go, or to study trail maps, send to park headquarters for a copy of the catalog of books and maps offered for sale by Pacific Northwest National Parks and Forest Association, the park's cooperating association.

And finally—Prepare to slow the pace of your usual pattern of living and absorb the marvelous sights and tantalizing sounds Nature has blessed this land with. This will be a vacation you will long remember!

Sources of Information

Superintendent
North Cascades National Park
2105 Highway 20
Sedro Woolley, WA 98284-1799
Phone: 206-856-5700

Diablo Lake Resort
Box 176
Rockport, WA 98283
Phone: 206-386-4429

Ross Lake Resort
Rockport, WA 98283
Phone: 206-386-4437

Lake Chelan Chamber of Commerce
Box 216
Chelan, WA 98816
Phone: 800-4CHELAN (WA residents only) or 509-682-3503

Lake Chelan Boat Company
Box 186
Chelan, WA 98816
Phone: 509-682-4584

Chelan Airways
Box W
Chelan, WA 98816
Phone: 509-682-5555

North Cascades Lodge
Box 1779
Chelan, WA 98816
Phone: 509-682-4711

Stehekin Valley Ranch
Box 36
Stehekin, WA 98852
Phone: 509-682-4677

Department of Wildlife
State of Washington
600 Capitol Way North
Olympia, WA 98504
Phone: 206-753-5700

Public Affairs Office
Washington State Department of Transportation
Transportation Building KF-01
Olympia, WA 98504-5201
Phone: 206-753-2150

Seattle City Light, Skagit Tour Desk
1015 Third Avenue
Seattle, WA 98104-1198
Phone: 206-684-3030

"Keep these bits of primitive America for those who seek peace and rest; keep them for the hardy climbers of the crags and peaks; keep them for the horseman and the pack train; keep them for the scientist and student of nature; keep them for all who would use their minds and hearts to know what God had created ... "

—Statement made by Horace M. Albright to National
Park Service personnel upon his resignation as
Director of the National Park Service, 1933

SLEEPING BEAR DUNES
NATIONAL LAKESHORE

Long ago, in the land that today is Wisconsin, a mother bear and her two cubs were driven into Lake Michigan by a raging forest fire. They swam and swam, but soon the cubs tired and lagged far behind. Mother bear finally reached the opposite shore and climbed to the top of a bluff to watch and wait for her offspring. But the cubs became exhausted and drowned. Faithfully, the mother kept her vigil. When she, too, died, the Great Spirit Manitou marked the spot with a solitary forested dune overlooking Lake Michigan, and where the cubs drowned, created the two Manitou Islands.

—Chippewa Indian legend

Today, it takes a bit of imagination to see the form of a gigantic sleeping bear in the outline of Sleeping Bear Dune. As recently as the turn-of-the-century, however, its resemblance to a shaggy, curled up bear was striking. Since that time the dynamics of wind and wave have reshaped the dune and continue to do so. Sleeping Bear currently is two-thirds of its height in 1900, has lost much of its cover of trees and shrubs, and is rapidly drifting into oblivion as an independent dune.

Sleeping Bear country, like much of Lake Michigan's eastern shore, is sand country, thanks to the abundant supply of mixed sand, gravel, silt, and rocks left by the glaciers that for at least a million years waxed and waned over the land. Along the shoreline and back about a mile from the lake, the combination of onshore prevailing winds and powerful wave action sorts this glacial drift into three components. The silt and clay, fine and light-weight, blow high in the air and dissipate over a wide area. The gravel and rocks are moved little if at all. Sand particles, however, are fine enough to blow and bounce along the surface, coming to rest in and building sand dunes.

Some of these dunes rise hundreds of feet from the water's edge to ridges parallel with the shore extending thousands of feet along the water. Some perch like scattered drifts of snow over the high headlands and tablelands deposited by the glacier. Many are in never-ending motion, with the wind constantly rearranging them, sculpting, increasing, diminishing, destroying—a ceaseless interplay of sand, grasses, and shrubs.

Constant change has been the lot of the Great Lakes area. The glacial period with its massive lobes of ice bulldozed what had been broad, low, river valleys into deep basins that each period of glacial retreat filled with huge lakes of melt-water. Geologists believe that among the many prehistoric episodes were three distinct stages of particular importance to the creation of today's Sleeping Bear area.

Each stage is called by the name given by geologists to the lake they believe dominated at the time.

► Lake Algonquin. At this stage, about 11,000 years ago, the conformation of today's Great Lakes had already been roughed out. Glaciers still covered most of today's Lake Superior and prevented melt water from draining to the north. Drainage water, augmented by the melting glacier, built up before the ice front and flowed to the south and to the sea. The level of the water at this time was 605 feet above the sea.

► Lake Chippewa. In this stage, about 9,500 years ago, glacial melting had opened lower level outlets to the north and the water fell to 230 feet above sea level. The Manitou Islands at this stage were connected to the mainland.

► Lake Nipissing. With the removal of the weight of glacial ice, the earth's crust to the north rebounded upward, raising the elevation of the northern drainage channels until water level returned to 605 feet above sea level and began to drain again through the south outlets. Today, the water level in Lake Michigan is at 580 feet above sea level.

Lake Michigan is vast. Like ocean waters, the lake, at times, is treacherous; at times, serene and beautiful. Anyone who spends time on its waters or along its shores cannot fail to be fascinated with this fresh-water sea. The Sleeping Bear Dunes National

Lakeshore includes a sixty mile stretch of shoreline of northeastern Lake Michigan and two of its islands, and several inland lakes, once a part of Lake Michigan. The National Park Service, which administers the lakeshore, has been charged with the responsibility of preserving the waters and lands of this part of Lake Michigan in their natural setting, and protecting them "from development and uses which would destroy the scenic beauty and natural character of the area."

The lakeshore's coastline runs from Good Harbor Bay on the north to three miles south of the Platte River. Its borders are split at two points by the towns of Glen Arbor and Empire. A portion of the lakeshore borders Glen Lake. North Manitou Island and South Manitou Island, historically important landmarks several miles offshore, are part of the lakeshore.

The lakeshore's authorized boundaries include a strip of land in Benzie County between State Route 22 and U.S. Route 31 over which an automobile corridor overlooking Crystal Lake on the south and Platte Lake on the north has been proposed. The land is now privately owned and it will probably be several years before the future use of the land will be determined.

Flora and Fauna of Sleeping Bear Dunes National Lakeshore

Bayfront areas of Sleeping Bear country have vegetation typical of a sand dune dominated environment. There are four distinct zones paralleling the shore front, reminiscent of the plant succession occurring along our seacoasts.

The Beach Zone supports few plants in its wave pounded, sun baked sands. It is, however, the source of sand for the next plant community.

The Dune Zone with its hot sun, strong winds, and shifting sands nurtures a community of plants that thrives in these conditions. Beach grass, sand cherry, sandreed, wormwood, and beach pea are found here. The plants begin to change these conditions, casting shade, slowing the movement of sand, and enriching the soil.

The Shrub Zone is really a belt of older dunes farther inland. Here, more distant from the lake, the wind slackens, and shrubs such as common juniper, bearberry, buffaloberry, and sand cherry prosper in the improved growing conditions created by the dune plants that preceded them. They continue the change toward shadier, richer, and more stable growing conditions.

The Pine-Oak Forest lies inland from the other three zones and was, successively, a beach, a dune, and a shrub zone. It is open woodland. This community seems to be stable over the short term, but there is evidence that it may eventually yield to the beech/maple forest.

The climax woodland of the lakeshore is the beech/maple forest, which frequently includes black cherry, red oak, and white ash. Inland ponds and lakes support aquatic and swamp plants.

The varied habitats of the Sleeping Bear Dunes area support a diverse population of wildlife. White-tailed deer and an occasional black bear are the only large mammals of the 48 species resident in the park. Racoon, porcupine, and rabbits are common species in most areas of the lakeshore, as are fox, squirrels, and mink. Seventeen species of amphibians, fifteen of reptiles, and 76 species of fish occur in the park.

Bird life numbers around 264 species. Frequenting the plateau and dune areas are vesper sparrows, horned larks, the ubiquitous goldfinch, and the marsh hawk (northern harrier). Red-eyed vireo, redstart, and ovenbird frequent the hardwood forests. On the lake and in the marshes and swamps, shorebirds, grebes, herons, ducks, and loons can be seen. Pine grosbeaks, chickadees, crossbills, and pine siskins are winter park residents. Bald eagles, a threatened species, and peregrine falcons, an endangered species, are reported occasionally in the Sleeping Bear area.

The People of Sleeping Bear Country

Lake Michigan and its climatic effect on the land adjacent to it has drawn waves of people to its waters, islands, and shores for thousands of years. Probably as long as 10,000 years ago, ancient people traveled through land now inundated by the waters of Lake Michigan. Finding artifacts and other evidence submerged in water hundreds of feet deep is a very difficult task. Research continues and, undoubtedly, more will be known in the future.

Archeologists do know that by 2000 B.C. a favorable lakeshore environment attracted prehistoric natives to Sleeping Bear country to hunt deer in the fall and winter, and smaller animals in the summer. They also fished in Platte Lake, Glen Lake, and Crystal Lake, which were then shallow bays of Lake Michigan. There is evidence people were living on South and North Manitou Islands at that time, although when white men arrived, natives had a special reverence for the islands as the embodiment of the Great Spirit, and it was thought that the Indians chose not to go there.

French explorers were the first white men to visit Lake Michigan, beginning in the early 1600s. During that period, Indians of the Ottawa and Chippewa tribes were periodically visiting Sleeping Bear country to hunt and collect maple sap and wild rice. They had many legends to explain awesome natural phenomena including various versions of the well-known story about the "Bear Lying Down."

The French learned much from the natives. Indians helped them adapt to Great Lakes country, teaching them the value of corn, birchbark canoes, and the trails they had made. By the 1700s, the French were familiar with the Sleeping Bear landmark, calling it "L'ours qui dort."

French explorers paved the way for fur trappers and traders, French, English, and Americans, who came seeking the smaller fur-bearing animals of north Michigan's woodlands. By the mid 1800s, this wave of entrepreneurs had pushed on to more productive territory, and the next influx of people had begun.

The American frontier was pushing westward, and commercial ships were plying the Great Lakes, carrying goods to fill the needs of cities and towns springing up in the mid-west. Lake Michigan became a major artery, and the favored route was through the Manitou Passage between the islands and the shore. All of the Great Lakes can be treacherous, especially when high winds churn the cold water, fog eliminates visibility, and the passage between shallow waters is narrow. South Manitou Island offered the only harbor of refuge from Mackinac Straits to the north and the city of Chicago at the southern end of the lake.

Lighthouses and life-saving stations were built on the Manitou Islands and at Sleeping Bear Point to guide the ships through the Passage and rescue those that came to grief. And many did. At least fifty shipwrecks have been identified. The lighthouse and lifesaving station at South Manitou Island and the lifesaving station (later becoming the Coast Guard station) at Sleeping Bear Point have been preserved and are important stops for lakeshore visitors who want to fully comprehend the essence of Sleeping Bear country's past.

Wood-burning steamships needed replenishment of their fuel, and the forests of the islands and nearby mainland offered a ready supply. Cordwood docks were built on South Manitou Island first, then on North Manitou Island and on the mainland near Sleeping Bear Point. Communities like Glen Haven built up near the sawmills; and lumbering became the leading economic activity of Sleeping Bear country in the late 1800s and early 1900s.

When the area was logged off, people turned to farming. The climate along the eastern shore of Lake Michigan is ideally suited for fruit growing, especially cherries, with milder winters and a longer fall growing season than farther inland. Even today, this is the prime agricultural activity of the area, as visitors can readily see when they travel the roads through the lakeshore and see acre after acre of fruit orchards.

Buildings associated with life in earlier times are visible today at the village of Glen Haven and the historic D. H. Day farm.

Like it did for the Indians of a century or more ago, Sleeping Bear country still has seasonal appeal. Tourists discovered the pleasures of relaxing and enjoying the summer breezes, white sand beaches, and lake waters early in the 1900s, and many bought vacation homes bordering the lakes. The practice continues to this day. Some of these houses are within the borders of the National Lakeshore and, with certain restrictions, they continue in private ownership.

But when did the nation decide to set aside and save a significant portion of Sleeping Bear country for the benefit of all its citizens? That action was taken as a result of a survey Congress instructed the National Park Service to make in the 1950s. The fifties were a decade when the nation became very much aware of the need to acquire, preserve, and in some cases, develop for recreational purposes, more of its land and water resources while they were still salvageable.

Following a study of the U.S. side of the Great Lakes, the National Park Service reported that certain islands and lake shore-fronts merited special protection. Two national lakeshores were created in 1966: Pictured Rocks, on the southern shore of Lake Superior, and Indiana Dunes, on the southeastern shore of Lake Michigan. Senator Philip A. Hart led the forces pushing legislation to establish a national lakeshore surrounding the unique Sleeping Bear Dune. There was considerable opposition among many va-cation home owners in the area, but finally in 1970, the law creating Sleeping Bear Dunes National Lakeshore was enacted.

Why Go to Sleeping Bear Dunes National Lakeshore?

▸ To see a unique American landscape where huge sand dunes have been coursing over the land for thousands of years;

▸ To relax, swim, or picnic at an uncrowded "sugar sand" beach and scan the horizon for passing ships;

▸ To walk on a lakeshore beach, head down, searching for a Petoskey stone, a fascinating marine fossil with a distinct hexagonal pattern, originally formed in a coral reef over 300 million years ago;

▸ To hike alone under the dense shade of a beech-maple forest—or traverse a moving sand dune to view a "ghost forest"—or walk a quiet island path to the "Valley of the Giants," the name given to a grove of virgin white cedar trees more than ninety feet tall;

▸ To test your physical fitness by climbing a 130 foot high sand dune; then, feeling like the King of the Mountain, crossing the rolling dunes for a sweeping view of Lake Michigan, the islands, and many miles of shoreline;

▸ To hoist camping gear and supplies on your back and spend a few days in the wilderness of an almost deserted island;

▸ To canoe, kayak, or float on the gentle, shallow waters of a tree-lined river;

▸ And, in winter, to cross-country ski through a red and white pine forest, a gently curving meadow, or a steep downhill path.

Whether you seek a relaxing or a physically challenging experience on your vacation, you will find that Sleeping Bear Dunes National Lakeshore has much to offer.

How to Get to Sleeping Bear Dunes National Lakeshore

Empire, where Lakeshore headquarters and the park's main visitor center are located, is in the northwestern portion of Michigan's Lower Peninsula and very much off the beaten path. The main north-south roads nearest to the lakeshore are U.S. 131 from Grand Rapids, and U.S. 31, which roughly parallels the Lake Michigan shoreline for a considerable distance. Roads that lead to State Route 22, the main road through the lakeshore, are State Route 72 west from U.S. 31 at Traverse City, and State Route 115 west from U.S. 31 at Benzonia. Write to the Michigan Travel Bureau for a Michigan State map and other information useful for traveling through the state .

There is no entrance fee at the National Lakeshore.

Where to Stay

Non-Campers. Vacationers have been going to the Sleeping Bear area for many, many years, and the communities around the lakeshore are well-prepared to accommodate visitors in the summer. Most motels, resorts, and rental cottages are operated seasonally, but a few are open during the height of the winter season to provide for cross-country and downhill skiers. One resort, a condominium, specializes in lodgings for wintertime guests. For information on overnight accommodations, write to the Empire Business Association, the Glen Lake-Sleeping Bear Chamber of Commerce, the Benzie County Chamber of Commerce, and the Leelanau County Chamber of Commerce. If you plan to visit Sleeping Bear Dunes National Lakeshore out of season, be sure to specify that you need information about places that are open year-round.

There is a wide range of restaurants, but many are open only in the summer. There is even a restaurant in Empire that appeals to bird lovers. Just outside the dining room window, well-stocked bird feeders are constantly patronized by a great variety of birds, including hummingbirds.

Campers—Recreational Vehicles and Tents. The National Lakeshore maintains two campgrounds. The D. H. Day Campground, bordering Lake Michigan, is two miles west of Glen Arbor on State Road 109. The campground has water but no hookups. It is open year-round. There is a $6 per night campsite fee. Campsites are available on a first come, first served basis, except group campsites which must be reserved in advance. Park rangers frequently conduct programs at campgrounds during the summer.

The Platte River Campground, located in a wooded area near the Platte River, 11 miles south of Empire, is currently undergoing a complete renovation. When completed it will have all new facilities, including an amphitheater, flush toilets, and water and electric hookups for trailers and recreational vehicles. It will also have areas restricted to tent camping and remote walk-in sites. Visitors interested in staying at Platte River Campground, which is convenient for fishing and canoeing in the river, should check with Lakeshore headquarters in advance to see if renovation is completed and the campground is open.

There are many private and Michigan State campgrounds in the vicinity of the lakeshore. Some of them take reservations, including the KOA campground on National Lakeshore property, which provides full hookups. When the renovated Platte River Campground is reopened, the KOA Campground will be removed. For a list of campgrounds within the Sleeping Bear area, write to lakeshore headquarters.

Campers—Backcountry. Walk-in camping is permitted at certain designated campsites on the mainland and on North and South Manitou Islands. Free permits are required. They can be obtained at the visitor center in Empire, at the D. H. Day and Platte River Campgrounds, and at ranger stations on the islands.

What to Do at Sleeping Bear Dunes National Lakeshore

Summer is the ideal time to go to Sleeping Bear Dunes National Lakeshore. Temperatures range from the seventies to the nineties, June through August, rain is infrequent, and opportunities for enjoying Nature's bounty are many. Sleeping Bear Dunes has its fall and winter partisans, however. Fishermen come in the fall seeking to catch coho and king salmon, and cross-country skiing is popular in mid-winter.

On your first visit to the lakeshore, stop at the Philip A. Hart Visitor Center on State Route 72 in Empire. It is open daily from 9 a.m. to 6 p.m. in July and August, for shorter periods at other times. It is closed on Thanksgiving and Christmas. Exhibits explain the centuries-long natural phenomena that led to the present state of Lake Michigan, the dunes, and the forests of northern Michigan. There are also displays of goods, tools, and crafts associated with the lives of the people who have lived and worked in Sleeping Bear country in the past one hundred years. The Center shows movies about the Great Lakes and an outstanding orientation slide program. A variety of publications, postcards, etc. are offered for sale.

Be sure to check out the Ranger-conducted programs offered daily in July and August, such as reenactments of a turn-of-the-century shipwreck rescue (in which visiting children play a role), Junior Ranger programs, and bird, wildflower, and dune walks. Participating in some of these programs adds immensely to the enjoyment of your visit to the lakeshore.

The Pierce Stocking Scenic Drive. Named for a lumberman who so loved the woods, dunes, and lakeviews of Sleeping Bear country that he wanted to share it with others, this road was originally built by Pierce Stocking. The 7.4-mile drive is a must for visitors to Sleeping Bear country. A self-guiding brochure explains what you are viewing at each of the twelve stops, including a covered bridge, Glen Lake, a beech-maple forest, Sleeping Bear Dune, and Lake Michigan. Take your time, enjoy the scenery, and absorb the natural surroundings. You may want to take a picnic lunch with you. There are two picnic areas. The 1.5-mile Cottonwood Trail originates from one of the parking areas.

Hiking. The most obvious, dramatic, and probably the most strenuous hike at the lakeshore—a mecca for lovers of sand dunes—is the Dune Climb Trail. Beginning at the Dune Climb parking lot, hikers climb through loose sand 130 feet to the top, then travel 1.5 miles along open, rolling dunes, and graveled surfaces laid down by glaciers at least 11,000 years ago, to Lake Michigan. Advice on how to prepare for this hike is given in a brochure available at the visitor center in Empire.

Beach-goers accustomed to warnings about the damage to the natural build-up of stabilizing vegetation that is caused when people tramp on sand dunes may be suprised to learn that climbing this dune is permitted. The Park Service explains that this policy is based on recognition that dune climbing is traditional at this location. It is hoped that by concentrating this activity at this one place, there will be less impact on other parts of the dunes. At other sand-built hillsides where vegetation has begun to hold the sand in relative stability, visitors are cautioned not to disturb the dune grass.

Less-hardy souls will enjoy picnicking near the parking lot, and watching the antics of people coming back down the face of the dune. At times a ranger is there to show you a scale model of the dune system.

There are trail maps for many other maintained, mainland lakeshore trails, e.g. the Alligator Hill, Old Indian, Pyramid Point, and Empire Bluff Trails. The Pyramid Point Trail ends at a high overlook of Lake Michigan that is a popular launch site for experienced hang gliders. Mainland trails vary in length from three-quarters of a mile to thirteen miles. Some of the trails on the Manitou Islands are longer and more rugged. Brochures are also available to guide cross-country skiers on the several trails maintained in winter for their enjoyment.

Beach-Going. Beach-loving visitors head for the shores of Lake Michigan to relax, picnic, and stroll the beach. Two roads from Route 22, Esch Road and Lake Michigan Road near the Platte River, provide easy access to the lake. You can also get to the lake at the public beach in Empire, at North Bar Lake Road, at the Maritime Museum, and at the Cannery in Glen Haven. Some people prefer to swim at Glen Lake where the water is warmer.

Visit South and North Manitou Islands. A park concessioner offers day-long trips to South Manitou Island from a dock in the town of Leland, a few miles northeast of the lakeshore's northern boundary. Round trip rates are $14 for adults, $10 for children; $16 for adults and $12 for children with camping gear. The trip crosses the waters of the Manitou Passage, taking one and one-half hours each way. Reservations are necessary. The boat runs daily in June, July, and August; five days a week in May, September, and through Columbus Day weekend in October.

Snacks are available on the boat, but there is no food service on the island, so take your lunch with you. There are picnic tables near the docking area. Once there, you can join one of the guided tours in an open-air vehicle, or hike on trails. Fees for the vehicle tours are $5 for adults and $2 for children. If you prefer to explore on your own, a map will show you the various trails—to the Valley of the Giants, a stand of large white cedar trees including the "national champion," an overlook of a shipwreck, historic buildings, the lighthouse, and the visitor center.

Backcountry campers must register if they plan to stay in one of the three campgrounds.

Boat trips to North Manitou Island run during the same months but less frequently. These trips are for campers only, since after discharging passengers the boat immediately heads back to Leland. Special rates and schedules apply during hunting season in the fall. For details, contact Manitou Island Transit.

Canoe on Quiet Rivers. Canoes, kayaks, and floating tubes may be rented on the Platte River in the southern section of the lakeshore. The river flows gently in its lower reaches, taking approximately two hours to reach Lake Michigan. More adventurous canoeists may prefer a longer, faster trip in the upper reaches of the river. Reservations for canoe trips are recommended. Rentals are also available on the Crystal River at the northern end of the park.

Fishing. Fishing for trout, pike, bass, and salmon is the preferred activity of many park visitors. Area stores sell the required Michigan State fishing license.

Hunting. Hunting for deer, rabbit, squirrel, ruffed grouse, and waterfowl is permitted in season, except in the vicinity of Pierce Stocking Scenic Drive. Both firearms and bow hunting are allowed. Michigan state hunting regulations apply. Sporting goods stores in the area sell hunting licenses.

Visit Historic Sites. A visit to the Sleeping Bear Point Coast Guard Station Maritime Museum located beyond the end of State Route 209, just west of Glen Haven, is a lively, visual Great Lakes history lesson. The building, originally a lifesaving station, was moved one-half mile from its first location at Sleeping Bear Point to its present site in 1931. Drifting sands threatened to bury some of the buildings of the station complex, and high surf sometimes made launching rescue boats difficult. The main building and boathouse contain exhibits depicting a surfman's life and work, and equipment used by the Great Lakes lifesavers. Every afternoon during July and August, rangers demonstrate rescue operations.

On South Manitou Island, visitors may walk to the lighthouse and other historic sites. North Manitou Island campers may hike past abandoned buildings associated with the small settlement that once existed there.

NOTE. *There is no off-road driving at the lakeshore. Pets may be taken to the lakeshore if they are on a leash, but they may not go on the Dune Climb, Glen Lake Beach, or the Manitou Islands. Parking and restrooms are equipped for the physically handicapped in some locations, e.g. the visitor center in Empire, the Maritime Museum, and the Pierce Stocking Scenic Drive stops. Each of the two lakeshore campgrounds has one site suitable for the handicapped. Advance arrangements can be made to accommodate persons with disabilities on the boat trip and the auto tour of South Manitou Island. There are other special provisions for persons with hearing or visual impairments. For details on all these provisions, write to lakeshore headquarters for the brochure, **Park Facilities Accessible to the Disabled.***

If You Have the Time

  ► Visit the Empire Historical Museum and Country School. The museum features exhibits recreating the life of Empire residents at the turn-of-the-century and offers for sale reproductions of old Christmas items and toys.

  ► Browse through the galleries, craft, and antique shops in Glen Arbor and Leland.

  ► Drive to Traverse City, 23 miles east of the lakeshore, and visit the floating Maritime Museum on the "Madeleine," a replica of a mid-nineteenth century Great Lakes schooner. For information, contact the Maritime Heritage Alliance.

  ► If you are an experienced skin diver or SCUBA diver, contact the Maritime Bottomland Preserve Committee for information about diving to see the shipwrecks and natural underwater features in the Manitou Passage.

Tips for Adding to Your Enjoyment of Sleeping Bear Dunes National Lakeshore

1. Send to lakeshore headquarters for a park brochure and information of special interest to you, e.g., brochures on hiking or cross-country ski trails, park facilities accessible to the disabled, or campgrounds in the Sleeping Bear Dunes area.

2. Decide early where you want to stay overnight and write to the appropriate Chamber of Commerce or Business Association for information on motels and other types of lodging.

3. If you would like to read more about the history or the natural resources of Sleeping Bear country before you go there, send to park headquarters for a catalog of publications and maps offered for sale by the Eastern National Park and Monument Association, the lakeshore's cooperating associatiion.

4. Send to the Michigan Travel Bureau for a Michigan State map and other travel information.

5. If you would like detailed information about the boat trip to South or North Manitou Islands, renting watercraft on the Platte or Crystal Rivers, or diving in the Manitou Passage, write to Manitou Island Transit, Riverside Canoe Trips, Crystal River Canoe Livery, or Maritime Bottomland Preserve Committee, respectively.

6. Take your camera and binoculars with you.

And finally—As the nomadic Indian, the French explorer, the burly logger, and the courageous life-saving boatman did before you, stand on a high bluff overlooking Lake Michigan, drink in the fresh air, savor the far-reaching maritime scene, and relish the ever-changing natural wonders wrought by the Great Spirit.

Sources of Information

Superintendent
Sleeping Bear Dunes National
Lakeshore
Box 277
Empire, MI 49630
Phone: 616-326-5134

Glen Lake-Sleeping Bear
Chamber of Commerce
Box 217
Glen Arbor, MI 49636
Phone: 616-334-3238

Empire Business Association
Box 65
Empire, MI 49630
Phone: 616-326-5337
616-326-5181

Benzie County Chamber of
Commerce
Box 505
Beulah, MI 49617
Phone: 616-882-5802

Lelanau County Chamber of
Commerce
Box 627
Leland, MI 49654
Phone: 616-256-9895

Michigan Travel Bureau
Michigan Department of Commerce
Box 30226
Lansing, MI 48909
Phone: 800-5432-YES

Crystal River Canoe Livery
Box 133
Glen Arbor, MI 49636
Phone: 616-334-3090 or
616-334 -3831

KOA Kampground
M-22 at Platte River
Box 234A
Honor, MI 49640
Phone: 616-882-4723

Manitou Island Transit
Box 591
Leland, MI 49654
Phone: 616-256-9061
or: 616-271-4217

Maritime Heritage Alliance
Box 1108
Traverse City, MI 49685-1108
Phone: 616-941-5577

Manitou Bottomland Preserve
Committee
Northwest Michigan Maritime
Museum
Box 389
Frankfort, MI 49635
Phone: 616-352-7251

Riverside Canoe Trips
M-22 at Platte River
Honor, MI 49640
Phone: 616-325-5622

PICTURED ROCKS
NATIONAL LAKESHORE

Ye who love the haunts of Nature,
Love the sunshine of the meadow,
Love the shadow of the forest,
Love the wind among the branches,
And the rain-shower and the snow-storm,
And the rushing of great rivers
Through their palisades of pine-trees,
And the thunder in the mountains,
Whose innumerable echoes
Flap like eagles in their eyries;—
Listen to these wild traditions,
To this Song of Hiawatha!
                    —From Longfellow's ***The Song of Hiawatha***

Things are different, now, in the land of Hiawatha. Today it is called Pictured Rocks National Lakeshore. The hand of the white man caused many changes—traps and bullets decimated the game animals; the axe harvested the dark forests; the steamship, the train, the automobile, and the aircraft relegated the birch canoe and the Indian trail to their place in history.

But the white man's changes are really shallow; game is regenerating, forests are renewing, and the mechanics of civilization are being tempered by a growing appreciation of nature, and the joys and satisfactions of being a part of the ecological as well as the social scene.

The land has changed little. Hiawatha's Gitche Gumee, the Big-Sea-Water, is now called Lake Superior, but it still rules the land around it, exacting its toll of men and the vessels that challenge it. The brilliant-colored pictured rocks are today the rocky doorways and deep abysses in which Hiawatha's dastardly adversary, Pau-Puk-Keewis, took refuge only to be slaughtered by the lightning (Waywassimo) and Hiawatha's magic mittens (Minjekahwun).

And today's Grand Sable, or great dunes, stretching for miles along the south shore of Lake Superior, are little changed from legendary times when they were heaped there by the whirlwind dancing at Hiawatha's wedding to Minnehaha.

This land is fraught with history. This is the so-called upper peninsula of the state of Michigan. Historically, it was by-passed during the early development of the United States, but this country was rediscovered in the mid 1800s, and became a residual area of exploitation of its natural resources.

Pictured Rocks National Lakeshore lies on the southeastern shore of Lake Superior between the communities of Munising and Grand Marais, Michigan. Some forty miles long, the lakeshore is a shorefront strip of federal park land up to three miles wide. Also part of the lakeshore, a buffer zone created to control activities incompatible with the park's natural setting runs along the landward side of this shorefront strip.

The shorefront includes three distinctive areas, each having its own characteristic scenery, geologic masterpieces, and intriguing history. Back from the shorefront are deep woods, extensive basins and lakes, and miles of trails for hiking, camping, and in winter, skiing, snowshoeing, and snowmobiling.

The Pictured Rocks escarpment is the centerpiece of the lakeshore, the feature that gives the park its name. It extends eastward from near Munising along the shorefront about fourteen miles. It is a vertical cliff fifty to 200 feet high rising out of the waters of Lake Superior. An exposed face of ancient layered sandstone, the escarpment is a marvelous array of turreted castles, arches, caves, and architectural imagery formed by the relentless carving of the lake's waves in the varying hardness of the sandstone layers. It is, however, the color that is so fascinating and gives the formation its name. Vibrant colors are splashed across the lakefront face like paints from an artist's palette. Dazzling streaks, patches, and swaths of reds, browns, greens, and yellows are interspersed with veining of slate blue and deep red and white mottlings. The imagination readily finds a variety of pictures and images.

Two or three miles northeast of Grand Portal Point, and about one-third of the way along the park's shoreline, Pictured Rocks escarpment turns inland and is lost to sight in the surrounding terrain. The shoreline beyond becomes a long stretch of beach,

Twelvemile Beach. Here, another vista unfolds—a vast sweep of white sand and pebbles where hikers can experience solitude and the allure of ever-new beach surfaces. Inland from the beach is Beaver Basin, where expiring glaciers carved a wide melt-water channel that became dry land as the level of Lake Superior dropped to its present level. Dry land that is, except for extensive wetlands and the Beaver Lakes that remain today, a focus for hiking and camping in a delightful, forested habitat in any season, and a "winter wonderland" when the snow is on the ground.

Beyond Twelvemile Beach and reaching to the end of the park are the Grand Sable Banks and Dunes. Unlike the Pictured Rocks escarpment, the banks and dunes were formed by the glaciers. Here the banks rising out of Superior consist of glacial outwash, gravels and sands deposited in a crevasse as the ice carrying them melted along this line. Here are sand dunes, called "perched" dunes by geologists for their location atop the banks. Consisting of sand moved inland by prevailing winds and finer particles blown from the underlying banks, the dunes have been reworked by the wind into U-shaped configurations. The sand dunes on top of the gravel banks form the Grand Sable Banks and Dunes, reaching over 300 feet above the level of the lake's surface.

The varied habitats provide a wide range of species of plant, animal, and bird life. Trees in Pictured Rocks National Lakeshore represent a transition between northern beech-maple hardwoods and the boreal, or spruce-fir forest. Birch, aspen, and mountain ash abound in patches and groves, with white pine and hemlock, and, in some locations, red pine, spruce, tamarack, and white cedar giving the feeling of the "northwoods."

About sixty species of wild flowers have been identified in the park. Many are the ordinary garden-variety plants such as skunk cabbage and violets, but some are the more deep woods species such as wakerobin, hepatica, trailing arbutus, and wood anemone.

Deer, black bear, and an occasional moose are the only larger mammals regularly seen in the park. Most of the smaller species found in the northern hardwood habitat occur here, as well as the lesser known pine marten, fisher, and the industrious beaver. Bobcats and coyotes are relatively common, and timber wolves are likely occasional visitors.

Bird life, especially the migrant song birds, is extensive and varied. With the lake on one side and streams, marshes, and woods on the other, shore birds, sea birds, and song birds abound. And birds of prey vary with the season. The habitat provided by the park in the Pictured Rocks escarpment area has been chosen for a location to attempt reintroduction of the peregrine falcon, the epitome of a wild, natural, winged predator. All but rendered extinct a few years ago by the unbridled use of pesticides poisoning the food chain, this remarkable flyer has responded well to reintroduction in other upper midwest areas. A three-year program has been instituted in Pictured Rocks National Lakeshore to attempt restocking of the area with this famous hawk. Within the park's Beaver Basin the American bald eagle has returned to nest under the protection of the national lakeshore.

The People of Pictured Rocks

> *"History records that no great armies clashed and that no stirring words were ever spoken here. History is measured in the tread of a moccasin, the cadence of a voyageur's paddle, the black scar of a fire built on a rock slab, or an arrowhead kicked loose from its resting place."*
>
> —*Pictured Rocks National Lakeshore,*
> National Park Service brochure.

This land of "painted" and fantastically shaped rocks, a great and dramatic sand dune, and dark, cool forests is a place where, for the most part, people came to look for something special, found it, then departed. Only a few stayed. Even the earliest American wanderers left little here to mark their passage through the forests and brief pauses along sheltered bays. When enough food was harvested to serve their needs for the coming winter, they moved on.

Frenchmen were the first white men to reach the southern shore of Lake Superior. Whether motivated by curiosity, the spirit of adventure, the glory of king and country, personal profit, or a desire to spread Christian gospel, each one had his own vision of the rewards to be gained by visiting this land. Settling down on the peninsula was not their intention.

Lured by the promise of a generous supply of beaver for the lucrative European fashion market, French trappers and traders were the most persistent travelers in the seventeenth century. They got along well with the Indians who summered in the area, the Chippewas (white man's version of Ojibwas). They must have been fascinated with the unusual natural formations bordering the lake, for they gave them descriptive names that still apply to some of the lakeshore's landmarks: Grand Sable, Le Grand Portail, La Chapelle, Grand Marais.

A geologist who surveyed the area one hundred years after the heyday of the French explorers and traders recorded his impressions of how the adventurous voyageurs must have reacted to the Pictured Rocks:

> *"To the voyager coasting along their base in his frail canoe they would, at all times, be an object of dread; the recoil of the surf, the rockbound coast, affording for miles no place of refuge; the lowering sky, the rising wind,—all these would excite his apprehension, and induce him to ply a vigorous oar until the dreaded wall was passed. But in the Pictured Rocks there are two features which communicate to the scenery a wonderful and almost unique character. These are, first, the curious manner in which the cliffs have been excavated and worn away by the action of the lake, which for centuries has dashed an ocean-like surf against their base; and, second, the equally curious manner in which large portions of the surface have colored by bands of brilliant hues. It is from the latter circumstance that the name by which these cliffs are known to the American traveler is derived from the former, and by far the most striking, peculiarity."*

> —*Foster and Whitey Report of the Geology of the Lake Superior Land District. 1850*

Not until after Michigan became a U.S. possession and subsequently a state in 1837 did settlers venture into the Upper Peninsula, and then not in great numbers. For many years before that time, wars between the French and English, then between the English and the newly-formed American government, left in doubt just who was in control of the area. One of the first duties of the American surveyors and Indian agents was to make clear to the Indians just who was now in charge. The Indians were not numerous and, after some initial cultural resistance, gradually they left or became assimilated into a new way of life.

Soon, new commercial enterprises drew people to the upper Great Lakes area—iron mining, logging, commercial fishing, and shipbuilding. It was a logical sequence. New England forests were dwindling and lumber was needed to build homes and stores in the cities and towns of the mid-west. Charcoal made from wood was needed to stoke iron furnaces. There was a plentiful supply of both white pine and hardwoods in the forests of the peninsula. And ships were needed to transport ore and lumber.

Heavy logging did not begin in the Upper Peninsula's more remote Pictured Rocks area until the 1880s. By then the supply was diminishing in lower Michigan and improvements in cutting and processing methods made it profitable to move farther north.

To get the logs from the high, forested terrain above the rocks, where it was cut, to the sawmills, one method used was the log slide. One famous incline was called the Devil's Slide. It was built into a slope of the Grand Sable Dunes, starting 300 feet above the lake and sloping down at a 35 degree angle. Once in the water, logs were made into rafts and floated to the sawmills. At one time, Grand Marais was a booming sawmill town. Lumbering and the manufacturing of forest products are still significant commercial enterprises in the Pictured Rocks area today.

Commercial shipping on the Great Lakes and especially in the vicinity of Pictured Rocks has always been hazardous. An irregular shoreline, offshore reefs, frequent sudden storms, and heavy fog are factors that have brought many ships to their doom. A lighthouse was built at Au Sable Point in 1874. Its Fresnel lens, the state-of-the-art lighting system at the time, was visible for eleven miles. Nevertheless, shipwrecks continued. In 1905, there were 38 shipwrecks within the waters bordering the Pictured Rocks coastline.

In 1933, the Munising Coast Guard Station was built at Sand-Point, an historic location where Indians once camped and Methodists held camp meetings. After nearly thirty years of rescue work, the station closed in 1961, and the station is now the site of lakeshore headquarters.

Diving to explore the remains of some of the ships wrecked between the lakeshore's coastline and Grand Island is both a scientific and recreational activity in lakeshore waters today. Wrecks are protected by the Alger Underwater Preserve, one of five Michigan Bottomland Preserves.

Glimpses of various sites associated with Pictured Rocks history can be had by visiting the remains of the Schoolcraft Iron Company's furnace at Munising, adjacent to the interpretive center at Munising Falls, the Au Sable Point Light Station (both of which are on the National Register of Historic Places), the Log Slide Overlook, and the Maritime Museum at Grand Marais, housed in a former Coast Guard Station.

Word about this picturesque and fabled land on the southern shores of Lake Superior began to spread in the late nineteenth and early twentieth centuries, possibly because many readers were intrigued with Longfellow's epic poem, *The Song of Hiawatha,* mentioned earlier. Occasionally tourists took one-day trips on excursion boats from various Michigan resorts to see Pictured Rocks and Grand Sable Dunes.

The state of Michigan expressed interest in establishing a park around the Pictured Rocks as early as 1924. Plans were drawn up for state parks to encompass many of the renowned coastal features, but there was no funding to buy the land. Still people came to sightsee and to hike or camp in the woods. By the mid-fifties there were summer cottages and two State Forest Campgrounds. In 1957-58, the National Park Service made a survey of the Great Lakes shoreline and cited the Pictured Rocks shore as being of national significance. A recommendation was made to establish a 100,000 acre national park that would include the entire watershed.

After several years during which discussion centered on the proposed size of the park, legislation was passed in 1966, providing for the creation of a National Lakeshore—the first in the nation that was smaller in size than originally planned, it is divided into two zones—a shoreline zone and an inland buffer zone.

The primary location for recreational activities is the shoreline zone, approximately 33,500 acres. Except for a small parcel owned by a local government entity, the land in the shoreline zone is totally federally owned. The inland buffer zone was established to protect the character and existing use of the land. Much of the land within this zone is privately owned, mostly by the forest products industry and individual land and home-owners. The National Park Service has responsibility to see that forest lands in the buffer zone are managed scientifically, and local zoning authorities regulate development and other land uses.

Why Go to Pictured Rocks National Lakeshore?

People go to the lakeshore during all seasons and for different reasons. Some make the trip to marvel at the scenery. Others enjoy the solitude of long woodland hikes on foot, skis or snowshoes. Many visitors are attracted to the area because of Great Lakes maritime history.

Most of the traveling public has yet to discover Pictured Rocks National Lakeshore. All but about ten percent of the lakeshore's visitors come from Michigan and five neighboring states. Pictured Rocks is in far north country—away from highly-traveled north-south and east-west major highways. It is in land you've read about in stories, poems, and history books, and have seen pointed out on weather maps when below zero temperatures, heavy snowfall, and gale-force winds prevail. It is an intriguing land one should plan to visit for several days.

Over half of the park's visitors come during the short, cool summer season. Winters are long and cold. Yet when the waterfalls turn to giant icicles, the lakes and ponds are covered with ice many inches thick, and the trails are laden with deep, fresh snow, increasing numbers of winter sports enthusiasts come from all over the midwest to invigorate their spirits and test their physical fitness by participating in a variety of outdoor winter activities.

How to Get to Pictured Rocks National Lakeshore

To reach Pictured Rocks National Lakeshore, located in Alger County in Michigan's Upper Peninsula, a traveler must leave super highways and cities far behind. Detroit, Grand Rapids, and Lansing are a day's drive away. Munising is 120 miles from the Mackinac Bridge where the nearest Interstate Highway, I-75, crosses the Straits of Mackinac to link the lower and upper peninsulas of Michigan with Canada at Sault Ste. Marie.

You can approach the lakeshore from the east at Grand Marais, or the west at Munising. Grand Marais is on State Route 77, 42 miles north of U.S. Route 2 which follows along the southern border of the Upper Peninsula. To travel to Munising, leave State Route 77 at Seney and drive west on State Route 28, or stay on U.S. Route 2 as far as Manistique and take State Route 94 north about forty miles.

If you must travel a great distance to reach the lakeshore, consider flying either to a major city or to the Upper Peninsula communities of Marquette or Escanaba and renting a car. Chicago is 375 miles away, Detroit, 413 miles, and Duluth, 295 miles. Send to the Michigan Travel Bureau for a Michigan map and other information about traveling in the state.

There is no entrance fee at Pictured Rocks National Lakeshore.

Where to Stay

Non-Campers. Both Munising and Grand Marais, which are small, thriving communities, offer services to non-camping lakeshore visitors. There are a variety of motels, cabins, and resort areas at moderate prices, as well as restaurants and sandwich shops in each place. Some motels overlook Lake Superior. For specifics, write to Alger County Chamber of Commerce and Grand Marais Chamber of Commerce.

Campers. Camping among the tall pines, firs, white birches, and maples, along quiet lakes, ponds, and streams, and nearby sweeping beach shores, is among the lakeshore's rewarding experiences. Three lakeshore campgrounds are accessible by car. Little Beaver Lake, the smallest campground, is alongside a remote inland lake. Twelvemile Beach Campground is located on a sandy bluff above the Lake Superior beach. The drive to the campground takes you through a breathtaking beautiful stand of tall white birch trees. Hurricane River Campground is situated at a point where the Hurricane River flows into Lake Superior. The Au Sable Light Station, currently being restored, is a short one and one-half mile hike away. The trail to the light station takes you along the beach where the remains of ships wrecked in troubled waters are visible.

There are a total of 61 designated campsites in these campgrounds. All have water, picnic tables, grills, and vault toilets. Sites are available on a first come, first served basis. A $5 per night fee is charged for each campsite. Most sites accommodate small recreational vehicles, but there are no hookups.

Often in July and August, all campsites are filled on weekends, so plan to arrive early in the week. However, there are numerous campgrounds in the vicinity of the lakeshore—in Hiawatha National Forest, Munising City Tourist Park, Lake Superior State Forest, and privately-owned campgrounds.

Backcountry Camping. Hiking along the park's Lakeshore Trail from one end of the lakeshore to the other is enjoyed by many people. Thirteen campgrounds and seven group campsites are spread every few miles along this and other trails for backpackers. Only two sites, Mosquito River and Chapel Beach, have toilets. Free permits are required for backcountry camping. If you plan to do this kind of hiking, send for the lakeshore brochure on backcountry camping. It includes a map of backcountry campsite locations, and regulations that apply to backcountry camping.

What to Do at Pictured Rocks National Lakeshore

Pictured Rocks National Lakeshore is a quiet place, a place where a person goes to relax, to enjoy the bounties of nature, to wonder about the past, and to put the structured life aside for a while. As the spirit moves, a visitor engages in activities in this frame of mind.

When you arrive in Munising, stop first at the Visitor Information Center operated jointly by the National Park Service and the U.S. Forest Service. It is located at the intersection of Michigan 28 and H 58 in Munising and is open daily except on Thanksgiving, Christmas, and New Years Day. You will be able to get up-to-the-minute information about the places you want to go, buy publications, see exhibits, and find out about ranger-conducted programs. When *your* spirit moves, here are some of the things to do at the lakeshore.

Visit Scenic Areas. Pictured Rocks National Lakeshore is not just for the rugged outdoorsman. The scenery is so grand, and much of it easily accessible, that even persons with limited mobility can enjoy the views. First, there are the Pictured Rocks. You can see them by driving on a paved road to the Miners Castle Overlook at the end of Miners Castle Road. The trail to the overlook is wheelchair accessible. Take a side trip from the road to Miners Falls. A half-mile, tree-lined trail from the parking area leads to a platform close to a 75-foot waterfall which drops into a cool, dark canyon.

For the most dramatic and fascinating view of the Pictured Rocks, and such rock formations as Grand Portal, Battleship Rock, Miners Castle, Chapel Rock, Rainbow Cave, and Lovers Leap, take the boat trip from Munising. It's a two to three hour trip. The colors are especially impressive in the late afternoon when the sun's rays shine on the rocks. A narrator points out the various formations, waterfalls, and the old wooden lighthouse on Grand Island. At one point, the boat goes close to the Rocks for picture-taking opportunities. Cruises are normally operated from the first of June until October 10. Tickets for the boat trip are $14 per person. For departure times, contact Pictured Rocks Boat Cruises in Munising.

Waterfalls are among the grandest scenic attractions at Pictured Rocks National Lakeshore. One of the most accessible is the Munising Falls, only one and one-half miles from the center of Munising. A short walk from the parking lot, past a park interpretive center, on a paved, wheelchair accessible trail, leads to the site. A special feature here is the opportunity to walk *behind* the falls. It's a marvelous picture-taking opportunity. Other waterfalls along hiking trails are Chapel Falls, a 1.3 miles walk from unpaved Chapel Road, and Sable Falls, not far from H-58.

A drive along H-58 takes you past Kingston Lake, across the Hurricane River, along Grand Sable Dunes and Grand Sable Lake. A side road from H-58 leads to the overlook of a former log slide, from which there is also a view of the Au Sable Light Station to the west and Grand Sable Banks to the east.

Hiking. There are numerous trails for day hiking to explore forests, lakes, waterfalls, dunes, and the beach. There are short walks, e.g. the Munising Falls trail (one-quarter mile) and the Hemlock Trail loop through 200 and 300 year old white pines near Little Beaver Lake (.7 miles) and the quarter of a mile walk along the beach at Sand Point. There are longer hikes, e.g. the Beaver Basin Loop Trail which takes you past old "sea caves," around the Beaver Lakes to Lake Superior, and the nine-mile Chapel Loop Trail. The newest trail is the Sand Point Marsh Trail built by the Youth Conservation Corps in the summer of 1989. It is a half mile, handicapped accessible boardwalk through lakeshore wetland. Interpretive signs explain the significance of what you see.

The 42.8 miles Lakeshore Trail between Munising and Grand Marais, which hugs the Lake Superior shoreline, is part of the

North Country National Scenic Trail that winds from the Vermont-New York state border to western North Dakota. Further information about the North Country Trail can be obtained from lakeshore headquarters.

Beach-Going. Twelvemile Beach is a great place for solitary walking, searching for unusual, colorful rocks, and picnicking. Though lake waters are cold, swimmers frequent Sand Point Beach near Munising and the beach at Grand Sable Lake.

Visit Historic Sites. Persons with a special interest in Great Lakes maritime history enjoy visiting the Maritime Museum at Grand Marais, once a base of the U.S. Coast Guard operations on this section of Lake Superior. Exhibits at the museum include artifacts from the Au Sable Point Light Station, the Life Saving Service which preceded the Coast Guard at Grand Marais as rescuers of men and ships foundering on Lake waters, items from various shipwrecks, and items associated with Grand Marais' commercial fishing industry. Hikers may also visit the Au Sable Light Station. Ranger-led hikes to this site are regularly scheduled in summer.

Fishing. A Michigan fishing license is required to fish in Lake Superior and the inland lakes and streams of the lakeshore. In the spring, salmon and trout are the prime catches. At other times of the year, fishermen look for trout, bass, and perch. Fishing licenses may be obtained at local hardware, bait, and sporting goods stores.

Hunting. Hunting for bear, upland birds, and deer in the woods and along the lakes and streams of Michigan's Upper Peninsula is a time-honored tradition. The law authorizing the creation of a national lakeshore at Pictured Rocks specifically allowed hunting to continue within the borders of the lakeshore in accordance with the migratory bird laws and Michigan state regulations. The Beaver Basin region is the primary site for this fall-centered activity.

Winter Sports. A deep blanket of snow covers the lakeshore for five months of the year, drawing many people to the park to engage in winter sports. Cross-country skiing, snowshoeing, snowmobiling, and ice fishing have become increasingly popular. The lakeshore maintains groomed cross-country ski trails in the Munising and Grand Marais areas. Brochures marking the trails also rank them from easy to difficult. Some trails that are not groomed are more appropriate for snowshoes. Snowmobiling is allowed on unplowed roads that are normally open to vehicles in other seasons. Most people bring their own snowmobiles. Snowmobiles may be rented in Munising and in Christmas, a community about three miles west of Munising.

The lakeshore permits winter camping in the park campgrounds, but cautions that only people fully prepared for extreme weather conditions should plan to camp during this season. Most motels remain open in winter, but if you plan to come to the lakeshore in winter, be sure to ask what facilities are open year-round when inquiring about overnight lodging.

SCUBA Diving. Diving among the shipwrecks and colorful rocks that lie within the Alger Underwater Preserve, located in the waters of the lakeshore in Munising Bay and around Grand Island, is a popular activity. A brochure identifies such wrecks as the Bermuda, a wooden-hulled schooner lost in the 1880s, the Superior, a sidewheel steamer wrecked in 1856, and the Smith Moore, a wooden hulled steam barge that sank in 1889. Charter boats for divers are based in Munising. For more information, contact the Alger Underwater Preserve.

NOTE: *No off-road driving is permitted at the lakeshore, and bicycles and all-terrain vehicles are not permitted in the backcountry. Though hunting is permitted during Michigan's hunting season, guns must be unloaded and in a case or car trunk, or disassembled while in or on any motorized land vehicle. Pets are permitted on roads and in developed areas such as campgrounds and parking lots, but they are not allowed in the backcountry. If you plan to take a pet with you to the lakeshore, send for a copy of A Notice to Pet Owners which outlines specific areas where you may take your pet. All campgrounds have campsites and toilets accessible to physically handicapped persons, and several viewing sites are accessible to people with limited mobility.*

If You Have the Time

▶ Visit Grand Marais Historical Museum on the town waterfront, a short walk from the lakeshore's Maritime Museum, and take a look at the life of a lighthouse keeper's family a half-century ago.

▶ Drive west on M-28 from Munising and stop at Grand Island Scenic Overlook, a camping spot for Indians, voyageurs, and missionaries, where they rested before and after canoeing past Pictured Rocks. Nearby is the historical site of Bay Furnace, where there are remains of a huge smelting furnace that operated on this site over a hundred years ago.

▶ Visit Hiawatha Folk Craft and Art Center just south of M-28 at Au Train, where local craftsmen and women demonstrate pottery-making, woodcarving, basket-making, and other art forms.

▶ Visit the Seney National Wildlife Refuge on State Route 77, three miles north of Germfask. Located in the Great Manistique Swamp, the open marshes attract Canada geese, loons, sandhill cranes, bald eagles, waterfowl, and various mammals, including deer, bear, beaver, and coyote. The Visitor Center, open May 15 to September 30, features dioramas, exhibits, and nature-movie -slide shows. You can take a seven mile self-guided auto tour of the refuge from July 1 to October 31, walk nature trails, and enjoy picnics at designated areas. For more information, write to the Refuge.

Tips for adding to your enjoyment of Pictured Rocks National Lakeshore

1. Plan early for your trip to the lakeshore. Send for the Park Service brochure and information of special interest to you, e.g. backcountry camping regulations, cross-country ski and snowmobile trails, regulations about pets.

2. If you do not plan to camp, write to the Chamber of Commerce in Munising and Grand Marais for information on overnight lodging.

3. Send to the Michigan Travel Bureau for a Michigan state map and other travel information.

4. If you would like to read about the Great Lakes, Indian legends, historic shipwrecks, and the wildflowers, birds, trees, and fish of the Pictured Rocks area, send for the publications list of the lakeshore's cooperating association and order books and maps that may be of special interest to you.

5. If you plan to take the Pictured Rocks boat cruise, check at the Chamber of Commerce or stop at the cruise office to check on

departure times and make reservations. Special arrangements may also be made for persons with limited mobility.

6. When you arrive at the lakeshore, check the schedule of ranger-led interpretive programs and plan to attend those of special interest to you.

And finally—As you cast your eyes over the Big Sea Waters, gaze up at white foamy waters cascading over high rocks, or softly tread woodland paths, let your thoughts roam. Perhaps you'll feel the presence of a Chippewa stalking a deer, hear the deep baritone of a singing voyageur, catch sight of a wooden sailing ship pressing against a howling wind, or listen to the screech of a once-mighty white pine tree trunk sliding down the banks of the Grand Sable.

Sources of Information

Superintendent
Pictured Rocks National Lakeshore
Box 40, Sand Point Road
Munising, MI 49862-0040
Phone: 906-387-3700

Michigan Travel Bureau
Box 30226
Lansing, MI 48909
Phone: 800-5432-YES

Alger County Chamber of
Commerce
Box 405
Munising, MI 49862
Phone: 906-387-2138

Grand Marais Chamber of
Commerce
Box 139
Grand Marais, MI 49839
Phone: 906-494-2766

Alger Underwater Preserve
Box 272
Munising, MI 49862
Phone: 906-387-2138

Pictured Rocks Boat Cruises
Box 355
Munising, MI 49862
Phone: 906-387-2379

Refuge Manager
Seney National Wildlife Refuge
HCR-2, Box 1
Seney, MI 49883
Phone: 906-586-9851

APOSTLE ISLANDS
NATIONAL LAKESHORE

Some islands are constantly at war with the sea, defiantly
resisting its onslaughts, bending under lost battles, but retreating
grudgingly. You sense the ceaseless conflict, the powerful presence
of the sea, in the battered shorelines—and in the faces and deter-
mination of the island dwellers.

Other islands seem to have the upper hand. The sea is the
battle-loser, its waters shoaled by the island's plant life, its edges
pushed back by natural and man-made barriers. The waters may
threaten, but the confident island residents prevail (at least for a
while), and the sea can only nibble at its island adversaries.

The mood is different in the Apostle Islands archipelago. In this corner of the great freshwater sea called Lake Superior, you sense harmony rather than battle, accommodation rather than confrontation, and a dynamic equilibrium between the islands and sea that the residents have come to respect as a fact of life in this age old struggle between land and sea.

Not that the sea does not do battle with island and man. The hundred-odd shipwrecks that have occurred in this area attest to that. But residents of the one populated island, Madeline Island (not part of the lakeshore), and the nearby mainland, seem to accept the sea as it is, enjoy the wondrous sailing it provides in warm weather, and utilize its frozen surface in winter to drive their cars between their island and mainland. (Cars are not permitted on the National Lakeshore islands.)

Apostle Islands National Lakeshore is at the northernmost tip of Wisconsin at the western end of Lake Superior. The lakeshore includes 21 of the 22 Apostle Islands and twelve miles of nearby mainland shoreline on the Bayfield Peninsula. Although the name, Apostle Islands, is attributed to the early explorers and traders, it is folklore that the group of islands were so named because it was thought there were only twelve islands, the same number as the Biblical Apostles.

The islands within the lakeshore range in size from three-acre Gull Island to 10,000-acre Stockton Island. They are scattered in a loose cluster north and east of the Bayfield Peninsula. Outer Island, some 24 miles from Bayfield, is the farthest offshore.

Six working light stations on Apostle Islands provide guidance for the ship traffic in the western end of Lake Superior. Keeping the light has been serious business in this area throughout recent history and continues to be today—although the lights are now automated.

At first glance, and from a distance, the Apostles appear quite similar- wooded, low-lying patches of green imbedded in the azure blue of lake waters in summer, a dark green rising above the dazzling expanse of ice in winter. In fact, however, the islands hold a treasure house of terrain and scenery, sandstone cliffs, beaches, bogs, and forests.

Like most of the Great Lakes area, the Apostle Islands are the result of hundreds of millions of years of building up of sandstone, rising and falling of the level of the land, and glaciation. The glaciers advanced and retreated over the land many times, scouring lake beds, planing off mountains, and, like gigantic conveyor belts, pouring rocks, clay, and gravel into moraines and till. The last glaciers to remold the land in this area retreated from the Apostle Islands archipelago about 12,000 years ago. The islands are mounds of glacial till piled on the underlying bedrock of sandstone left after the glacier widened Precambrian stream valleys between them and the deeper depths of the lake beyond. The milder effects of erosion have further sculpted the islands and continue to do so.

Tucked along the shorelines of Apostle Islands National Lakeshore is some striking evidence of that erosion. Here the layer of ancient Devils Island Sandstone is exposed to the wave action of Lake Superior and wondrous caves, tunnels, and arches rise out of the water. These caverns can be explored by boat on calm days on the north shore of Devils Island, Swallow Point on Sand Island, and at the mainland's Squaw Bay cliffs.

In the winter the sea caves become ice caves that can be explored on foot over the frozen surface of the lake. The scene in winter is particularly dramatic, with the red sandstone cliffs, the glaring white ice, and the cobalt sky contrasting with the dark shadows of the caves. Within, the caves are hung with ribbons and curtains of stalactites while the floor of ice is mounded and peaked with stalagmites—all formed of ice that is renewed each year. Like many other wonders of nature, the ice caves should be explored with great caution, especially on Sand and Devils Islands. Park rangers should be consulted before setting out, since lake conditions in summer and ice conditions in winter vary from hour to hour.

Several of the islands have sparkling beach strands where you can squirm your toes in the sand, sunbathe, beachcomb, and (if you insist) swim in the shallow water. A lakeshore brochure, *Sandscapes of the Apostles Islands* describes the beach environment and identifies activity you should avoid to prevent damage to these fragile habitats.

A variety of shore birds such as spotted sandpipers patrol the beaches, while loons, mergansers, and a few other duck species dot the waters just offshore. Clumps of American beach grass and beach pea spot the lower dune areas, and beach heather, juniper and blueberry help to stabilize the higher dunes. Even trees like white pine, red pine, and paper birch are established in some dune areas, further advancing the stabilization of these "sandscapes," or sandy ecosystems.

The Apostle Islands straddle the transition zone between the boreal forest of balsam fir, white spruce, and paper birch, and the northern hardwood forest of sugar maple, yellow birch, white pine, hemlock, and yew. All but small pockets of the forests are second growth from 30 to 125 years old, since most of the area was commercially logged repeatedly, except for North Twin, Devils, and Raspberry islands. Fires, too, have taken their toll over the years, and the changes in forest cover were followed by destructive browsing of whitetail deer.

The forests are returning to the islands, however, and there are miles of trails through splendid groves. You can walk through uplands and wetlands, each with its own community of flowers, herbs, and trees. Remainders of the climax forest that somehow survived the loggers' axes tower over the younger second growth trees, while underfoot is a veritable ground carpet of green, mostly ferns and clubmosses. Like exclamation points, wildflowers seem to accent the green carpet around them—bunchberry with its tiny, greenish-yellow flowers and white whorl of bracts and cluster of red berries, and clintonia with its pale yellow bell-shaped flowers and dark blue, bead-like, (and poisonous) berry.

Although not plentiful, black bears, otters, whitetail deer and, rarely, coyotes are sighted on some of the islands. Beavers are plentiful on Stockton and Outer Islands. Black bears are strong swimmers and readily cross the channels between islands and mainland. Sightings are infrequent, but Stockton Island has a permanent population of reproducing bears. In at least one instance a bear became such a nuisance on campgrounds that he had to be relocated. Deer population which flourished after the last logging on the islands, peaked long ago and has decreased as the new forest cover matured and restricted the food supply. Only a handful of deer are on the islands today.

Birds that nest in the Apostle Islands number at least 95 species, including yellow-bellied sapsuckers, hermit thrushes, ruby-throated hummingbirds, and bald eagles. Eagle nesting is increasing on the islands, with six successful nestings in 1989. Two islands, Gull and Eagle, are bird sanctuaries closed to visitors to protect nesting activities. Herring gulls and double-crested cormorants establish large rookeries there each year. Many other migrants pass through the area and add further interest for the devoted birdwatcher.

The People of the Apostle Islands

Like other islands and coastlines of the western Great Lakes region, from the beginning, people were attracted to the Apostle Islands during particular seasons: when it was time to harvest food, or when moderate temperatures provided welcome relief from warmer, more humid climes.

Recent archeological research has revealed evidence that before the Europeans arrived, tribes of woodland Indians occupied at least 45 seasonal camps on various islands of the archipelago. These Native Americans hunted, fished, collected maple sap for sugar, and gathered berries. On one of the sites, Manitou Island, archeologists have found numerous artifacts—bones, fragments of stone tools, and remnants of trade goods. Ongoing research is expected to turn up more signs of past cultures on the Apostle Islands.

Indians of the Chippewa (Objibway) tribe were settled on Madeline Island when French traders arrived looking for beaver skins in the mid 1600s. In the 1800s, commercial fishing in the cold, deep waters of Lake Superior superceded the fur trade. It was a rough life for the hardy fishermen. Fishing was a year-round occupation, and in the long, cold winters fishermen had to cautiously make their way across vast stretches of ice to set their nets.

The stone-cutters came toward the end of the nineteenth century. As a result of the Great Chicago fire in 1871, they quarried the islands' top quality brownstone and sent it to mid-western cities that sought more durable building materials for major edifices. Lakeshore headquarters and its prime mainland visitor center are located in one of Bayfield's brownstone buildings built originally to house the County Courthouse in 1883.

Loggers set up operations on some of the islands by the 1870s. White pines, hardwoods, hemlocks, and white cedar needed for building material, fuel, and tanning operations, were plentiful on the islands. Transportation was not a major problem. The softwoods were floated and hardwoods were shipped over lake waters to the mills on the mainland. Occasionally, island hikers come across remnants of logging camps now almost buried within new-growth forests. When the bottom fell out of the building market during the Great Depression of the 1930s, logging ceased on the Apostle Islands and the process of natural reforestation began.

A number of farms were established on several of the Apostle Islands in the late 1800s. At first, prospects for success seemed promising. Produce could be shipped by boat to the communities sprouting up on the mainland shores, and there was a ready market in the commercial enterprises located on the islands. But conditions changed. Railroads reached northern Wisconsin and land transportation competed with water transport. In time, island quarries ceased operation and logging diminished. When farming on the islands was no longer profitable, many farmers gave up and moved to the mainland.

Before the Soo canals were built at Sault Ste. Marie connecting Lake Huron with Lake Superior, shipping was confined to intra-lake operations. But after 1855 it was possible for large commercial vessels to transport goods over the 1,000-mile waterway from the east to the western end of the Great Lakes. Highly visible navigation aids were needed for ships plying the often treacherous waters of Lake Superior. The response to this need brought a new, culturally significant group of people to the Apostle Islands—the lighthouse keepers and their families.

Over a 34 year period, six light stations were built on the islands. The first one was supposed to be constructed on Long Island to mark the south channel for ships approaching the islands from the east, but it was built by mistake on Michigan Island to the northeast. Another station was built on Long Island the following year. Successively, stations were built on Raspberry Island to guide ships heading for the LaPointe and Bayfield Harbors through the west channel; on Outer Island providing light visible to ships bound for Duluth and Superior; on Sand Island on the west side to guide ships coming east from Duluth and planning to enter the west channel; and lastly, on Devils Island on the north at the point where ships bound for Duluth make their final course corrections.

Fresnel lenses, the most powerful lens available at the time, were installed in all light stations. It was the lightkeeper's daily chore to trim and adjust the wicks, clean and polish the glass and brass parts, and maintain the clockwork mechanism so that the light would never fail to serve as a dependable guide to passing ships from one-half hour before sunset to one-half hour after sunrise.

The light stations are now fully automated and the era of the lonely lighthouse keeper, a dedicated servant to humanity, is only recalled in exhibits, publications, and visits to the sites. The Fresnel lens once installed in the Michigan Island light station is now on display at the lakeshore's visitor center in Bayfield.

All six light stations of the Apostle Islands are listed on the National Register of Historic Places. For a closer look at the life and times of manned lighthouses on the Great Lakes, take the guided tour of the Raspberry Island lighthouse complex conducted in summer by park rangers.

The city of Bayfield was founded in 1856, and by the late 1800s people were coming to the area in steamships and trains to escape the hot, humid city summers. Tourism had begun. Resorts were built at Bayfield, and summer homes were constructed on Madeline Island for the increasing number of summer visitors. Recreational boating and sport fishing became important factors in the Bayfield economy—and they still are.

During the 1960-1970 decade, public pressure convinced Congress to provide more national parks for public recreation, and to set aside rapidly diminishing, relatively undisturbed natural areas for preservation. Many new units were added to the National Park System. Among them were four national lakeshores on the Great Lakes. Legislation creating the Apostle Islands National Lakeshore was enacted in September 1970. Initially, the lakeshore included twenty of the 22 Apostle Islands. In 1986, Long Island was incorporated into the lakeshore. The largest island, Madeline Island, where year-round residents as well as summer residents had lived for many years, remains outside the lakeshore.

Currently, the lakeshore is engaged in a lengthy, formal process of planning for the future. Consideration by both the public and the Park Service is being given to the type and number of new facilities needed, access and costs of transportation to the islands, the suitability of designating some of the islands as wilderness areas, and how to best manage the lakeshore's natural resources, including wildlife habitat.

Why Go to Apostle Islands National Lakeshore?

▶ To sail over the clear, cool, deep waters of Lake Superior and to explore little-known, forested, tranquil islands reshaped 10,000 to 20,000 years ago during the last great glacial advance;

▶ To fantasize about life in the north lake country in centuries past when the harsh elements of nature determined where and how people lived;

▶ To join a park ranger on a guided walk and gain an understanding of the effect that all growing things—every native plant and tree, each wild animal, bird, and fish, and all human beings—have on the quality of life throughout the land;

▶ And to have fun in the out-of-doors sightseeing, sailing, kayaking, wind surfing, hiking, fishing, cross-country skiing, snowshoeing, or whatever activity helps you to clear your mind and refresh your spirit.

How to Get to Apostle Islands National Lakeshore

The mainland portion and islands of the Apostle Islands National Lakeshore are at the northernmost tip of Wisconsin. Park headquarters and visitor center are in the city of Bayfield on Wisconsin Route 13, twenty miles north of Ashland. Ashland, on U.S. Route 2, the farthest north east-west highway in Wisconsin, is 65 miles east of Superior, the nearest major city.

To drive to the lakeshore, you traverse mile after mile of sparsely populated areas. Coming from the east, you go through Bad River Indian Reservation, and from the west, through Chequamegon (pronounced Show-wa-me-gun) National Forest. Send to the Wisconsin Department of Transportation for a Wisconsin state map and other travel information.

There are no entrance fees to Apostle Islands National Lakeshore.

Where to Stay

Non-Campers. Bayfield has been a popular tourist center for many years. The city has a wide variety of motels, inns, resorts, and guest houses, plus many restaurants, art and craft galleries, and shops. Some lodgings overlook the town's waterfront, providing constantly changing views of Lake Superior. Send to Bayfield Chamber of Commerce for information about overnight lodging in the vicinity of the lakeshore.

Camping Accessible by Vehicle. There are no national lakeshore campgrounds on the mainland, but there are numerous campgrounds maintained by the city of Bayfield, the Red Cliff Indian Reservation, the Forest Service, Bayfield County, and private individuals. Some have showers, electricity, and hookups. For a list of mainland campgrounds, rates, and services offered, write to lakeshore headquarters. For information about camping in the

Chequamegon National Forest, twelve miles south of Bayfield, contact the District Ranger at Washburn.

There are two fine campgrounds on Madeline Island, the largest of the Apostle Islands and the only one not within the lakeshore. Big Bay State Park has 55 sites, and applications for reservations may be made by mail. For information, contact Big Bay State Park. A Town park, which has 45 sites, is maintained by LaPointe Township. Both parks have swimming available but no electricity. Madeline Island is accessible by car ferry from Bayfield.

Camping on the Islands. Camping is permitted in designated campsites on most of the Apostle Islands. There are developed sites for group and family camping, and sites in the backcountry. Undesignated camping is permitted on all but five islands. Access to the islands is by private boat, regularly scheduled Apostle Islands Cruise Service boat, or Apostle Islands Water Taxi.

Camping permits are required. They are free and may be obtained at park visitor centers or ranger stations. They are issued on a first come, first served basis. Sites for group camping (ten or more people) must be reserved in advance.

If you plan to camp on the islands, send for a copy of the park brochure, *Camping in the Apostle Islands.* It gives details of campsites and regulations governing camping on the islands.

For information on boat transportation provided by park concessioners, and reservations, write to Apostle Islands Cruise Service and Apostle Islands Water Taxi. Try to get a regularly scheduled boat trip because water taxis are expensive unless there is a sizeable group to share the cost.

What to Do at Apostle Islands National Lakeshore

Start by going to the visitor center located in the old brownstone courthouse building in Bayfield. It is open daily from 8 a.m. to 6 p.m. from Memorial Day through Labor Day., and for shorter periods until the end of October. See the audiovisual programs and exhibits about the lakeshore's natural and cultural history and recreational opportunities. Check out the publications, maps, nautical charts, posters, and other items for sale. Inquire about park programs offered at various times during the summer, and about guest lectures presented on Wednesday evenings.

Take a drive through the Red Cliff Indian Reservation to the Little Sand Bay Visitor Center, the only other lakeshore facility on the mainland. Here there are more exhibits and audiovisual programs, a dock, a boat launch ramp, and picnic tables. Tours of the nearby Hokenson Brothers Fishery, a complex of buildings used in a family commercial fishing operation thirty to sixty years ago, are offered hourly during the summer. There is also a visitor center on Stockton Island, accessible by boat only.

Boating. A visit to this lakeshore would not be complete without boating on Lake Superior to or among some of the Apostle Islands. Morning and afternoon narrated cruises are offered by the park concessioner at specified times. Morning cruises provide views of nineteen of the 22 islands. One afternoon cruise stops at Stockton Island where passengers may disembark either to stay for several days of camping, or to enjoy a two hour stay on the island, hiking on trails and exploring beaches. The boat goes on to Manitou Island where passengers may visit a historic commercial fish camp before the ship returns to Stockton Island to pick up passengers. Another cruise makes a similar trip to Raspberry Island to see the lighthouse. The morning Grand Tour cruises run from early June through the first week in October. The Stockton Island and Raspberry Island cruises start in early July and end the fourth week in August. Fees for the boat trips are $16.95 for adults, $8.50 for children.

If you are an experienced sailor and look forward to sailing on Lake Superior, ask the Bayfield Chamber of Commerce for information about sailboats available for charter.

Sea kayaking is a popular activity along the coastlines of various Apostle Islands. Because weather and wind conditions can suddenly turn hazardous and the lake water is very cold, lakeshore officials strongly advise visitors not to use open boats or canoes between the islands. Swimming in the lake is not recommended. Hypothermia can overwhelm even a strong swimmer within minutes.

Hiking. Hiking on island trails that vary from one-quarter mile on South Twin Island to a 9.4 mile trail on Stockton Island is is one of the many enjoyable ways to immerse yourself in the lakeshore's beautiful natural surroundings. Trails go through open meadows, hardwood forests, along logging roads and bay shores, and to abandoned quarries. Park naturalists lead nature walks. Self-guiding brochures illustrate the trails on Stockton Island, Basswood Island, and Oak Island.

Fishing. Deep sea fishing for lake trout and exotic salmon lures many a sport fisherman to the Apostle Islands. Finding the fish can be tricky, however, because the fish move about to different places, varying with the season, as they seek preferred water temperatures. The best chance for a successful fishing trip for a person unfamiliar with Great Lakes water is to book a guided charter fishing trip on one of the many charter fishing boats in Bayfield and nearby communities. There is no inland fishing on the islands. A Wisconsin state fishing license and a Great Lakes trout-salmon stamp are required for fishing in Lake Superior. They are available at local stores, the Bayfield office of the Wisconsin Department of Natural Resources, and from the Department's office in Madison.

Visit Historic Sites. Most of the lakeshore's historic sites are on the islands. Visitors and campers who boat to various islands can see the remains of logging camps, fish camps, and abandoned sandstone quarries, and view still-functioning light stations. The Hokenson Brothers Fishery near the Little Sand Bay Visitor Center is the one interpreted historic site on the mainland. The Fishery is listed on the National Register of Historic Places, as are several island structures, including logging camps, quarries, and two archeological sites.

SCUBA Diving. A direct and close encounter with a significant piece of Great Lakes shipping history awaits the experienced SCUBA diver. The cold, clear waters surrounding the islands has preserved several major shipwrecks in the Apostle Islands; two shipwrecks within the lakeshore boundaries are in remarkable condition. The Noque Bay, a 205-foot schooner barge which burned to the waterline in October 1905, lies in fifteen feet of water in Julian Bay off Stockton Island. This is a popular dive site and on clear days the wreck is visible to non-divers and snorkelers. In shallow water near Long Island, the 195-foot schooner Lucerne, lost in a howling November storm in 1886, sits upright in the sand. Shipwrecks are protected by law. Removal or disturbance of artifacts is prohibited.

Free permits are required for SCUBA diving in lakeshore waters. Permits and information about other fascinating dive sites may be obtained at park headquarters.

Winter sports. Things quiet down at the lakeshore in winter; nevertheless, winter sportsmen enjoy many facets of outdoor recreation: cross-country skiing, snowshoeing, ice fishing, and winter camping. Even in summer a visitor is alerted to another winter sport popular in the Bayfield area by the roadside signs marking snowmobile crossing. However, snowmobiling is not permitted on lakeshore islands or the park's mainland property.

Hunting and Trapping. The lakeshore's enabling legislation permits hunting and trapping within the lakeshore, in accordance with Wisconsin law. For information about regulations that apply, check with lakeshore headquarters.

NOTE: *Off-road driving is not permitted at the lakeshore. Pets must be on a leash and under physical control at all times. The main visitor center and rest rooms in Bayfield are accessible to persons with a physical handicap as are the cruise boat and rest rooms on the boat. Special printed material and cassette tapes are available for use by persons with hearing or visual impairments.*

If You Have the Time

▸ Visit the Buffalo Art Center on the Red Cliff Indian Reservation. It includes a museum of Lake Superior Chippewa with many fine examples of contemporary Indian art, and a gift shop. There is a modest entrance fee for the museum.

▸ Visit the Cooperage Museum and Gift Shop, a working barrel museum close to Bayfield's waterfront.

▸ Take the fifteen minute car ferry ride from Bayfield to LaPointe on Madeline Island, drive around the island, browse through the shops, have a meal, and visit Madeline Island Historical Museum. Madeline Island was the home of Chippewa (Ojibway) Indians and the site of a French trading post at the close of the eighteenth century and, subsequently, British and American trading posts. The stockaded museum complex, operated by the Wisconsin Historical Society, contains many exhibits relating to fur trading, logging, commercial fishing, and missions of times past. The museum is open June 15 to September 15. There is a modest admission charge. For car ferry information, contact Madeline Island Ferry Line, Inc. For more information on Madeline Island, contact Madeline Island Chamber of Commerce.

▸ Drive the marked route through Bayfield's many apple orchards, especially if you are there in springtime when apple blossoms are a spectacular sight, or in the fall, when activities associated with a bountiful apple harvest are in full swing.

▸ Take a walking tour of Bayfield's Historic District.

Tips for Adding to Your Enjoyment of Apostle Islands National Lakeshore

1. Send to lakeshore headquarters for a park brochure and information of special interest to you, e.g. camping on the islands, campgrounds on the mainland, SCUBA diving permits and regulations.

2. Send to the Bayfield Chamber of Commerce for information on overnight lodging in the Bayfield area and, if you want to sail or fish, information on sailboat chartering and charter fishing trips.

3. If you would like to read more about Apostle Islands, Chippewa (Ojibway) history, lighthouses on the Great Lakes, or natural history of the area before you go to the lakeshore, send to park headquarters for the publications list and order form of the Eastern National Park and Monument Association, Apostle Islands office.

4. Take with you binoculars, camera, and warm clothing, even in summer.

And finally—Stand high on the hillside overlooking Bayfield Harbor, drink in the fresh, clear air of the north country, and let your gaze sweep across the distant view—the vast, deep blue water of Lake Superior dotted in every direction with furry little green islands, and a few watercraft that, from this vantage point, look like bathtub toys. This is an experience you will long remember.

Sources of information

Superintendent
Apostle Islands National Lakeshore
Route 1, Box 4
Bayfield, WI 54814
Phone: 715-779-3397

Wisconsin Department of
Transportation
3617 Pierstorff St.
Madison, WI 53704
Phone: 608-246-3265

Bayfield Chamber of Commerce
42 South Broad Street
Box 138
Bayfield, WI 54814
Phone: 715-779-3335

Wisconsin Department of Natural
Resources
101 South Webster Street
Box 7921
Madison, WI 53707
Phone: 608-266-2621

Big Bay State Park
Box 589
Bayfield, WI 54814
Phone: 715-779-3346

Apostle Islands Cruise Service
Route 1, Box 237E
Bayfield, WI 54814
Phone: 715-779-3925

Apostle Islands Water Taxi
Box 691
Bayfield, WI 54814
Phone: 715-779-5153

Madeline Island Ferry Line, Inc.
Box 66B
LaPointe, WI 54850
Phone: 715-747-2051

Madeline Island Chamber of
Commerce in Old LaPointe
Box 274B
LaPointe, WI 54850
Phone: 715-747-2801

Washburn District Ranger
USDA Forest Service
Box 578
Washburn, WI 54891
Phone: 715-373-2667

"... a magnificent realm of woods, most of which, by railroads and trails and open ridges, is also fairly accessibly not only to the determined traveler rejoicing in difficulties, but to those (may their tribe increase) who, not tired, not sick, just naturally take wing every summer in search of wildness."

—John Muir describing four early national parks in his book,
Our National Parks, 1901

VOYAGEURS NATIONAL PARK

This was the twelfth "pipe" of the day for the brigade, and the aroma from many clay pipes wafted through the ominously calm air above the heavily laden canoes. The few-minute break after an hour's steady paddling was near an end. Small talk had dwindled in the unusual midday calm on Rainy Lake and a sense of foreboding sobered the normally effervescent voyageurs. A sharp expletive from the brigade's Guide drew everyone's attention. The guide had reared up in the bow of his canoe and pointed up the lake. There, a half-mile ahead, an echelon of ripples in the calm water led all eyes to a swimmer—a bull moose making his way across the lake. Every canoe came alive in the water as paddles driven by hardened muscles pushed the water

141

behind. *The brigade became a synchronized fleet with the same objective arising from the single thought of each voyageur—no dried fish for supper tonight! No chewing on pemmican! No thick rubbaboo, either! God has sent us a moose—fresh, tasty, red meat! The water literally boiled away behind the huge north canoes!*

The guide let them exhaust their initial excitement in the sprint. Then, calmly, he guided the brigade past the swimming moose, and, with paddling now back to a mile-eating cadence paced by a French chanson, they faced the coming storm. The Guide knew that the time lost in chasing, killing, and butchering the moose might make the difference between a secure night camp or the loss of his crew and their precious cargo in an afternoon storm. And his paddlers knew it, too.

Thus it was, day after day, along the Voyageurs' Highway—the excitement and challenge of the primitive "pays d'en haut," the dreary food to eat, the crushing loads to portage, and the indomitable light-heartedness of the voyageurs.

Voyageurs National Park is in the heart of the Voyageurs' Highway, the canoe route stretching along and above the Canada–U.S. border for 3,000 miles from Montreal in the east to Fort Chipewyan, on Lake Athabasca in the west. The park adjoins 55 miles of the Canada–U.S. border, the "customary waterway" of the fur traders chosen by the treaty of 1783 as the boundary between the two countries. Most of the park's land surface is on the Kabetogama (pronounced Cab-uh-'toe-gi-mah) Peninsula, on the southern shore of Rainy Lake, and along the south and west shores of Lakes Namakan and Sand Point.

The park, like the Voyageurs' Highway, is predominantly a land of water. Nearly forty percent of its 219,000 acres are lake and stream. With its hundreds of islands and over thirty lakes it forms a seemingly endless network of waterways ranging from maze-like bogs to huge Rainy Lake with 35-mile reaches of open water.

Also like the Voyageurs' Highway, Voyageurs National Park lies along the southern edge of the Canadian Shield, a rock formation under half of Canada as well as other areas in the northern hemisphere. It is the world's largest area underlain by Pre-Cambrian rocks (rocks estimated to be from 2.5 to 4 billion years old and mostly devoid of fossils).

Unlike the rocks to the south, the Canadian Shield is a strata of hard, granitic rock. When the glaciers came eons later they planed off the high spots, scored and smoothed down the surface, and carried away all that lay on its surface, but the rocks of the Shield remained substantially in place. The softer rocks to the south were dredged away and vast grooves plowed out that became the beds of the Great and lesser lakes.

About 10,000 years ago, when the last period of glaciation ended, water filled the grooves and the lake country began. So it was that chains of waterways were formed along the southern edge of the Canadian Shield, from mighty Lake Superior to the Athabasca River. And the early Americans, with their invention of the canoe, that masterpiece of the forest formed into an incomparable vehicle for transportation, turned that water route into a transcontinental highway.

The earliest European explorers, guided by friendly natives, used the waterway as they pushed westward into the primitive land. Early fur traders used it to reach the homes of the furbearers. Then came the heightened demand for fur, the European markets avid for animal pelts, especially beaver. As the trapping grounds moved westward, so did the traders, until in the late eighteenth century the fur brigades began, the voyageurs were recruited, and the Voyageurs' Highway rang to the French chansons of "A la Claire Fontaine," "C'est l'Aviron," and "En Roulant ma Boule."

Things have changed since that time in the Voyageurs National Park area. In summer there are motor boats. In winter there are snowmobiles. And the visitors who pass through, like the voyageurs did, may not be as colorful. But the land and water still form that liquid tapestry of nature and remote vignettes of primitiveness that the boater, the hiker, the skier, and the snowshoer find fascinating. Thanks to mile after mile of wilds surrounding the park in all directions, it supports one of the most, if not the most, primitive habitats in the U.S. Elk and woodland caribou that used to roam this area are now gone. Today, however, the signs are strong that health is returning to the wildlife populations. Moose are maintaining their numbers, the beaver are flourishing, and the black bears are becoming a nuisance. Deer are numerous enough to have raised the question of whether the deer to forage ratio is a stable one.

The forests of the park are predominantly southern boreal. Pines, spruce, firs, aspen, and birch intermingle or grow in vast pocket groves. Under their canopy are found many of the furbearers that have become scarce in the lower 48 states—marten, lynx, mink, and fisher. Birdlife also is healthy, with bald eagles commonly seen and a dozen or more pairs mating and producing offspring. About one hundred species of songbirds, wildfowl, and shorebirds are common in the park.

Two of the deep northwoods predators are occasional visitors in the park. You will probably never see him, and never hear him, but the wolverine is known to pass through, probably just to sample life south of the border. You'll probably not see the other predator either, the archetypical denizen of the wild country. But maybe you will hear him calling in the nighttime to his mate or to assemble his pack, for the timber wolf is resident here. An estimated thirty to forty wolves range in and about Voyageurs National Park.

The People of Voyageurland

Here you are on the verge of the twenty-first century. Yet when you ply the waters and walk the trails of Voyageurs National Park, an aura of the past overwhelms you. This is a land of roaming woodland Indians, joyous, rigorous, rousing French-Canadian voyageurs, fortune-seeking miners, enterprising lumbermen, and nature-loving countrymen. And you are part of the next wave of people to value this beautiful piece of the earth.

It's known that ancient people roamed over northern Minnesota searching for big game—woolly mammoths, musk ox, and bison—to bring down with their spears. No artifacts from that era have been found within the park's boundaries, but it seems logical that these wide-ranging hunters found their way to this area.

There is some evidence of the next identifiable group of people who frequented this land, Indians who used more sophisticated hunting tools made of stone and copper. But the greatest archeological finds have been associated with people who lived here about 3,000 years ago, Indians of the woodland culture, the Laurel and, later, the Blackduck. Hundreds of their temporary campsites have been located along park lakeshores. Just west of International Falls, at the confluence of the Big Fork and Rainy Rivers, a tremendous Indian burial mound of this era, one hundred feet across and more than forty feet high, and many smaller mounds remain for anyone to see.

The Indians who followed the mound-builders, the Dakotas and the Cree, were displaced by the Ojibways who moved westward from eastern Canada and northeastern United States. These are the woodland Indians of poetry and legend, the ones who built canoes out of white cedar and birchbark, and moved about with the seasons to plant and harvest food, a spiritual people who told great stories about the encounters of their ancestors with the Great Spirit as manifested in animals and natural surroundings. They used the lake and river waterways to transport their people and their belongings, and were already familiar with the water highway from the St. Lawrence River to the Northwest Territories when white trappers and traders used it to make a different kind of living.

French explorers paddled westward from Lake Superior around the 1700s, looking for a route to the Pacific. Soon the fur traders arrived, seeking beaver skins for the European market.

Along the route, fur trading posts were built, including one designated as Fort St. Pierre, built in 1731 on the north side of Rainy Lake across from the site of present-day International Falls.

The British took over the land from the French in 1763. By then, fur trappers were being forced farther and farther west to set their traplines. Competition was strong among the trading companies and one, the Northwest Company, instituted a new system for trading guns, ammunition, beads, axes, and other goods for the highly-prized furs. Instead of waiting for the trappers to bring furs to mid-west trading posts, they set up a long distance transport system. They employed brigades of French-Canadian men to travel the water highway in specially designed canoes to bring goods directly to the trappers and then return east with the furs. Thus the era of the Voyageurs began.

For about fifty years these light-hearted, colorfully-dressed men paddled and portaged their canoes over the lakes and riverways that became so identified with them that their route was dubbed the Voyageurs' Highway. The men were very strong and short of stature (to get maximum strength in minimum space). They canoed fifteen to eighteen hours a day, singing French songs and pushing their paddles to the strong cadence of their own music. On portages around falls and rapids and over stretches of land mass, each man carried 180 pound loads, sometimes more, on his back and shoulders.

By the mid 1800s, European taste had switched to other products for making their fashionable hats and other items of clothing, and the demand and price for beaver nosedived. The day of the Voyageur was at an end.

For several decades thereafter, land on the U.S. side of Rainy Lake was almost solely the province of the Ojibway Indians. Then one day in 1893 a lone prospector found a vein of gold on Little American Island, an island now within the park. Word got out. Gold fever struck and hundreds of fortune-seekers poured into the area. They came via railway, stagecoach, and steamboat to Rainy Lake City where the ore was hauled for processing. The city quickly became a bustling community of 500 people. Mines were opened on other islands—Dryweed and Bushyhead, and the search was on. It didn't last. The difficulty and costs involved in extracting the gold were too much. Less than $5,000 worth of gold was all that was mined. After three years, Rainy Lake City was deserted as people moved homes and belongings to Koochiching, since renamed International Falls. The Little American Mine is part of a Gold Mine Historic District listed on the National Register of Historic Places. The mine shaft on Bushyhead Island is visible from boats passing to the south of the island.

Shortly after the gold boom, lumbering of the northwoods of Minnesota reached the land bordering and within the present-day park, and the timbering period began. Over forty logging camps were set up to facilitate the harvesting of white pine. Next came the paper mill industry. Mills were built on both sides of Rainy Lake, at International Falls, and at Fort Frances in Canada, to convert pulpwood to paper. Productive, prosperous paper mills depend on a large, sure supply of trees to keep in business. When paper companies began to guarantee their source of raw material by buying up large tracts of forested land, the stage was set for a conflict that continued for many decades.

A National Park—End of a Long Campaign

It took eighty years for the determined people of Minnesota to convince Congress to authorize a national park along Minnesota's border with Canada. As early as the last decade of the nineteenth century people recognized the uniqueness of the land and waters of northern Minnesota, and sports fishermen and tourists began to come to the area, staying at resorts that were built along the lakeshores. The seeds of the environmental movement had been sown.

In 1891, the Minnesota State Legislature passed a resolution urging Congress to create a national park along a one hundred mile border of Rainy River and Rainy Lake. The rationale was that preservation of forested land would help to retain moisture in the atmosphere and benefit nearby agricultural lands. No action was taken by the federal government, but the state established a state park that year, the first of numerous state parks and forests to come.

Environmental awareness was raised in the next several years, and a citizens' group was formed in 1899 to lobby Congress for a national park. Many interests joined the battle on both sides—

lumbermen, local residents, conservationists, and federal and state officials. The outcome was a compromise—the establishment of a forest reserve, later named the Chippewa National Forest, in 1902. Legislation permitted some logging under controlled conditions and allowed recreation activities along two beautiful lakes, Cass Lake and Leech Lake.

The campaign for a national park continued and it was not over until 1971. Compromises were made between the various interests, and steps on the road to eventual success were taken. The Superior National Forest was created in 1909. In the 1920s, roadless areas were set aside within the forest and measures were taken to protect shorelines. The Boundary Waters Canoe Area was designated for wilderness preservation within the Superior Forest. In the 1930s, National Park Service studies acknowledged that the Kabetogama/Rainy Lake area was a possible site for a national park. Minnesota park interests kept up the pressure and the idea again received tentative endorsement when the Park Service updated its earlier survey in 1960.

When a new governor, Elmer Anderson, took office in 1961, he gave high priority to the campaign for a national park. In June 1962, he gathered together a group of people representing all the powerful interests concerned, among them conservationists, paper company officials, and the Director of the National Park Service, Conrad Wirth, for a boat trip along Kabetogama Lake. The strategy worked. Amid the comradery of a fishing, sightseeing venture on the beautiful lake, agreement was reached that a national park should be established along the Kabetogama Peninsula. Even the name, Voyageurs, suggested by renowned ecologist and writer, Sigurd Olson, met with approval.

There followed a lengthy period during which answers to questions were developed, the opposition's arguments were counteracted, Congressional support was built, Congressional hearings and debate took place, and details relating to the park's proposed borders were ironed out. The bill authorizing Voyageurs National Park became law in 1971, but the park was not formally established until 1975, when enough land had been acquired from the state and private landholders to make it a viable operation.

Why Go to Voyageurs National Park?

▶ To watch the early rays of a sunrise over Rainy Lake turn dark islands silhouetted against the vanilla-lemon-peach light into countless patches of green floating in deep blue water;

▶ To feel like a voyaguer paddling a "canot du nord" on Black Bay, singing rhythmic French songs as you glide along wild rice beds;

▶ To watch a bald eagle swoop down from its high perch to catch its supper at the water's edge;

▶ To search for deer or moose tracks as you hike along forest paths;

▶ To listen to the haunting tremolo of a loon in the evening quiet;

▶ To catch a lake trout, a walleye, or, if you're lucky, a sturgeon;

▶ To skim over lake waters in a kayak, canoe, motorboat, houseboat, or guided tour boat;

▶ To take the kids exploring for a beaver pond;

▶ To hear a far-off wolf howl while you lay snug in your sleeping bag;

▶ To feel the bite of the wind on your face as you snowmobile over frozen lake waters and island trails;

▶ To take the best photographs of your life!

This is only a sample of the many exciting and wondrous experiences to be had at Voyageurs National Park. When you've had them all, check with park rangers. They have 101 ideas!

How to Get to Voyageurs National Park

Voyageurs National Park is clearly a "destination" park. A traveler purposely sets out to visit this park, for it is not a short side trip on the way to other places. International Falls, where park headquarters is located, is 289 miles from Minneapolis/ St. Paul, 163 miles from the Duluth/Superior area. Roads leading to the park traverse through national and state forests and along many of the state's "10,000 lakes." U.S. Route 53, the chief northwest/southeast route, borders the tracks of the DW&P (Duluth, Winnipeg, and Pacific) Railroad for a good stretch of the road.

There are four main centers of access to lake waters: Rainy Lake Visitor Center, eleven miles east of International Falls on paved Minnesota Highway 11; Kabetogama Lake Visitor Center, three miles north of U.S. 53 on paved County Route 122; Ash River, 11 miles east of U.S. 53 on unpaved County Route 129; and Crane Lake, 25 miles east of U.S. 53 at Orr on paved County Route 23. Rainy Lake Visitor Center is open year-round, though for fewer hours in winter. Kabetogama Lake Visitor Center is open seasonally. There is a Ranger Station at Crane Lake.

There are no entrance fees to Voyageurs National Park.

Where to Stay

Non-Campers. The only overnight lodging within the park is the historic Kettle Falls Hotel, a twelve bedroom wooden structure recently refurbished. The structure was built originally in 1913 to provide accommodations for lumbermen and commercial fishermen meeting at the Kettle Falls dam. The hotel and surrounding area are listed on the National Register of Historic Places.

Kettle Falls Hotel is now operated by a park concessioner, a member of the family that operated the hotel for over seventy years. The hotel complex includes a dining room serving daily visitors as well as hotel guests, an old-time bar, boat rentals, fishing guide services, and individual cabins. It is accessible only by boat or seaplane. The hotel is open from mid-May to the end of September. Prices are in the expensive range. For more information and reservations, write to the Kettle Falls Hotel.

The lake waters of northern Minnesota have attracted sportsmen and tourists for nearly a century. Long before there was a national park in the state, resorts, lodges, and private campgrounds serviced visitors. Today a great variety of resorts, lodges, campgrounds, and rental houseboats provide accommodations for travelers. Most of them are on the lakeside, so that even if you are not a camper, you can relax in a quiet, remote, woodland setting. Most facilities are open from May to October. A few stay open in winter.

Send to park headquarters for an *Accommodations Guide,* which lists all the lodging accommodations at Rainy Lake, Kabetogama Lake, Ash River, and Crane Lake, and the services they offer (water transportation, marine services, aircraft services, fishing guides, and outfitting services).

For information about accommodations and services in the city of International Falls, write to the Greater International Falls Chamber of Commerce.

Camping on the Mainland. There are no national park campgrounds on the mainland, but there are many privately-run campgrounds in the vicinity of all four lakeside centers as well as in International Falls. Many provide electricity, hookups, and dump stations. The park's *Accommodations Guide* and the Chamber of Commerce's *Official Tourist Vacation Guide* give details.

There are Kabetogama State Forest campgrounds at Ash River and on Lake Kabetogama. For information, contact the Department of Natural Resources Tourist Information Center.

Camping on the Islands. A truly lakeshore-woodland experience awaits the camper at any one of the park's 120 boat-in campsites. Sites are located on tiny, unnamed islands, in sheltered bays, and along small lakes on the Kabetogama Peninsula.

If you don't have your own boat, water transportation to the islands is available from concessioners in several locations.

Some campsites are closed temporarily to camping and houseboat anchorage early in the season to protect nesting sites of bald eagles, osprey, and common terns.

Campsites are available on a first come, first served basis. Campers are required to pitch tents only on tent pads, where they are provided. There is a fourteen day limit at any one site. There is no fee for use of a campsite. For other information and regulations relating to camping, write to park headquarters.

What to Do at Voyageurs National Park

Visitors go to Voyageurs National Park primarily in two seasons—summer and winter. Moderate climate and an unlimited expanse of deep blue lake waters, dotted with innumerable intriguing islands waiting to be explored, lure most people in summer. Here are the primary activities engaged in during the summer months.

Boating. Whether in a motorboat, canoe, kayak, sailboat, or houseboat, plying the waters of Voyageurs appeals to the curious sightseer, the energetic paddler, the relaxed sailor, and the vacationer seeking to regain personal vitality by a complete change of outdoor scenery and a slower daily pace. Many people take their own boats to the park and launch them at park or commercial launch ramps. Resorts and marinas rent watercraft of all types, including houseboats. Both the park *Accommodations Guide* and the Greater International Falls Chamber of Commerce provide information about boat rentals and marina services.

People preferring to let someone else "do the driving" can take a guided trip on "The Pride of Rainy Lake" or the "Betsy Anna," tour boats operated by the park concessioner. "The Pride" departs at specified times from Rainy Lake Visitor Center for two and one-half hour cruises on Rainy Lake, and for day-long cruises among many of the islands to Kettle Falls. Passengers can disembark and eat lunch in the Kettle Falls Hotel dining room, or on their big front porch, or have a picnic. A guide on the boat provides information about the history and natural resources of the area, and the wildlife you may see enroute. The concessioner also offers dinner cruises at certain times in summer.

The "Betsy Anna" departs from Kabetogama Lake Visitor Center at various times for short naturalist-led cruises on the lake and longer trips to Kettle Falls.

Reservations are suggested for all boat trips. Rates range from $6.50 to $29.50 for adults, $3.75 to $18.00 for children. For schedule information, rates, and reservations, contact Voyageurs National Park Boat Tours, Inc. or inquire at park visitor centers.

A special treat for park visitors who like to canoe is to join a ranger-led group and paddle a 26-foot Voyageur North Canoe. Check at the Rainy Lake Visitor Center for times and other information.

Fishing. During all seasons, but especially in summer, you will see sports fishermen assembling their gear and swapping stories at resort centers and campgrounds in the park's four major lakeside centers. The lakes of northern Minnesota are famous for their walleye, northern pike, and small-mouth bass. Other fish caught in lake waters are muskie, perch, sauger, lake trout, and crappie.

Be assured if you are not there to catch fish, you can still enjoy it served in most area restaurants.

Fishing is permitted from docks at campsites and trailheads. Fishing guides are available at all four resort locations. See the *Accommodations Guide*. A Minnesota state fishing license is required for fishing in park waters. An Ontario fishing license is needed when fishing on the Canadian side of Rainy, Namakan, or Sand Point Lakes. The licenses may be obtained from local sporting goods stores, bait shops, and resorts. They may also be obtained from the Minnesota Department of Natural Resources.

The park encourages sports fishermen to follow a "catch and release" policy, a responsible sport fishing method of perpetuating the lakes' natural fish population.

Hiking. Hiking through the boreal forest, above marshes, and along beaver ponds, studying the plant life and listening for sounds of native wildlife, is one of the best ways to enjoy the solitude of Voyageurland.

The park maintains 32 miles of hiking trails. A trail guide for the two-mile Nature Trail to Locator Lake can be purchased at the visitor centers or picked up at the trailhead. To reach the trailhead at the northwest edge of Kabetogama Lake, launch your boat at the Kabetogama Lake Visitor Center or the Woodenfrog campground, or seek transportation from one of the nearby resorts. Before you go, stop at the visitor center and see if a Park Service canoe or rowboat is available for use on Locator Lake.

The Cruiser Lake Trail, accessible only by boat, is a ten mile hike from Kabetogama Lake to Rainy Lake. It winds through the peninsula's wilderness and along several small lakes, a trek providing rewarding experiences for the dedicated backpacker. Ask park rangers for a copy of the trail guide. Shorter nature walks are led periodically by park naturalists.

Swimming and Waterskiing. They are permitted in the park's waters. However, visitors are urged to swim only in protected coves where the bottom slopes gradually to deep water. Waterskiers must be towed only by boats operated by experienced drivers, accompanied by experienced observers.

Winter Sports. Minnesotans have learned to enjoy the out-of-doors during their long periods of below zero winter weather, by indulging in a variety of sports. Snowmobiling, cross-country skiing, and snowshoeing are so popular in Voyageurland that as soon as the ice is thick enough, the park plows and maintains the Rainy

Lake Ice Road from the Rainy Lake Visitor Center on Black Bay to Cranberry Bay, a distance of seven and one-half miles. Snowmobile portage trails between lakes and other frozen waterways are designated at various points on the Kabetogama Peninsula. Cross-country skiers and snowshoers usually enjoy their sport along the lakeshores. Black Bay Ski Trail, across from the Rainy Lake Visitor Center, is groomed specifically for their use. Fishermen continue to catch walleye and lake trout in mid-winter through holes in the ice.

NOTE: *Off-road driving is not permitted except on frozen lake surfaces. Hunting is prohibited in the park. Carrying firearms is not permitted except under special conditions. Pets on leashes are allowed in developed areas, on land within 100 feet of the shores, and on the surfaces of Rainy, Kabetogama, Namakan, Sand Point, and Crane Lakes. They are prohibited on park trails, in the backcountry, and on interior lakes. Both visitor centers and the Oberholtzer Nature Trail are accessible to persons with a physical handicap.*

If You Have the Time

▶ Spend a few hours in International Falls and see the city's ten foot high digital thermometer erected in recognition of the city's reputation as the Nation's Ice Box, and the imposing statue of Smokey the Bear and two cubs in the center of the town park. Visit the park's Koochiching County Historical Museum full of exhibits of Indian artifacts and items associated with life in northern Minnesota in earlier times.

▶ Drive across the bridge to Canada and visit Fort St. Pierre, a replica of an early fur trading post, and other museums and shops in the town of Fort Frances. Passports are not required, but other forms of identification may be necessary when you go through U.S. and Canadian customs.

▶ Visit the Grand Mound History Center, a seventy acre woodland site preserving prehistoric burial mounds. The Interpretive Center, operated by the Minnesota Historical Society, is located seventeen miles west of International Falls on State Highway 11. It is open May 1 through September 1.

▶ Take a guided tour of Boise Cascade's paper mill at International Falls, offered Monday through Friday from June through August.

Tips for Adding to Your Enjoyment of Voyageurs National Park

1. Send to park headquarters for a park brochure and information of special interest to you, e.g., overnight lodgings in the four lakeside resort areas, island campsites and camping regulations, fishing guides, and tour boat trips.

2. Contact the Greater International Falls Chamber of Commerce for information about lodging, campgrounds, and services in International Falls.

3. Write to the Minnesota Office of Tourism for a Minnesota state map and other information about traveling in the state.

4. If you want to read more about the park or the area's natural resources and wildlife before you go, ask the park for a publications catalog of the Lake States Interpretive Association, the park's cooperating association.

5. If you want information about canoeing in the Boundary Waters Canoe Area, just east of the park, write to the Superior National Forest.

6. Take camera, binoculars, and warm clothing.

7. When you arrive at the park, make a park visitor center your first stop. Find out about ranger-led programs and get a copy of *Rendezvous,* the park's newspaper, for up-to-date information.

And finally—Take a few moments to muse about those Minnesotans who so loved this country they waged a life-long campaign to save it as it was, so that we, too, can experience the wonder of traveling through the lakes and forested islands of the soft-treading woodland Indians and the high-spirited voyageurs.

Sources of Information

Superintendent	Greater International Falls
Voyageurs National Park	Chamber of Commerce
Box 50	Box 169B
International Falls, MN 56649	International Falls, MN 56649
Phone: 218-283-9821	Phone: 218-283-9400

Minnesota Office of Tourism
375 Jackson St.
250 Skyway Level
St. Paul, MN 55101
Phone: 1-800-657-3700

Kettle Falls Hotel, Inc.
Box 1272
International Falls, MN 56649
Phone: Summer: 218-374-3511
Winter: 218-286-5685

Voyageurs National Park Boat
Tours Inc.
Rt. 8 Box 303, Dept. F-9
International Falls, MN 56649
Phone: 218-286-5470

Boundary Waters Canoe Area
Superior National Forest
Box 338
Duluth, MN 55801
Phone: 218-720-5324

Department of Natural Resources
Information Center
500 Lafayette Road
St. Paul, MN 55155-4040
Phone: 800-657-3700 (Ask for
DNR) or 800-652-9747 (within MN)

CAPE LOOKOUT
NATIONAL SEASHORE

The islands of Cape Lookout National Seashore—Portsmouth Island, Core Banks, and Shackleford Banks—are links in a chain of islands off the North Carolina coast called the Outer Banks. These islands, however, are as different from the rest as day from night. There are no bridges to them, no paved roads, no motels, condominiums, restaurants, or fast-food places, and no year-round human inhabitants. Only shorebirds, a few animals, and various forms of sea life inhabit the beaches, dunes, salt marshes, grassland flats, and the few hammocks of dense vegetation.

Except for Portsmouth Village on Portsmouth Island, most of the physical evidence of former residents is gone. Some of it—

abandoned cars and trucks, and shanties once used by fishermen and hunters—has been removed. A few structures are in occasional use under special arrangements provided for in the park's enabling legislation. The rest has been destroyed by fire or has succumbed to wind and wave action as the sea staked its claim.

The islands are all within the one hundred year flood plain. Once they were the home of a hardy group of people. The Bankers eked out a living from the sea. When times changed and that was no longer possible, they left.

Family cemeteries remain. A few village structures—homes, the post office, the schoolhouse, the church—still stand, well preserved, in the little village of Portsmouth at the northern tip of the seashore—across Ocracoke Inlet from the village of Ocracoke.

Strolling on a quiet path through Portsmouth village, past the old life-saving station, across the tidal flats to the beach, you can feel the essence of island living. And wonder about the independent, proud spirit of those who dared to live there.

Cape Lookout National Seashore is not very big. Its total acreage is just over 28,000 acres. The islands are narrow ribbons of sand, varying in width from 600 feet to one and three-quarters miles. They are one of the few places where you can view sand dunes never disturbed by man. Winds come from the northeast in autumn and winter, the southwest at other times, constantly reshaping the land. The islands are migrating toward the mainland as the shores erode on the ocean side an average of one and one half feet a year.

Not many people have discovered Cape Lookout National Seashore. To get there, you have to plan. You need to check out the ferry schedules, bring your own food and water, and prepare for weather changes. But if you find pleasure in taking a solitary walk on a remote beach, primitive camping, ocean fishing, or touching base with a vignette of maritime history, this seashore should rank high on your "must do" list.

The People of Cape Lookout

Coree Indians once inhabited Shackleford Banks and Lookout Point, but most of what is known about life on the islands of Cape Lookout National Seashore starts with the eighteenth century. While the Outer Banks islands paralleling the North Carolina coast served as protective barriers from the onslaughts of the sea, they and the shallow inlets through them were an obstacle to ships transporting commercial products to and from the mainland.

In 1753, the legislature authorized the establishment of the town of Portsmouth on the southern border of Ocracoke Inlet to help solve this problem. Here, it was planned, the cargo of heavily-ladened ships could be unloaded and stored in warehouses, then transported to the growing cities along the coast in lighter, shallow-draft boats. (The term "lightering" is used to describe this procedure). The larger ships, unburdened of much of their cargo, could then proceed through the inlet. Early on, private interests built warehouses on nearby Shell Castle Island (made up entirely of oyster shells) which became the prime storage area.

For nearly one hundred years, the pilots and other residents of Portsmouth derived their livelihood from the work involved in this operation or the support of those who were. The town also was the site of a marine hospital and, for a brief period, a small fort.

During the Civil War, most residents fled Portsmouth and Confederate and Union troops each spent time there. After the war, some residents came back but the fickleness of the sea, upon which the town's prosperity was dependent, settled its fate. During a mid-century storm, a better inlet had broken through at Hatteras Inlet farther north. Major commercial shipping no longer passed through Ocracoke Inlet and the economic well-being of Portsmouth came to an end.

To the south, in and along the Core Banks, Lookout Point, Lookout Bight, and Shackleford Banks, maritime-related activity was of a different sort.

Nature did not provide the early island settlers with soil for a bountiful harvest of land crops, but she was generous when it came to food from the sea. Early colonists engaged in "the taking of whales." At first their methods were primitive. A 1709 account relates: "Whales are very numerous on the coast of North Carolina ... where these Whales come ashore, none being struck or killed with a Harpoon in the Place, as they are to the Northward ... all those Fish being found dead on the Shoar, most commonly by those that inhabit the banks and sea-side where they dwell ..."

New England whalers frequented the waters of North Carolina. Some of them decided to settle down in the area. Soon the local fishermen, at first perhaps guided by the experienced New Englanders, were taking to their boats and hunting for their prey. After a whale was killed, it was towed to the beach where try-pots were set up for boiling the blubber as the whale was cut up.

The whalers liked to name the whales. One was called "Mayflower" because it was caught on May 4. Another was called "Haint Bin Named Yet."

The town of Diamond City on the east end of Shackleford Banks for a time thrived as the center of North Carolina whaling. Eventually the waters along the coast were whaled out and by 1900, battered both by the loss of a productive livelihood and severe hurricanes, everyone had gone. Some took their houses with them to Harker's Island, Beaufort, Morehead City, or Salter Path.

Cape Lookout Bight is a natural fish trap and around the turn of the century mullet fishing was an active commercial enterprise.

From June until late fall, crews of mullet fishermen set up their operations on the Outer Banks, fanning out with their nets to catch the fish on both the sound and ocean sides as they migrated northward. Commercial fishing is still important to the economy of coastal North Carolina.

Early seafarers sailing along the North Carolina coast both feared and appreciated the configuration of Cape Lookout. On the one hand, dangerous shoals extended out from the cape about ten miles. Low-lying land and frequent fog hampered the visibility, adding to the hazardous conditions. "Promontorium tremendum," horrible headland, was what Cape Lookout was termed by a late sixteenth century map maker.

But if a vessel safely traversed the perilous waters and made it around the sandy point that curved to the west, forming Lookout Bight, a safe harbor awaited. This spot became a favored rendezvous site for fighting ships from pirates and Spanish privateers to British warships in the American Revolution and the War of 1812. Union ships planning blockades of southern ports during the Civil War and Europe-bound convoys of World Wars I and II also rendezvoused there.

Responding at last to the long-known hazards of the shoals off Cape Lookout, Congress authorized the building of a lighthouse. It was completed in 1812. It was not the most effective lighthouse on the Atlantic coast and there were many complaints about its poor visibility and lighting system. By 1859, a new tower had been built and a "state-of-the-art" Fresnel lens installed. In 1873, a distinctive black and white checker design was painted on the tower, serving as a useful day marker, which it does to this day. In 1950, the lighthouse, under the jurisdiction of the U.S. Coast Guard, was automated.

For those whose ships did not find safe passage, there was one last hope. As on other key barrier islands, courageous men, members of the U.S. Life-Saving Service, frequently risked their lives in daring rescue efforts. For about fifty years, starting in the late 1800s, they braved the perils of the sea and, from three life-saving stations—at Portsmouth, at Cape Lookout, and about halfway between on Core Banks—they rowed their surfboats through stormy seas to save the crews of foundering ships.

Core Banks may have been sparsely populated in the early decades of the twentieth century, but it was not forgotten. Because of this particular location along the Atlantic coast and the excellent harbor at Lookout Bight, at different times the island was of special significance to shipping interests, the military, and fishermen.

After many years of study to determine the best location for a "Harbor of Refuge" for large vessels facing severe weather along the Carolina coast, work began in 1914 on the construction of an extensive stone breakwater further enclosing Lookout Bight. The prospect of turning Cape Lookout into a major seaport brightened with the news that the Norfolk and Southern Railway Company planned to extend the rail line from Beaufort to Shackleford Banks and over to Cape Lookout if the federal government built the breakwater.

Work stopped on the project before it was completed, however, when World War I erupted. It was never finished and plans to extend the railroad to the banks were dropped.

World War II was a very real and present danger to the people living on the banks. The sights and sounds of warfare on the seas were with them constantly in the early months of the war when German U-Boats prowled the coastal waters, sometimes scoring direct hits on American merchant ships.

The Army placed guns at strategic points to protect the entrance to the harbor at Cape Lookout; Coast Guard cutters patrolled the ocean; and volunteers backed them up. Some flew Civil Air Patrol planes and some, members of the Home Guard, used their own boats to patrol the coastal waters and perform whatever tasks the Navy asked of them.

Those were the bad times; but between wars, there were lots of good times. It was a favored spot for many North Carolina mainlanders to vacation. The fishing was great at the point, near the abandoned breakwater, and farther north at Drum Inlet. Private and party boats congregated, especially on weekends. After the fishing, there was square dancing and listening to songs sung by favorite balladeers.

Recreational fishermen and hunters came in increasing numbers to the shores of Core and Shackleford Banks after World War II. The regulars built overnight shanties, some on land they did not own. They ferried cars, trucks, and oversand vehicles to the islands so they could follow their prey. When the cars broke down, they were abandoned and parts of the islands looked like junkyards.

The Islands Become a National Seashore.

In the sixties, officials of the state of North Carolina looked into the feasibility of creating a state park on Cape Lookout. They concluded it would be too expensive. Yet the islands offered a rare opportunity to establish a public recreational site in a remote, predominantly natural, maritime environment. The National Park Service was approached, North Carolina's Congressmen introduced the legislation, and in May 1966, Cape Lookout National Seashore was authorized.

In the years that followed, the seashore took on two major tasks. First, a clean-up operation. Twenty-five hundred abandoned vehicles and over 300 squatter dwellings had to be removed from the sands and grasslands. Marine helicopters were called in to airlift rusted cars and trucks to acceptable disposal sites. Deteriorating structures were torn down and burned. By 1986, the job was done and most of the land reverted to its natural, sea-buffeted state.

Equally important was the second project—acting quickly to acquire and preserve the remaining structures of the village of Portsmouth so that the village could be restored and serve as an authentic, living demonstration of the daily life of the Bankers in the early days of the twentieth century. This task, well under way, is ongoing.

The last three permanent residents left in 1971, but a few of the former residents retain the right to use their houses during their lifetimes. They often return to the village for short stays in good weather. Some serve as volunteer National Park Service guides. They welcome your questions about life on a remote island with no telephone or electricity but plenty of seafood and self-created entertainment. When you go there, if you see a gentle, smiling lady sitting on her front porch, enjoying the cool sea breezes, stop by and visit. She'll tell you the returnees agree that "Being here is like going to heaven without dying."

Why Go to Cape Lookout National Seashore?

▶ To breathe the fresh sea air and walk in solitude on a beach where sands, sea oats, sea shells, sea birds, and every living thing is just as nature has created it;

▶ To step back in time and quietly wander through a maritime village as it appeared nearly one hundred years ago;

▶ To look up at a tall diamond-patterned lighthouse and picture its light beaming through the night to warn a lonely sailor on watch of the dangerous shoals extending ten miles out to sea;

▶ To cast a line in the surf and reel in the day's tasty catch;

▶ To catch a glimpse of a wild horse grazing along the banks of an island wilderness.

How to Get to Cape Lookout National Seashore

Access to all parts of Cape Lookout National Seashore is by boat only. Up-to-date information about island conditions can be obtained from seashore rangers at three places—the temporary Cape Lookout National Seashore headquarters at Beaufort, North Carolina, the temporary visitor center on Harker's Island, or at the visitor center at Ocracoke, a unit of the Cape Hatteras National Seashore.

Beaufort is on U.S. Route 70, one hundred miles east of U.S. I-95. If traveling by boat, use the Intracoastal Waterway which passes near Beaufort. To get to the Harker's Island Visitor Center and the dock for the boat to the lighthouse area, leave Route 70 about halfway between Otway and Smyrna and take SR 1332 and SR 1335 south for eight miles. To reach Ocracoke, take State Route 12 to the southern boundary of Cape Hatteras National Seashore. If you are not familiar with the roads in North Carolina, send to the North Carolina Travel and Tourism Division for a free map of North Carolina.

If your destination is Portsmouth, take a boat from Ocracoke. Reservations are necessary. Information about schedules and fees can be obtained from seashore headquarters or at the Cape Hatteras Visitor Center at Ocracoke. When you return to Ocracoke, if you want to visit other parts of Cape Lookout, take the car ferry to Cedar Island. Reservations are necessary. The ferry lands at SR 12 which leads to U.S. Route 70.

Ferries to the lighthouse and the Lookout Bight area run from Harker's Island. Ferries equipped to transport four-wheel-drive vehicles as well as passengers run from Davis to near Great Island, Core Banks, and from Atlantic to an area north of Drum Inlet. From Drum Inlet, it is possible to drive in a four-wheel-drive vehicle on designated routes to Portsmouth. Davis and Atlantic are on Route 70.

Ferries operate from spring until fall at specified times. Small boats also transport people from various points to Shackleford Banks. No motorized vehicles are allowed on Shackleford Banks.

All ferries are operated by seashore concessioners. Contact seashore headquarters for a list of ferry and boat concessioners and their rates which range from $10 to $40 per person. Then check schedules and make reservations directly with the operators.

Except for the cost of the ferry trip, there are no entrance fees to Cape Lookout National Seashore.

Where to Stay.

Non-Campers. There are several motels, inns, and bed and breakfast places in Beaufort, a lovely, old, coastal town where the seashore's administrative headquarters is located. Harker's Island and Ocracoke also have accommodations. For information about Beaufort and Harker's Island, write to the Carteret County Chamber of Commerce. For information about Ocracoke, write to the Dare County Tourism Bureau. The North Carolina Travel and Tourism Division also publishes an *Accommodations Directory.* The directory lists many hostelries that are locally-owned.

Camping on the Islands. You have a choice. For a primitive overnight stay, you can bring all your supplies, including water, and pitch a tent on the islands, or you can stay in one of the few simple structures available for rent by concessioners. Cabins are basically fishing camps. There is no electricity. For information and advice about overnighting on the islands, contact seashore headquarters. For information about cabins, contact the two concessioners, Alger Willis Fishing Camps, Inc. and Morris Marina, Kabin Kamps and Ferry Service.

Camping on the Mainland. The Carteret County Chamber of Commerce provides information about drive-in campgrounds in the vicinity of the seashore, and the North Carolina Travel and Tourism Division will send you a copy of its *Camping and Outdoors Directory* on request.

What to Do at Cape Lookout National Seashore

Go prepared. There is little shade on the islands. Take a shirt, a sun-shielding hat, and an effective sunscreen lotion to protect you from the sun, and insect repellent to ward off biting insects. There are a few shade shelters at various points along the banks.

Bring food and drink. Water is available only in Portsmouth and there are no services. Comfort stations are located at Portsmouth, the lighthouse area, and on Shackleford Banks.

Remember the hour the boat leaves for the return trip. When you leave, do your part to keep Cape Lookout an unspoiled seashore and take your trash with you.

Once you go to the islands of Cape Lookout, you are pretty much on your own. Plan to do some or all of the following.

Visit Portsmouth. Take a brochure from a box near the boat landing. It will serve as your guide on a walk through the village. Follow the path, bordered with red cedars, yaupon hollies, and wax myrtle, to the village. Stop at the visitor center in the first restored house you come to. Then take a leisurely stroll. Pass the cemeteries and the post office, which was a lively center of community gathering for two decades in mid-century until postal service to the island was cancelled because of a decline in village population.

Go into the old Methodist Church and sign the guest register. The church, a significant force in the life of village residents, was destroyed by fire in 1913, but money was raised from many sources to rebuild it the next year. Even today, on special occasions, former village residents congregate at the church and reminisce about life and events on the island in an earlier time.

After exploring the village, head for the U.S. Life-Saving Station and the beach. Pause at the station and picture the disciplined routine of the station's keeper and his men as they constantly kept watch and patrolled the beaches, prepared to put their lives on the line in rescue operations.

Portsmouth Village is listed on the *National Register of Historic Places.*

The Beach. For years to come, you will cherish memories of the time you spend on the beach—the feeling of remoteness, the treasures washed in from the sea, the fantasies conjured up as you gaze out over the Atlantic Ocean. There are many things to do on Cape Lookout's beaches—sunbathe, swim, surf, picnic, fish, walk the beach, and gather a variety of shells, such as sand dollars, moon snails, Scotch bonnets, and lettered olives.

If you are a bird watcher, in spring and fall look for migrating birds. In summer, terns, black skimmers, plovers, egrets, and heron nest at the seashore. At times you see the eastern brown pelican and the peregrine falcon, both on the endangered species list. Atlantic loggerhead turtles, on the list of threatened species, come up on the beaches at nesting time. Visitors will be warned to stay away from these areas when this occurs.

Do not pick sea oats. The spreading roots of these golden-tasseled grasses hold the sand and are one of the few natural stabilizing forces. They are protected by law.

You can enjoy all these experiences at any of the three islands of Cape Lookout National Seashore. But first you must get there. Boat landings are on the inland side of the islands. Beyond the Life-Saving Station on Portsmouth Island, a sign will point to a path for a mile-long walk over the tidal flats to the pristine beach.

The ferry from Harker's Island lands a short distance from the dramatic diamond-patterned Cape Lookout lighthouse. The lighthouse keeper's quarters now serve as a visitor contact station and, from time to time, rangers conduct interpretive programs there. Check with seashore headquarters for a schedule of such programs. The lighthouse is still an active aid to navigation and is not open to the public.

Walk on both the sound and ocean sides of the island and observe the difference in sand and sea life on the shores. If you want to go out to Lookout Point, where shell-collecting is especially appealing, you can take the three-mile walk along the beach or ride the motorized jitney operated by a concessioner for a modest fee.

For variation in scenery, you may choose to take a boat to Shackleford Banks, which is an eight mile island running east to west. Facing the prevailing winds, the blowing sand builds the dunes as high as 35 feet. Behind the dunes, near the western end of the island, there is a maritime forest. The designation of Shackleford Banks as an official wilderness area is under consideration. Until such action is taken, the island is being managed as a natural zone. No motorized vehicles are allowed on the island. Over one hundred wild horses run free.

Fishing. Fishing for drum, speckled trout, flounder, bluefish, Spanish mackerel, and pompano continues to be great sport at Cape Lookout. No license is required for salt water fishing, but fishing regulations of the state of North Carolina apply. For details, contact North Carolina's Department of Natural Resources and Community Development, Wildlife Resources Commission.

Hunting. Hunting for pheasants, rabbits, and waterfowl takes place on the islands under federal and state regulations. Hunting licenses may be obtained at local sporting goods stores and from the state Wildlife Commission.

NOTE: *Off-road vehicles, like all vehicles on the islands, must be driven only on designated paths. Pets are prohibited on ferry boats. They may be taken to the islands in private boats so long as they are on a leash at all times. As yet there are no special facilities for persons with a physical handicap either at the visitor centers or on boats transporting people to the islands. Many of the seashore's buildings are in temporary quarters, and as new facilities are built and old ones are restored, such facilities will be provided.*

If You Have the Time

▸ Spend a few hours in the old coastal town of Beaufort. Stroll along the waterfront boardwalk, visit the craft shops and art galleries, and take a walking or bus tour of the town's historic district.

▸ Visit the North Carolina Maritime Museum in the heart of Beaufort. There are models, aquariums, and a boat shop carrying out the museum's theme, "Down to the Sea."

For information about the Beaufort Historical Restoration Site and the Maritime Museum, contact the Beaufort Historical Welcome Center. Phone: 919-728-7317

Tips for Adding to Your Enjoyment of Cape Lookout National Seashore

1. Send to seashore headquarters for one of the seashore's brochures and information of special interest to you, e.g. overnighting on the islands and a list of concessioners for boat transportation.

2. Make reservations for boat transportation before you go.

3. If you need one, send to the North Carolina Division of Travel and Tourism for a state map and other information about traveling in North Carolina.

4. Send to the Carteret Chamber of Commerce for information about overnight lodging at Beaufort and Harker's Island, and to the Dare County Tourist Bureau for information about lodging at Ocracoke.

5. Take sun-shielding clothing and insect repellent with you.

And finally—When you get to the beach, watch the waves roll in and break on the shore. See how the seabirds and sand crabs poke about looking for a tasty morsel brought in from the sea. Listen to the sounds of the sea in a seashell. Take a stick and write a message in the sand. Scan the horizon and imagine how far it is to the nearest point of land. This is what a visit to Cape Lookout National Seashore is all about.

Sources of Information

Superintendent
Cape Lookout National Seashore
415 Front Street
Beaufort, NC 28516
Phone: 919-728-2121

NC Travel and Tourism Division
430 N. Salisbury St.
Raleigh, NC 27611
Phone: 800-VISITNC

Carteret County Chamber of Commerce
Box 1198
Morehead City, NC 28557
Phone: 800-NCCOAST
or 919-726-6831

Dare County Tourist Bureau
Box 399
Manteo, NC 27954
Phone: 919-473-2138

North Carolina Dept. of Natural
Resources and Community
Development
Wildlife Resources Commission
512 N. Salisbury St.
Raleigh, NC 27611-7687
Phone: 919-733-7191

Ferries between Cedar Island and
Ocracoke:
Phone: Ocracoke: 919-928-3841
Cedar Island: 919-225-3551

Alger Willis Fishing Camps, Inc.
Box 234
Davis, NC 28524
Phone: 919-729-2791

Morris Marina, Kabin Kamps and
Ferry Service
Star Route Box 76J
Atlantic, NC 28511
Phone: 919-225-4261

CUMBERLAND ISLAND
NATIONAL SEASHORE

In the early days there were vast reaches of wide, sloping beaches where the tide gently deposited the sea's bounty, whole and unbroken, on the glistening sands. There was the deep shade of live oak forests draped with silver-gray clusters of Spanish moss. Wide salt marshes teamed with the incubating young of creatures of the sea and with the birds and animals that prey on them. Brackish ponds and bogs dotted openings in the forest cover where birds, reptiles, insects, and mammals competed for food and for life.

Above all, there was solitude.

They are all still there at Cumberland Island National Seashore. There have been changes, but they are few. The live oak

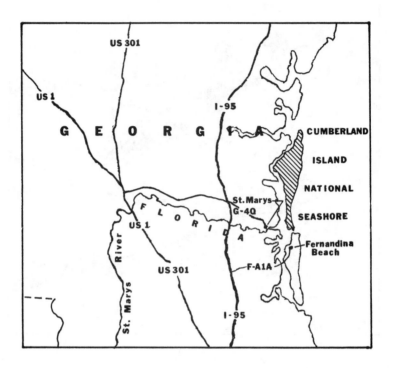

forest is a younger one, for many years ago the old forest trees were timbered off. On the beach, the sea now deposits bits of flotsam and jetsam along with nature's harvest. A few wild horses and pigs roam over the island. And occasionally, a hiker passes by.

But the beach is still mesmerizing. The live oak forests remain a delicate balance of light and shadow. The marshes and bogs continue to be an intramural battleground of nature's creatures. And, as they have for hundreds of years, the dunes march across the landscape engulfing the edges of the forest.

Solitude can still be found on Cumberland Island. A person can lay aside the pressures of a high tech world for a while, walk along a quiet beach or through a cooling forest, become absorbed in the antics of a chirping bird or a foraging animal, and let the world go by.

Cumberland Island is the largest and southernmost of the Sea Islands off the coast of Georgia. It is broader, more stable, and more lush in vegetation than the Outer Banks Islands of North

Carolina. The area known as Big Cumberland Island, the site of the national seashore, is approximately sixteen miles long and varies in width from one-half mile near the southern tip to three miles.

The Cumberland River and Cumberland Sound, part of the Intracoastal Waterway, separate the island from the mainland. On the south, the entrance to St. Marys River divides it from Amelia Island in Florida. To the north lies Little Cumberland Island across salt marshes and Christmas Creek. Technically within the boundaries of the seashore, Little Cumberland Island is being maintained as a natural preserve by the island's private property owners under terms of an irrevocable trust. So long as the trust is not violated, the federal government will not acquire land on Little Cumberland Island. To the east is the Atlantic Ocean.

Wide, sweeping beaches gradually slope into the ocean on the east side of the island. One prominent dune ridge, up to forty feet in some places, extends north and south on most of the island. Fresh water ponds, fertile salt marshes, and cool, dense, maritime forests support a rich variety of animal, seabird, plant, and marine life.

Though the island is subject to a modest amount of erosion due to the worldwide rise in sea level and blowing winter winds, it rarely is subjected to the devastating effects of violent maritime storms. The mild temperatures characteristic of southern coastal islands attract visitors in all seasons.

Much of Cumberland Island remained in its primitive state when the seashore was established. In 1982, Congress designated nearly 9,000 acres in the central and northern portions as a national wilderness area. Another 11,718 acres were declared potential wilderness. These lands will become wilderness areas when all existing rights and uses incompatible with wilderness status have expired.

The People of Cumberland Island

By the time the Spanish pushed north from their colonial bases on the Florida coast in the 1560s, Timucuan Indians had been living along the Georgia coast for 3,000 to 4,000 thousand years. They made pottery and fashioned tools and decorative ornaments from shells. They hunted and fished and traveled in canoes. Cumberland Island was a hospitable place and the Tacatacoru tribe of Timucuans settled in Missoe, an Indian name for the island.

The Spanish built a fort on the island and called it San Pedro. They were not welcomed by the Tacatacorus and the first missionaries, the Jesuits, failed in their efforts to convert the natives to Christianity. But twenty years later the Franciscans took over mission work and by the beginning of the seventeenth century, the Indians were loyal, converted friends.

The English came to Cumberland Island as a consequence of their several decades of conflict with the Spanish to determine which nation would control the colonizing of the Georgia-Florida coast. When the English staked their claim, they called the island Cumberland, a name suggested by an Indian who had been cordially treated by the Duke of Cumberland when his English friend, Colonel James Oglethrope, took him to London.

Forts were built on the north and south ends of the island and by 1763, the English clearly had won out.

The first Dungeness was built during this period. Named for a royal estate on the Cape of Dungeness in Kent, the structure is believed to have been used in connection with the hunt for food for troops at Fort Prince William at South Point. Later islanders referred to the building as Oglethorpe's "hunting lodge."

Life was quiet on the island until General Nathanael Greene, outstanding American military leader in the Revolutionary War, bought a sizeable piece of land on the south end. It is believed he intended to harvest live oak timber for shipbuilding and build a family home there. He died before the home was built, but his widow, Catherine, had a four-story mansion constructed of tabby, a mixture of shells, lime, sand, and water. Twelve acres of flower gardens and tropical plants including dates, guavas, olives, and oranges surrounded the house. Under the supervision of Phineas Miller, Catherine Greene's second husband, the estate, called Dungeness, became one of the island's first major plantations, growing cotton and sugar cane.

The nineteenth century saw great changes on Cumberland Island. Until the outbreak of the Civil War, the island thrived primarily on lumbering and farming. Live oak timber was considered a prime material for shipbuilding. Plantations supplied high-grade long staple cotton. Hogs, cattle, and horses were kept, and food was grown for island inhabitants, including the numerous slaves essential to the plantation economy. Shell middens were tapped to build a base for a road running the length of the island and to form an essential ingredient of tabby.

Prosperity ended with the Civil War and the loss of slave labor. Many plantations deteriorated, including Dungeness. Property began to change hands. For the most part, the purchasers were people of means seeking private recreational retreats. Most well-known among the new landowners was Thomas M. Carnegie of the wealthy steel-producing family, who came to the island in 1881. He built a grand and glorious new Dungeness on the former Nathanael Greene property. He and his wife, Lucy Coleman Carnegie, enjoyed life on the island so much they expanded their holdings until they owned ninety percent of the island.

Over the years the Carnegies built a nine-hole golf course, a guest home with swimming pool, island homes for their children, and roads to remote areas. They also farmed vegetables and kept hogs, cattle, and horses.

Lucy Carnegie outlived her husband by many years. Before she died in 1916, she set up a trust to maintain her Cumberland Island property as an entity for the use of all her children until the last one died.

The Island Becomes a National Seashore

With the family's matriarch no longer on the scene, it became increasingly difficult to manage the Cumberland Island holdings. The various Carnegie heirs had different ideas. As early as the 1950s, one heir began to search for a way to save the island in its natural state for future generations to enjoy. Others sought ways to derive income from the property. Another went to court to prevent the Carnegie trust from leasing land for the mining of several kinds of ore known to be in the sands of the sea islands.

When the last surviving child of Lucy Carnegie died in 1962, the land was divided among the heirs. Each heir was free to make an individual decision about the future of his or her property.

Land developers began to cast their eyes on Cumberland Island. One succeeded in acquiring a small parcel and laid plans for the development of a high class resort. But more land was needed. He began to woo other property owners.

A 1956 National Park Service report had cited Cumberland Island as "one of the two most outstanding undeveloped seashore areas remaining along the Atlantic and Gulf coasts." The special attributes of Cumberland Island were also recognized by persons associated with conservation minded organizations and foundations.

The heirs who wanted to preserve Cumberland Island in a natural state entered into negotiations to transfer their property to the National Park Foundation, a private non-profit association. The Andrew Mellon Foundation provided the funds to acquire the land and hold it for eventual donation to the federal government.

Soon after the establishment of the Cumberland Island National Seashore was authorized in 1972, about 13,000 acres of former Carnegie land was donated to the seashore by the National Park Foundation, forming the bulk of the area now owned by the seashore.

A few island tracts remain in private ownership. So long as these lands are managed in accordance with the preservation ethic of Cumberland Islanders of the past, there will be no need for the federal government to acquire additional acreage.

Why Go to Cumberland Island National Seashore?

Cumberland Island is one of the National Park System's unexpected treasures. The same sights and sounds that drew vacationers a century ago remain for the enjoyment of seashore visitors today.

A visit to the island is an experience long remembered and one shared by only a few fortunate travelers. For in order to keep as much of the island as possible in a natural state, no more than about 300 persons are permitted to visit the national seashore at any given time. And those visitors can get there only by Park Service ferry or private boat.

Cumberland Island has special appeal for beach lovers who seek a quiet, awe-inspiring encounter with nature.

There is great beauty. A sea of tall, spindly, green to gold cordgrass borders the entire sound side, and here and there a snowy egret, white ibis, or great blue heron may be seen wading in the mud.

Centuries-old live oak trees form a dark, cool sunshade over spongy, brown trails traversed by hiker, white-tailed deer, nine-banded armadillos, and raccoons. Light greenish grey feathery Spanish moss drips down from massive branches to gently brush saw palmetto growing in great profusion.

Remote fresh water lakes and ponds support game fish and colorful pond lilies and attract osprey and waterfowl. In the forest, alligators, mink, and otters slip in and out of brackish sloughs (pronounced "slews").

A grand expanse of lightly colored, firmly packed, sandy beach, littered with great numbers of unbroken shells, gradually slopes to meet a gentle surf.

Cumberland Island National Seashore is a place where you are engulfed with beauty spiced with wonder, vistas that spur curiosity, and tranquility that evokes good humor.

How to Get to Cumberland Island National Seashore

Seashore headquarters, where you board the Cumberland Queen ferry, is at St. Marys, Georgia. St. Marys is nine miles east of U.S. I-95, just north of the Florida-Georgia border.

For a map of the state of Georgia, contact the Georgia Department of Transportation, or get one at one of the state's Visitor Centers on most major highways entering Georgia.

Going to Cumberland Island National Seashore is not a quick sightseeing trip. It's an adventure that should be planned and savored. Whether going for a few hours, a full day, or several days, make reservations well in advance for the ferry trip and, if you plan to camp, for a campsite. No food or supplies, other than water, are available on the island, so take along food, drink, sunscreen lotion, insect repellent, fishing gear, clothing for possible weather changes—whatever you may need while there.

To make reservations, both for the ferry trip and a campsite, phone the seashore reservation number 912-882-4335, between 10 a.m. and 2 p.m., Monday through Friday. At certain times the phone is extremely busy, so be patient and persistent. You may also make reservations in person at seashore headquarters which is open seven days a week.

Round trip boat fares are $7.50 for adults, $6.25 for senior citizens, $3.85 for children twleve years and under, plus Georgia state sales tax.

Reservations may be made up to eleven months in advance of the dates you plan to be on the island. Be forewarned—space on the ferry fills up quickly for the period from mid-March through April and on weekends. To save time and phone call expense, write the seashore before you make reservations for information on schedules, rates, and cancellation procedure.

The ferry does not run on Tuesdays and Wednesdays from October 1st to mid-March. However, special charters may be arranged on these days for groups of 46 or more.

There is no additional entrance fee to Cumberland Island National Seashore.

Where to Stay

Non-Campers. The only overnight accommodations on the island are at Greyfield Inn, a turn-of-the-century mansion that was once the home of members of the Carnegie family. Descendants of the family, who operate the inn, seek to recreate the atmosphere of graciousness and gentility of bygone days.

The inn has nine double rooms, all except one, with shared bathrooms. The rate, in the expensive range, includes three meals. Bicycles and guided walking and driving tours of the island are available for an additional fee. The inn is two miles north of Dungeness. Transportation to the inn from either Fernandina Beach, Florida, or the seashore's island docks, can be arranged. Advance reservations are a necessity. For further information, contact Greyfield Inn.

Overnight lodging is available in the town of St. Marys where seashore headquarters is located. St. Marys is a picturesque, historic coastal village. Situated almost directly across from the seashore's ferry dock is the Riverview Hotel. Built in 1916, in a style typical of southern hostelries, the hotel offers a limited number of accommodations in a modest price range. Contact the hotel for further information. Other information about lodging and the community of St. Marys may be obtained from St. Marys Tourism Council.

Accommodations are also available at motels along I-95.

Camping on the Island. A sixteen-site campground is located one-half mile from Sea Camp Dock. All food and equipment must be hand-carried from the dock to the campsite. Water, cold-water showers, and restrooms are available. Day use beachgoers may also use these facilities.

Maximum stay at a campsite is seven days. There is no fee. Campfires are permitted. During the summer, and on weekends during the winter season, check posted schedules for ranger-conducted programs.

There are four primitive camping areas for backpackers. One, a 3.5 mile walk from Sea Camp, is at Stafford Beach. Three are within the National Wilderness Area at distances of 5.5, 7.4, and 10.6 miles from Sea Camp. Fires are not permitted in primitive areas. Bring a camp stove. There are no restrooms. Trash must be carried out when you leave. Twenty is the maximum number of primitive campers at any one site for a maximum number of sixty at all sites.

Camping on the Mainland. Camping is available on the mainland at Georgia's Crooked River State Park year-round. There are spaces for motorized vehicles, pop-up campers, and tents. Water, electricity, dump stations, hot showers, grills, and picnic tables are provided. The park also has a swimming pool, a miniature golf course, and rental cabins. For information write the Superintendent, Crooked River State Park.

What to Do at Cumberland Island National Seashore

Plan to arrive at seashore headquarters about one-half hour before ferry departure time so that you can get your boarding pass, watch an audiovisual presentation about the seashore, check out publications and displays, and listen to a ranger orientation talk. In warm weather, be sure to take insect repellent. "No see-ums" (very tiny, biting insects) frequent the dock area in swarms.

After a 45 minute cruise down the St. Marys River and across Cumberland Sound, you will leave the boat either at the Dungeness Dock or Sea Camp Dock. There is a visitor center at Sea Camp.

It has restrooms and offers exhibits oriented to the island's natural history. A limited number of private boats may also dock for the day at Sea Camp Dock. Adjacent to the Dungeness Dock there is a museum featuring the island's cultural history. The Dungeness washhouse has been renovated to provide restrooms and an interpretive center.

The Beach. Whether you visit Cumberland Island for a few hours, a full day, or several days, you will want to spend time at the beach. From Sea Camp Dock it is a mile-long hike on a path through the forest and across a boardwalk through the sand dunes to a pristine beach that stretches as far as the eye can see. Sit on the clean, white sand, a blanket, or a log washed up on the shore, and let your eyes roam far out over the Atlantic Ocean. You may catch a glimpse of an ocean-going ship far out to sea, a boat trawling for shrimp, or a bottlenose dolphin. You surely will see seagulls and pelicans fly by. Soon the inner glow of complete relaxation will engulf you.

When you are ready to move, swim in the ocean or walk the beach. Take a container if you can't resist collecting coquina clam shells, whelks, conch shells, a starfish, or a sea-green bottle deposited on the beach by an ocean wave. See how close you can get to an oyster catcher, a sanderling, a sandpiper, or a tern skittering back and forth at the water's edge. You will enjoy the solitude, for there are no lifeguards and very few people in sight.

If you should see a Loggerhead sea turtle nesting on the beach, do not disturb it. The loggerhead is a threatened species. Adult females weigh between 200 and 400 pounds. They emerge from the ocean sometime between mid-May and mid-August to lay eggs in nests they prepare on the beach. A brochure describing the seashore's Caretta Caretta (Loggerhead Marine Turtle) research project may be obtained from the visitor centers.

Hiking. You can hike almost the length of the island on the main island road, a tree-shaded lane built in the days of the Carnegies, or on shorter trails through the forest, past ponds and inlets, and to the beach. A trail map is available at seashore headquarters. When walking, stay on trails. Poisonous snakes, including diamondback rattlers and cottonmouth moccasins, live on the island, and a few wild hogs still rumble through the woods and marshes.

You may be surprised to see a motor vehicle. Seashore visitors may not take them to the island, but island property holders still have the right to use their own vehicles on island roads.

Even if you are on the island for only a few hours, a walk on the Dungeness Trail can be a highlight of your visit. The trail follows a loop from one dock area across the island, along the beach, and back across the island to the other dock, a distance of about three miles. Take along a brochure that explains the natural and man-made features along the trail. Among the sights you will see is a high dune gradually pushing across the island—sands burying palm trees in the path, wild horses grazing in open meadows, and the ruins of the Dungeness built by Thomas and Lucy Carnegie in the late 1880s. Pause a while at the ruins, look at some of the estate buildings still standing, and visualize life on the island when this beautiful retreat brought joy and pleasure to a well-to-do, conservation-minded family.

Visit Historic Sites. Virtually all the island's known historic and cultural resources are listed on the National Register of Historic Places. Visitors can walk among the Dungeness ruins not far from the Dungeness Dock, and visit Greyfield, about a mile north of Sea Camp Dock. And from May to September, the seashore conducts weekly boat trips on Sundays to Plum Orchard, a lovely island home built for one of Lucy Carnegie's children. The exterior of the home, which is over ninety years old, has been restored by the Park Service. Volunteers have raised funds for interior renovation and have acquired authentic furnishings. For detailed information, write to the seashore.

To visit other historic sites, it is necessary to hike several miles or join a tour emanating from Greyfield Inn. One of the historic sites at the north end of the island is the High Point-Halfmoon Bluff Historic District, which includes cemeteries and a church associated with blacks who lived on the island during the plantation and turn-of-the-century periods.

Fishing. A Georgia State fishing license is necessary for fresh water fishing. Licenses may be obtained at Walmart, Inc. in St. Marys, or from the Department of Natural Resources, Game and Fish Division. State laws apply to fresh water fishing. No license is needed for salt water fishing. Fish most sought by sportsmen include channel bass, flounder, speckled trout, and whiting. Cast netting for mullet or bait-fish is often fruitful.

Hunting. As required by the seashore's enabling legislation, hunting is allowed. The seashore conducts deer hunts as part of the management of the deer population and in accordance with the hunting laws of the state of Georgia. These hunts are scheduled during certain periods in the fall and early winter. Persons permitted to take part in the hunts are determined by lottery. For detailed information, write the Superintendent, Cumberland Island National Seashore. Only persons directly involved in the hunt are allowed in the designated areas during those times.

NOTE: *There is no off-road driving at the seashore. Pets may not be taken on the ferries, so plan to leave them elsewhere when going to Cumberland Island. Access to the island via the ferry can be very difficult for persons with a physical handicap because of tide variations and the steepness of dock ramps. There are no special facilities on the island for persons with a physical handicap, but public buildings accommodate wheelchairs.*

If You Have the Time

Take a guided walking tour through St. Marys historical district emanating from Orange Hall, an ante-bellum mansion over 150 years old.

Tips for Adding to Your Enjoyment of Cumberland Island National Seashore.

1. Send to the park well in advance of your trip for a park brochure, the ferry schedule and rates, and other information of special interest to you, e.g. camping, hiking trails, trips to Plum Orchard, and hunting.

2. Make reservations for the ferry trip and a campsite as early as possible.

3. Send to Greyfield Inn, the Riverview Hotel, or St. Marys Tourism Council for information on lodging, and to Crooked River State Park for camping information, if needed.

4. If you would like to read more about Cumberland Island before you go there, send for the list of publications offered for sale by the seashore's cooperating association.

5. Prepare for varied weather conditions when you pack your clothing, and take insect repellent and sunscreen lotion with you.

6. Take binoculars and a camera with you to preserve memories of your visit to Cumberland Island.

And finally—Know that when you go to this enchanting island, you are a guest of all the natural creatures, big and small, that you may encounter. With that understanding, the fiddler crab skittering across the marsh, the armadillo scurrying in the brush, the logger-head turtle lumbering across the beach, the wild turkey roaming in the meadow, the black-crowned night heron nesting in the branch, the untamed horse grazing in the field, and many, many more hosts and hostesses welcome you to their home.

Sources of Information

Superintendent
Cumberland Island National
Seashore
Box 806
St. Marys, GA 31558
Phone: General information:
912-882-4336; Reservations:
912-882-4335

Georgia Department of
Transportation
2 Capitol Square, S.W.
Atlanta, GA 30334
Phone: 404-656-5336

St. Marys Tourism Council
Box 1291
St. Marys, GA 31558
Phone: 912-882-6200
or 912-882-4000

Greyfield Inn
Drawer B
Fernandina Beach, FL 32034
Phone: 904-261-6408

Riverview Hotel
105 Osborne St.
St. Marys, GA 31558
Phone: 912-882-3242

Crooked River State Park
3092 Spur 40
St. Marys, GA 31558
Phone: (912) 882-5256

Department of Natural Resources
Game and Fish Division
Law Enforcement Section
1200 Glynn Ave.
Brunswick, GA 31523
Phone:912-264-7237

"To build a railroad, reclaim lands, give new impulse to enterprise, and offer new doors to ambitious capital — these are phases of the ever-widening life and activity of this Nation. The United States, however, does more; it furnishes playgounds to the people which are, we may modestly state, without any rivals in the world. Just as the cities are seeing the wisdom and necessity of open spaces for the children, so with a very large view the National has been saving from its domain the rarest places of grandeur and beauty for the enjoyment of the world."

—**Introduction to National Parks Portfolio,** prepared by the Department of the Interior in 1916 to promote public interest and knowledge of nine national parks and monuments

BISCAYNE NATIONAL PARK

The coral reefs in Biscayne National Park form one of the most complex natural habitats known. Here, even the dividing line between what is flora and what is fauna is blurred. The reefs support animals such as sponges that are rooted in one spot, plants whose mobility (if aimless) is endless, and coral, that life-form shared by both plant and animal, that prospers as it clings to the dead skeletons of its forebears.

Observing the reefs can become mesmerizing. Looking through a glass bottom boat you become enchanted with the myriad life forms, sizes, and colors of the reefs of Biscayne.

For the snorkeler, the scene expands and intensifies. The colors and patterns of many of the more than 250 types of fish are

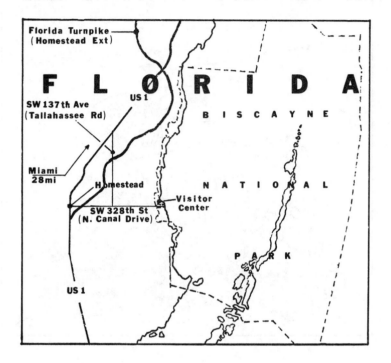

vivid, bizarre, and sometimes, downright fantastic. The fish all but ignore your presence so that you feel that you've entered an acre-sized tank of tropical fish.

The ultimate experience in this wondrous world is reserved for the SCUBA diver. Hovering between the top of the reef and the water surface above, the diver can swim among the waving, plant-like limbs and tufts of the soft corals like sea fans and sea whips, examine at close range the living surfaces of the hard corals like brain and finger coral, and join the schools of riotously-colored tropical fish.

The reefs are the crown jewel of Biscayne National Park. This is the northern end of the only living coral reefs in the continental United States. With the park's three other habitats, the mangrove forest, Biscayne Bay, and the offshore keys, they form a complete ecological system.

The park covers about 284 square miles along the southeast coast of Florida. Ninety-six percent of the park is water. A narrow strip of shoreline anchors the western edge of the park to the Florida mainland. The strip, some fifteen miles long, is mostly mangrove wetlands. Park headquarters and the main visitor center are at Convoy Point, a little south of the midpoint of the mangrove shoreline.

Biscayne National Park extends eastward from the mainland across Biscayne Bay to the ten fathom curve on the ocean side of the outer reefs, fourteen miles at the widest point. The irregular north and south boundaries are approximately 22 miles apart. A string of vegetated, coral islands bisects the park north to south. Between these islands, or keys, and the mainland lies Biscayne Bay, relatively shallow, and also bisected from north to south by the Intracoastal Waterway, where the water depth reaches its maximum of thirteen feet.

The mangrove shoreline habitat of the park has been preserved almost untouched by man. Here and there a drainage canal crosses it, with current-eroded channels and some signs of past dredging, but for most of its length it is an almost impenetrable forest of red and black mangrove branches, trunks, and roots. In several places the swamp forest is laced with a network of creeks, a canoeist's and birdwatcher's paradise. It is the nursery for a myriad of creatures at and near the bottom of the food chain, supplying Biscayne Bay with a constant flow of new generations of sea life. The mangroves protect the bay by filtering out pollutants from the land. They also protect the coast, serving as a natural line of defense against the winds and waves of storms.

Biscayne Bay is remarkably clear and healthy despite its proximity to the congested greater Miami area, nearby agricultural lands with attendant runoff of insecticide and fertilizer, and the discharge from drainage canals. The bay bottom and underwater life are readily observed from the water's surface.

The 44 keys in Biscayne National Park, the park's fourth habitat, are the legacy of coral reefs built tens of thousands of years ago when sea levels were higher. When sea levels receded, the reefs surfaced above the water. Today, lush jungles of gumbo limbo, Jamaican dogwood, strangler fig, torchwood, and mahogany cover some of the higher hammocks, the result of pioneer seeds and plants brought to the islands by the north-flowing air and ocean currents. This mix of forest cover is typical and common in the West Indies, but found in this country only in south Florida.

The ubiquitous mangroves also prosper here, on the tidal shores and across those islands that remain substantially water-logged. Inlets such as Hurricane Creek on Old Rhodes Key can create such a deep mood of timelessness for the boater enjoying their solitude that he might not be surprised to round a turn amid the mangroves and meet a band of brigands rowing a jolly boat flying the Jolly Roger!

The People of Biscayne Bay's Past

There is much yet to be learned about the people who once occupied these islands, located many miles offshore and covered with lush, creeping vegetation. Some signs of seasonal occupancy by pre-historic people have been found, and it is known that the Tequestas, Indians of the south Florida coast, visited the keys. However, catastrophic diseases and eventual amalgamation into other tribes has meant that no rich legacy of stories or direct descendents of these early Americans exist to tell us of their life on the keys.

But the legendary days of the Spanish galleons, privateers, and piracy have been well-documented, both in stories and in the physical evidence lying in the waters of the outer reefs. Heading back to Spain after loading their ships with gold, silver, and other valuable cargo from the New World, the captains chose to follow the Gulf Stream along the south Florida coast. Many ships, subjected to navigational miscalculation, violent storms, or both were wrecked on the reefs. A number of commercial schooners later plying the coastal waters met the same fate. To date, over fifty shipwrecks have been identified in park waters.

The remote, primitive islands surrounded by a vast expanse of water have made them prime sites for law-evading operations. Pirates (Caesar Creek between Elliott and Old Rhodes Keys is named for the famous pirate Black Caesar), rum-runners, drug smugglers, and importers of illegal aliens have all made profitable use of the bay islands' isolation.

For a short time in the 1800s and early 1900s, the larger islands supported commercial enterprises. Loggers cut down mahogany trees and farmers cleared land, grew and harvested pineapples, key limes, tomatoes, and grapefruit. Turtle hunters and sponge fishermen frequented the waters. Sponging is still practiced today in park waters.

For most of the twentieth century, however, the keys and waters of Biscayne have been the realm of the weekend sportsman and the vacationer. Modern means of water transportation now make the keys just a short boat ride away from heavily populated coastline cities.

In the 1920s and 1930s, private landowners built vacation retreats. Most visible remains of this era are on Boca Chita. Mark Honeywell (of the Honeywell Corporation) bought the island in 1937 and built a stone lighthouse on the northwest tip to help the captain of his ship take navigational bearings. However, once the light was lit, the Coast Guard ordered it extinguished because it was not an official navigational aid and might well confuse other ship captains. The picturesque structure still stands and is kept in good condition by park volunteers. It is open to the public on most weekends.

Another building associated with the recreational activities of the rich and famous of the past no longer stands. Carl Fisher built the clubhouse of the Cocolobo Club on Adams Key in 1920. Well-known industrial giants like Harvey Firestone and Presidents of the United States, Lyndon Johnson and Richard Nixon among them, were entertained there. Fire destroyed the clubhouse in 1974, but other buildings associated with the retreat remain and have been adapted for use by the park.

In the 1950s and 1960s, the people of the local area and state and federal officials concerned with the environmental health of south Florida, became alarmed at the threats to the life-nurturing coastline and the bay's fragile water and island resources posed by unregulated collection of coral and tropical fish and increasing real estate and commercial development. They sought ways to protect the area from further despoliation. The first steps were taken in 1960. Through a cooperative effort of the federal and state governments, both of which had jurisdiction over the waters involved, action was taken leading to the establishment of John Pennekamp Coral Reef State Park in waters bordering Key Largo.

In 1968, Congress established Biscayne National Monument in a portion of Biscayne Bay farther north. The monument's boundaries were expanded southward in 1974 to connect with the northern boundary of John Pennekamp Coral Reef State Park. To further protect the ecology of Biscayne Bay, in 1980, Congress extended the boundaries north almost to the southern tip of Key Biscayne and west to include a long strip of mangrove shoreline. At the same time its status was changed to a national park.

Now the islands and waters of Biscayne National Park are open to all. The natural underwater wilderness attracts snorkelers, divers, and boating spectators. The abundant supply of fish draws fishermen to cast their lines from the shore, the jetties, and boats. The mangrove-lined shores appeal to canoeists. And on the islands, day visitors and overnight campers walk nature trails, catch glimpses of rare birds and active wildlife, and, if they choose, enjoy solitude.

Why Go to Biscayne National Park?

▶ To leave the hustle and bustle of highly developed tourist centers, sit quietly at a picnic table on a mangrove-lined shore, and watch the boats go by;

▶ To don snorkeling or SCUBA gear and prowl among Elkhorn Coral, sea fans and plumes, or the remains of a sailing schooner;

▶ To peer through the glass bottom of a boat or bucket and view an underwater garden where brilliantly colored, striped, and diamond patterned fish swim among waving sea grasses and corals;

▶ To catch a glimpse of a brown pelican, a peregrine falcon, a Florida manatee, a sea turtle, a Schaus Swallowtail butterfly, or one of several other rare or endangered species that periodically frequent Biscayne islands and waters;

▶ To glide quietly in a canoe along the park's mainland shore and creeks while great blue herons and snowy egrets watch you from their dark green perches overhead;

▶ To fish for snapper, grouper, sea trout, and Spanish mackerel from a jetty or a fishing boat;

▶ To walk on a path through a jungle-like hardwood hammock to the eastern edge of an island, look out over the Atlantic Ocean, and wonder how many ships and what kind of treasures still lie beneath the very waters before you.

Biscayne National Park is still in the process of attracting a constituency beyond the local supportive community which, for years, has realized the importance of protecting the treasured coral reefs in its offshore waters.

To enjoy the total range of enjoyable experiences at the park, you need to get out on the water and you need to get over to the islands. Unless you have your own boat or rent one, a visitor is dependent on a concession-operated boat system. Guided boat trips are regularly scheduled, but they are sometimes cancelled because of inclement weather or a lack of sufficient number of reservations to make the privately-funded boat operation profitable. Park visitors should be aware of the possibility of cancellation when planning a boat trip.

Nevertheless, even a shore-bound visitor can enjoy a visit to Biscayne National Park. There are things to see and do at the Convoy Point visitor center, open daily from 9 a.m. to 5 p.m. during the peak season, late December to April. There are walks along the waterfront, picnic grounds on the shoreline, and canoes to paddle along the shore. Windsurfing is also popular.

There are no entrance fees to Biscayne National Park.

How to Get to Biscayne National Park.

Park headquarters and the mainland visitor center are located at Convoy Point, nine miles east of the center of Homestead, on North Canal Drive (SW 328th St.). Homestead is on U.S. Route 1 about an hour's drive from Miami. There is an exit to Homestead from the Florida Turnpike Extension. Detailed directions for driving to the park may be obtained from park headquarters.

If you are unfamiliar with the roads in Florida, send to the Florida Division of Tourism for an official state map, or get one from one of the state-run Florida Welcome Centers on major highways entering the state. If you prefer to reduce driving time, consider flying or taking the train to Miami and renting a car. Major airlines, Amtrak, and car rental agencies service Miami.

Where to Stay

Non-Campers. Homestead and Florida City, its adjoining neighbor, offer a wide range of motels, many of them affiliated with major motel-hotel chains. For a list of motels and bed and breakfast places and their rates, contact the Greater Homestead-Florida City Chamber of Commerce. There is a great variety of places to eat, from take-out service to gourmet dining.

Biscayne National Park is one of four units of the National Park System located in south Florida. The others are Everglades National Park, Big Cypress National Preserve, and Fort Jefferson National Monument. If you plan to make your trip a grand tour of all the national park facilities in this area, you may want to spend a night or more at the lodge or one of the cottages maintained by a concessioner during the peak season at Everglades National Park. They are located about sixty miles west of Biscayne National Park. For information, contact Flamingo Lodge Marina and Outpost Resort.

Camping on the Mainland. There are no park campgrounds on the mainland. Upon request, the park will send you a list of public and private campgrounds and mobile home parks in the vicinity of Biscayne National Park. The settings for the campgrounds at Everglades National Park and John Pennekamp State Park are especially appealing, but they are a considerable distance from Biscayne park headquarters. For more information, contact the parks.

Camping on the Keys. Park campgrounds are maintained on Elliott Key and Boca Chita Key. There is a group campsite on Elliott Key. Picnic tables, grills, and restrooms are provided. Campers must take their own drinking water to Boca Chita Key. None is available on the island. All campsites are available on a first come, first served basis. There are no fees. For a map showing locations of campgrounds and a copy of camping regulations, write to park headquarters.

Backcountry camping is permitted on Elliott and Sand Keys. A free permit is required. It can be obtained from any ranger or visitor center.

Be prepared to take all your trash with you when you leave. There is no trash pick-up on any of the islands.

To reach park campgrounds, it is necessary to have private boat transportation.

What to Do at Biscayne National Park.

Biscayne National Park has its summer season and its winter season. Late spring and summer bring afternoon showers. It is hot and humid, and the predominant visitor is the mosquito. But the water is warm and SCUBA divers, snorkelers, and fishermen, mostly from nearby cities and towns, come to the park to indulge in their favorite pastimes. Campers don their bug jackets, put on their sun-shielding hats and sunscreen lotion, and head for water-front campsites.

From December through April, the peak season, out-of-state snowbirds and vacationers join local residents for a variety of activities. Sunshine is abundant, the air is drier, temperatures are in the mid seventies and low eighties, and it's time for daydreams to become reality.

First stop for a newcomer to Biscayne National Park should be the visitor center at Convoy Point. This is where you can see exhibits and a slide show depicting the history of the park area, inquire about ranger-conducted canoe trips, make reservations for glass bottom boat trips and snorkeling/SCUBA trips, take a nature walk, browse through the bookstore, have a picnic, and ask park rangers and volunteers a host of questions. The visitor center is open from 9 a.m. to 5 p.m. during peak season, from 9 a.m. to 4 p.m. at other times.

Here are some of the most popular activities at the park.

Boating. By far, most of the boats you see in Biscayne Bay are privately owned. Nearby marinas provide boat slips and ramps for launching boats. Some marinas rent motor boats and sailboats. The nearest launch ramps are at two county parks, Homestead Bayfront Park, adjacent to the park's mainland site, and Black Point Park, a few miles north.

The average depth of the bay is four to ten feet, and boaters are urged to use the nautical chart for the area, check tide tables, and be especially watchful when nearing coral reefs. Boat propellers, anchors, and even human contact can easily damage the extremely fragile coral. Anchor only on sandy bottoms.

Elliott Key, eight miles from the mainland, has wet slips up to twelve feet in width. Docking is free and slips are available on a first come, first served basis. Two miles north of the harbor there is a marked anchorage area and another dock, University Dock.

There are docks on Adams Key bordering the passage through Caesar Creek to the reefs and on Boca Chita Key. Boaters may disembark at Elliott Key for camping, walking a nature trail, swimming at a pocket beach, and going to the visitor center, which is open on weekends during the peak season. Adams Key has rest rooms but no drinking water. Send to park headquarters for a brochure on boating within the park.

Viewing the Underwater World—Snorkeling, Diving, or Through a Glass Window. It's one thing to view parrotfish, angelfish, eels, brain and finger corals, and other fascinating sea life in an aquarium; it's quite another thing to see them in their natural setting. The prospect of seeing the park's underwater life close-up draws park visitors year round. You can lower a glass bottom bucket over the side of your boat and look at turtle grass, sponges, shrimp, and other tiny swimmers in tidal creeks and shallow waters, or you can don diving or snorkel gear and swim among brilliantly colored tropical fish, sea fans, sea whips, plumes, and elkhorn coral. Concession operated boat trips to the coral reefs for divers and snorkelers are scheduled regularly. Fees are in the $20–$25 range. Snorkel and SCUBA gear may be rented from the concessioner.

You can stay dry in a boat and still see all this from a concession-run glass bottom boat. Trips are scheduled seven days a week. Fees for adults are in the mid-teens, less for children. Advance telephone reservations are necessary for all boat trips. For information on departure times and rates, contact Biscayne Aqua-Center, Inc.

For more about diving at Biscayne National Park, send for *A Diver's Guide to the Patch Reefs.*

Canoeing. Bring your own canoe or rent one from Biscayne Aqua-Center and explore the shallow bay waters or mangrove creeks on your own. If scheduled, join a ranger-led canoe trip during the peak season. Reservations are required.

Fishing. There are more than 250 kinds of fish in the park's waters, making the bay and ocean a major attraction for both commercial and sports fishermen. Beyond the keys, fishing for marlin and sailfish is enjoyed all year. Spear fishing is permitted. With certain exceptions, all fishermen are required to have a recreational fishing license. Licenses are sold at local bait and tackle shops.

All of the water between the park's mainland shore and a line running north to south along the keys are within the Biscayne

Bay/Card Sound and Little Card Sound Lobster Sanctuary. The taking of lobsters is prohibited within the sanctuary. For further information, write for the park brochure on lobstering.

If you plan to fish at Biscayne National Park, write to the Florida Marine Fisheries Commission for copies of *Florida Recreational Saltwater Fishing Facts* and *Who Needs a Florida Saltwater Fishing License.*

NOTE: *No off-road driving is permitted in the park. Hunting and the carrying of loaded firearms and explosives is prohibited. Pets must be kept on a six foot leash and are restricted to certain areas. Visitor center restrooms and the shower stalls at Elliott Key are accessible to persons with physical handicaps and ramps make it possible for people with limited mobility to board the glass bottom boats.*

If You Have the Time

► Take a day to visit Everglades National Park. Stop at the main visitor center eleven miles west of Homestead; drive the park road and pause at times for magnificent views of this unique complex of land and water designated by the United Nations as an International Biosphere Reserve; walk the Anhinga, Gumbo Limbo, and other trails; and look for many of the park's native wildlife.

► Visit the John Pennekamp Coral Reef state park, about a 45 minute drive south of Homestead. Stop at the visitor center and see the dramatic aquarium full of tropical sea life, and the films about diving in Florida's waters. Swim at the beach or rent a motorboat, sailboat, canoe, or sailboard.

► Take time out for a swim at the beach at Homestead Bayfront Park.

Tips for Adding to Your Enjoyment of Biscayne National Park

1. Send to park headquarters for the park brochure and other information of special interest to you, e.g., boating, camping on the

mainland or the islands, diving, snorkeling, the coral reefs, birds, or endangered species in the park.

2. Send for a Florida state map.

3. Write to the Greater Homestead/Florida City Chamber of Commerce for a list of overnight lodgings in the vicinity of the park.

4. If you would like to read more about Florida's coral reefs, diving in the Florida keys, or the history and wildlife of the area before you go, send to park headquarters for a catalog and order form of the Florida National Parks and Monuments Association, the park's cooperating association.

5. If you intend to spend some time on the keys, take a sun-shielding hat, a bug jacket or insect repellent, and sunscreen lotion with you.

6. Take camera and binoculars. You may see an eagle, a great blue heron, a manatee, or colorful tropical fish through the glass!

And finally—Biscayne National Park was created by Congress so that this "rare combination of terrestrial, marine, and amphibious life in a tropical setting of great natural beauty" would be preserved and enjoyed by all Americans. This unusual combination of clear water, biologically productive coastal vegetation, primitive island habitat, and fantastic underwater beauty so close to a major center of population and commercial activity may not qualify the park officially as an "endangered species," but it could become one if people use its beautiful resources carelessly or fail to keep a watchful eye out for actions that could do them great harm. Perhaps, after your visit to Biscayne National Park, you, too, will value this precious oasis and do your part to save it for the benefit of future generations.

Sources of Information

Superintendent
Biscayne National Park
Box 1369
Homestead, FL 33090-1369
Phone: 305-247-7275

Greater Homestead/Florida City
Chamber of Commerce
43 North Krome Avenue, 2nd
Floor
Homestead, FL 33030

Florida Division of Tourism
126 West Van Buren Street
Tallahassee, FL 32399-2000
Phone: 904-487-1462

Flamingo Lodge Marina and
Outpost Resort
Box 428
Flamingo, FL 33030
Phone: 305-253-2241

Everglades National Park
Box 279
Homestead, FL 33030
Phone: 305-247-6211

John Pennekamp State Park
Box 487
Key Largo, FL 33037
Phone: 305-451-1202

Biscayne Aqua-Center, Inc.
Box 1270
Homestead, FL 33030
Phone: 305-247-2400

Florida Marine Fisheries
Commission
2540 Executive Center Circle West
106 Douglas Building
Tallahassee, FL 32301
Phone: 904-487-0554

"... To conserve the scenery and the natural and historical objects and the wild life therein, and to provide for the enjoyment of the same in such manner and by such means as will leave them unimpaired for the enjoyment of future generations."

—The mission of the National Park Service, described in the National Park Service Act, 1916

THE NATIONAL PARK SYSTEM

Legend has it that the idea emerged from a discussion around a campfire over one hundred years ago. Members of an exploring expedition in 1870 were extolling the wonders they had seen during their days of trampling through the forests and canyons, and around great waterfalls, spectacular geysers, and beautiful lakes and rivers in Yellowstone country. One person suggested that each should acquire a piece of the fabulous land that would eventually "become a source of great profit to the owners." Some of the group approved the idea, but one expressed opposition to private ownership of any part of the area, voicing the opinion that "the whole of it ought to be set aside as a great national park." According to one of those present, nearly everyone responded enthusiastically and pledged to work toward that end.

There is some doubt that the facts are exactly as recalled years later in a diary by a member of the exploring party. Nevertheless, within two years, in 1872, the nation had its first official national park—Yellowstone National Park. The first step had been taken in the development of a world renowned national park system. Today there are over 350 units in the National Park System—at least one in every state except Delaware, and in Puerto Rico, the Virgin Islands, Guam, and American Samoa.

Before Yellowstone became a national park, Congress, in 1832, had set aside Hot Springs in Arkansas as a reservation, primarily because of its reported medicinal benefits, and in 1864, a law was enacted to preserve the Yosemite Valley and a grove of Sierra redwoods in California for public use. The land was turned over to the state of California to administer. Years later, both the valley and the grove were ceded back to the federal government to become part of Yosemite National Park.

The concept of setting aside special pieces of the American landscape for preservation and the enjoyment of all the people is truly American. In his book, *National Parks, The American Experience,* Alfred Runte maintains that support for the earliest moves to save spectacular natural scenery in perpetuity stemmed from the sensitivity of the nation's writers, philosophers, and political leaders, mostly in the eastern part of the country, to the fact that the young nation had nothing to compare with the cultural history of Europe. There were no great cathedrals, castles, or marvelous landscapes with historical significance. There was Niagara Falls—but they were embarrassed with the commercial exploitation being made of this one well-known, outstanding natural feature.

In the mid to late 1800s, exploring parties returning from the West fascinated the nation with tales of fantastic natural scenic wonders, comparing them favorably with the European landscape. Seizing upon these reports, people began to develop a sense of national pride in their own unique landscape and gradually the move to save these lands from exploitation gained support. In support of the legislation to establish the National Park Service in 1916, one of the leading proponents referred to the parks as "the Nation's pleasure grounds and the Nation's restoring places ... it is the one thing we have that has not been imported."

Other factors contributed to the inevitability that a system of national parks would become an American institution. Democratic principles—government "of, by, and for the people," guided governmental decisions. There was a relatively prosperous economy in which people of means were motivated to give their support, both financially and politically, to the formation of an American conservation ethic. And the federal government had acquired a vast amount of undeveloped public land in the early years of the nation.

At first, it was the scenic value of specific sites—grand canyons, astonishing rock formations, great waterfalls, giant geysers, and stands of immense trees, hundreds of years old, that motivated the establishment of national parks. Once they were in operation, people were urged to visit the parks to see the magnificent scenery. Railroads extended their routes to park borders and gave the parks much publicity. Park managers rushed to build roads, lodges, and hotels. Newspapers and magazines printed enticing stories.

As the nation matured, there developed an awareness of the uniqueness of the human history of the land it now occupied. This led to the Antiquities Act in 1906, especially aimed at protecting magnificent cliff dwellings and Pueblo ruins discovered in the Southwest. The President of the United States was given the authority to declare as national monuments, certain historic landmarks and historic and prehistoric structures that are on federal land. He could also place areas of historic and scientific interest in this category.

Presidents have used this authority many times. Sometimes the purported rationale for designating an area as a national monument was to preserve an area of significant scientific interest, when the most inportant motivating factor was in actuality a desire to save it from exploitation until such time as Congress established it as a national park. This happened in Alaska in 1978 when President Carter designated vast areas in Alaska as National Monuments. Two years later Congress established them as either national parks or national parks and preserves. In Florida, Biscayne National Monument preceded by twelve years the establishment of Biscayne National Park in 1980.

The National Park Service

By 1916, so many areas had been set aside for preservation by different government offices, Congress decided that responsibility for managing most of them should be placed in one office. For this purpose, Congress established the National Park Service in the Department of the Interior. The Service was to manage 37 existing diverse areas and such additional parks, monuments, reservations, etc., as Congress should determine in the future.

In its enabling legislation, the Park Service was given the responsibility for promoting and regulating the various units within the System "to conserve the scenery and the natural and historic objects and the wild life therein and to provide for the enjoyment of the same in such manner and by such means as will leave them unimpaired for the enjoyment of future generations." The purpose of national parks had expanded. In addition to the preservation of outstanding natural scenery, the nation had now made a commitment to the preservation of cultural and historical sites and objects, and wildlife.

Today the National Park System includes much more than what can be considered traditional national parks and monuments. The Park Service manages a great variety of places and sites of natural and historical significance, and also units brought into the system specifically for recreational purposes. In addition to national parks and monuments, Park System units include:

▶ national preserves, established specifically to protect certain natural resources (Example: Big Cypress National Preserve, adjoining Everglades National Park in Florida);

▶ national seashores and national lakeshores, primarily created to protect waterfront areas and provide water-oriented recreation (Example: Cape Cod National Seashore in Massachusetts and Sleeping Bear Dunes National Lakeshore in Michigan);

▶ national rivers and wild and scenic riverways, designated to preserve land bordering natural, undisturbed waterways (Example: Delaware National Scenic River in Pennsylvania and New Jersey);

▶ national scenic trails, lengthy footpaths traversing areas of scenic beauty (Example: Pacific Crest Trail extending from the Mexican-California border through California, Oregon, and Washington to the Canadian border near Ross Lake, Washington);

▶ national historic sites including military parks and battlefields and historic parks (Example: Gettysburg National Military Park in Pennsylvania);

▶ national memorials, commemorating the achievements of great national leaders or events (Example: General Grant National Memorial in New York City);

▶ national recreation areas, administered primarily for active recreation activities, some around great dams built for irrigation and flood control purposes, others to provide recreation sites in urban areas (Examples: Lake Mead National Recreation Area in Arizona and Nevada, and Golden Gate National Recreation Area in California);

▶ national parkways, roads built primarily for driving through areas of scenic beauty (Example: Blue Ridge Parkway in North Carolina and Virginia);

► and two areas specifically designated for the performing arts, Wolf Trap Farm Park in Virginia and the John F. Kennedy Center for the Performing Arts in Washington D.C.

While the park system was expanding, new scientific evidence made it clear that to manage natural resources for maximum effectiveness, the total ecosystem of which the resources are a part had to be taken into consideration. In 1963, a team of distinguished scientists, chaired by A. Starker Leopold, a highly-regarded biologist, released a report titled *Wildlife Management in the National Parks*. The Leopold report emphasized the need to integrate biological management with all aspects of park management. Appraisals and recommendations of this report continue to influence park management policies.

Ecosystems seldom coincide with park boundaries. This has been a problem for park managers who have no control over land beyond park borders. They must therefore rely on the cooperation of their neighbors through a system of scenic easements and other methods.

With the burgeoning of the environmental movement in the 1960s, laws were passed that brought new perspectives to the management of the parks. In 1964, the National Wilderness Act provided for the creation of a system of national wilderness areas. Wilderness areas were defined as places "where the earth and its community of life are untrammeled by man, where man himself is a visitor who does not remain." Park staff had to analyze their roadless areas to determine the parcels that might qualify for such designation. Wilderness areas that are authorized by Congress have to be administered in ways to perpetuate the wilderness.

Laws to promote clean air and clean water have led to the scientific monitoring of the air and water within park boundaries. When park resources are suffering from pollution from sources either within or outside park boundaries, this must be reported.

The 1973 Endangered Species Act set up categories of "threatened" and "endangered" species. Parks must take special action to protect the birds, mammals, reptiles, and vegetation on the lists when they are found within park boundaries. And when plans are made to build new facilities within their borders, parks must prepare an environmental impact statement.

Parks are also required to research historical properties within their boundaries to determine if they are qualified to be placed on the National Register of Historic Places, a register created by the National Historic Preservation Act in 1966. Furthermore, all historic and archeological resources must be managed in accordance with special guidelines. Added to all this is the need to train park personnel in law enforcement, especially in those parks with remote coastal or international borders which attract drug smugglers.

So, just as the world has become more complex, so has the administration of national parks. Nevertheless, Park Service staff have not lost sight of one of their original purposes — to provide for the enjoyment of the people, now and in the future.

Primarily, this is the day-to-day responsibility of park ranger interpretive staff who plan exhibits, write trail guides, and conduct park activities to which all visitors are invited. These include campfire programs, ranger-led nature walks, geology car caravans, canoe and raft trips, Junior Ranger programs, rescue demonstrations, reenactment of historic events, and just plain meeting and talking one-on-one with visitors at all times.

Park Supporters

Right from the beginning, there have been devoted supporters of national parks. Prominent individuals, businessmen, journalists, naturalists, and education and political leaders were very involved in the early movement to establish parks. Among those who in later years made significant contributions was John D. Rockefeller, Jr. His contribution of a substantial amount of land or, in some cases, a sizeable sum of money, was an important factor in the establishment of Acadia National Park, Great Smoky Mountains National Park, Shenandoah National Park, and Grand Teton National Park.

Today there are many non-profit organizations focusing all their resources on the support of either the park system as a whole, a specific group of parks, or a single unit of the park system. The National Park Foundation raises money and awards grants for special park projects. The National Parks and Conservation Association has been promoting the park system and educating the public about the parks since 1919. There are 64 "cooperating associations" throughout the country who work with parks in a variety of ways. They publish interpretive material, sell publications and donate the profits to the parks for interpretive activities, conduct seminars, and fund research. Over $30 million has been contributed to the National Park Service by these organizations.

There are other organizations, like the Nature Conservancy, that support the parks by buying valuable land threatened with development and donating it to the park system. The Wilderness Society is especially supportive of efforts to save wilderness areas in the parks. Many other non-profit foundations award grants to fund park research and other projects.

And finally, a vast group of volunteers perform vital support services. Volunteers provide information to the public in visitor centers. They maintain trails and other park property. They help on research projects. In 1989, 55,000 people volunteered their services and accomplished tasks valued at approximately $21 million.

Redefining Park Service Policies and Goals

Any institution that has grown larger over several decades must pause periodically, take stock of its circumstances in view of changed conditions, and decide its priorities for the next few years. The Park Service has done this on several occasions. Among the most well-known plans resulting from such efforts was "Mission 66."

Having had its funding and its personnel severely cut back during World War II and again during the Korean conflict, the Park System's resources were greatly strained when post war visitation jumped from 6 million in 1942 to 33 million in 1950. In 1956, the Park Service embarked on a ten year rehabilitation program to get park facilities and resources in good shape by the time of the Park Service's fiftieth anniversary.

Park visitation has continued to climb. In 1981, noting that nearly 300 million visits had been recorded the previous year, the Secretary of the Interior decided it was time to halt the acquisition of additional park property, and to give priority to repairing the park physical resources, which again had been deteriorating. Major confrontations between the Secretary and environmental organizations went on during the years this Secretary was in office. Persons especially concerned with natural resource protection believed the Secretary was neglecting the government's responsibility for the preservation and protection of park resources. Eventually the Secretary left, but for several years there remained an uneasiness in the relationship between park supporters outside the federal government and the Administration.

In 1988, the National Parks and Conservation Association issued a nine volume report on the status of the park system titled *Investing in Park Futures, The National Park System Plan: A Blueprint for Tomorrow.* The report was the result of three years of research and the formulation of a host of recommendations. Included are recommendations concerning the protection of park natural resources, park research, park boundaries, proposed new parks, interpretive programs, and Park Service organization and staffing. The report acknowledges the valiant efforts of park staff to carry out the Service's mission during a time when budget resources have not kept up with the expansion of park responsibilities and the increase in park visitation. The report further recommends that the Park Service be made an independent agency which, they believe, would give it more clout in annual competition for federal funding.

A year later in 1989, the Commission on Research and Resource Management Policy in the National Park System, composed of scientific and educational specialists independent of the Park Service and the Association, issued a report, *National Parks: From Vignettes to a Global View.* The commission's recommendations once again stress the importance of incorporating the concept of ecosystem management in the operation of the park system.

For information on both of these reports, contact the National Parks and Conservation Association.

The Park Service is in the process of reanalyzing its mission, policies, and programs. A twenty-first century task force has been appointed to make recommendations on how the Park Service should prepare itself to meet the challenges of the twenty-first century.

The year 1991 will be the seventy-fifth anniversary of the establishment of the National Park Service. Undoubtedly other organizations and private individuals will mark the occasion by making their own recommendations of ways the Park Service can carry out its mission with the greatest effectiveness.

John Muir, one of the original environmentalists, and considered by many to be the father of the forest conservation movement, published a book, *Our National Parks,* in 1901. The book consists largely of articles he had previously written for *The Atlantic Monthly.* He described with passion the beauty and grandeur of the forests and parks he had spent many happy, inspiring hours hiking through. He urged people to visit the national parks and forests and "get them into their hearts" so that "their preservation and right use might be made sure."

This message rings true today. This book describes parks that were not part of the National Park System during Muir's lifetime. But when you visit them, you will still find places that will "get into" your heart and you, too, will become devoted to their preservation and "right use."

Sources of Information

The National Park Service
Public Inquiries Office
18th and C Streets, N.W.
Washington, D.C. 20013
Phone: 202-343-4747

The National Park Foundation
1850 K Street, N.W.
Suite 210
Washington, D.C. 20006
Phone: 202-785-4500

National Parks and Conservation
Association
1015 31st Street, N.W.
Washington, D.C. 20007
Phone: 202-944-8530

The Wilderness Society
1400 Eye Street, N.W.
Washington, D.C. 20005
Phone: 202-842-3400

The Nature Conservancy
1815 North Lynn Street
Arlington, VA 22209
Phone: 703-841-5300

Reading List

In addition to reading many government documents and interpretive brochures about the national parks, seashores, lakeshores, and recreation areas discussed in this book, we enjoyed reading other park-related publications, most of which are for sale at park visitor centers. Listed below is a selection of books and pamphlets we recommend if you would like to read more about the National Park System or specific parks.

The National Park System

Albright, Horace M., Russell E. Dickenson, and William Penn Mott Jr. *National Park Service, The Story Behind the Scenery.* KC Publications, Inc., Las Vegas, Nevada. 1987. 96pp. A fascinating step-by-step account of how the National Park System was established, as recalled by three former Directors of the National Park Service. Contains beautiful color photographs of various scenic and historic areas within the National Park System.

National Park Foundation. *The Complete Guide to America's National Parks. 1990-91 edition.* Distributed by Prentice-Hall, New York, New York. 1990. 596 pp. A comprehensive list of 375 national park areas with brief descriptions of visitor activities available.

Runte, Alfred. *National Parks: The American Experience. Second edition, revised.* University of Nebraska Press, Lincoln and London. 1987. 335 pp. A thoughtful and well-documented discussion of the history and the rationale for the establishment of a system of national parks in the United States, including an account of the conflicts between park "preservationists" and those who view the parks from a different perspective.

Big Bend National Park

Deckert, Frank. *Big Bend: Three Steps to the Sky.* Big Bend Natural History Association, Big Bend National Park, Texas. 1981. 40 pp. A naturalist's description of the river, desert, and mountains of Big Bend and all living things therein, as observed and experienced by a former Chief Naturalist of the park. Many beautiful color photographs.

National Park Service. *Big Bend. Official National Park Handbook.* U.S. Department of the Interior, Washington, D.C. 1983. 128 pp. The history and geology of Big Bend country, and an account of plant, animal, and bird life within the park. Many illustrations and color photographs.

Great Basin National Park

Houk, Rose. *Trails to Explore in Great Basin National Park.* Illustrations by Lawrence Ormsby. Great Basin Natural History Association, Baker, Nevada. 1989. 46 pp. A detailed description of seven main hiking trails in the park, including information on distance and elevation and a discussion of the geology and historical and natural resources of each trail. Includes maps, color photographs, and artistic illustrations.

Canyonlands National Park

Ambler, J. Richard. *The Anasazi: Prehistoric People of the Four Corners Region.* Photographs by Marc Gaede. Museum of Northern Arizona, Flagstaff, Arizona. 1989. 58 pp. A description of the culture and crafts at several developmental stages of the Anasazi, prehistoric Indians of the American southwest. Many color photographs.

Jones, Dewitt and Linda S. Cordell. *Anasazi World.* Graphic Arts Center Publishing Company, Portland, Oregon. 1985. 87 pp. Numerous color photographs of locations and dwellings associated with the Anasazi illustrate the story of this ancient people. Includes discussion of various theories explaining their disappearance.

Bighorn Canyon National Recreation Area

Lowie, Robert H. *The Crow Indians.* University of Nebraska Press, Lincoln and London. 1935. Bison Book edition, 1983. 350 pp. A story of the language, beliefs, and customs of the Crow Indians, written by an anthropologist who lived among them and became a trusted observer.

Coulee Dam National Recreation Area

U. S. Department of the Interior, Geological Survey. *The Channeled Scablands of Eastern Washington.* U.S. Government Printing Office, Washington, D.C. 1982. 25 pp. A fascinating detailing of the cataclysm that geologists believe formed the tortured landscape of eastern Washington state.

North Cascades National Park Complex

Blake, William A. *Stehekin: A Wilderness Journey into the North Cascades.* National Park Service, U.S. Department of the Interior, Washington, D.C. 1977. 45 pp. A useful guide for people who plan to visit Stehekin, with pictures depicting the life of the settlers in Stehekin and the beautiful scenery and natural resources of the lake, valley, and surrounding mountains.

National Park Service. *North Cascades. Official National Park Handbook.* U. S. Department of the Interior, Washington, D.C. 1983. 112 pp. A guide to the national park and recreation areas located within Washington's Cascades range. Includes history, information on trees, plants, animals, and fish, and tips for backcountry camping and mountain climbing. Maps, illustrations, and color photographs.

Weisberg, Paul. *North Cascades: The Story Behind the Scenery.* KC Publications, Inc. Las Vegas, Nevada. 1988. 49 pp. Spectacular color photographs of glaciers and snow-capped mountains illustrate the narrative describing the mountains, lakes, rivers, valleys, flora, and fauna of the land encompassed by the North Cascades National Park Complex. Written by a former backcountry ranger.

Sleeping Bear Dunes National Lakeshore

Weeks, George. *Sleeping Bear: Its Lore, Legends, and First People.* The Cottage Book Shop of Glen Arbor and the Historical Society of Michigan, Glen Arbor, Michigan. 1988. 58 pp. A story of the life and legends of the Indians who inhabited Sleeping Bear country from prehistoric times to the period when Europeans first explored the area.

Pictured Rocks National Lakeshore

Rawson, A. L. *Historic Legend of the Pictured Rocks of Lake Superior.* Originally published as an article titled "The Pictured Rocks of Lake Superior" in the May, 1867 issue of Harper's New Monthly Magazine. Reprinted by Avery Color Studios, Au Train, Michigan. 21 pp. Artistic pen and ink illustrations by the author illustrate this personal account of a nostalgic trip to visit, boat around, and camp on the shores of the Pictured Rocks more than a century ago.

Splake, T. Kilgore. *Pictured Rocks Memories.* Angst Productions, Battle Creek, Michigan. 1985. 45 pp. Black and white photographs and descriptions of key features of Pictured Rocks National Lakeshore.

Apostle Islands National Lakeshore

National Park Service. *Apostle Islands. Official National Park Handbook.* U.S. Department of the Interior, Washington, D.C. 1988. 64 pp. History, geology, and a description of the current status of the natural resources of the Apostle Islands. Maps, illustrations, and color photographs.

Voyageurs National Park

Breining, Greg. *Voyageurs National Park.* Photography by J. Arnold Bolz. Lake States Interpretive Association, International Falls, Minnesota. 1987. 56 pp. The islands, peninsula, and lakes of Voyageurs National Park appreciatively described as a land appearing essentially the same as it was when first seen by man. Includes spectacular scenic photographs and a reproduction of a famous painting of Voyageurs canoeing along the voyageurs highway.

Morse, Eric W. *Canoe Routes of the Voyageurs: The Geography and Logistics of the Canadian Fur Trade.* Minnesota Historical Society, St. Paul, Minnesota, and the Quetico Foundation of Ontario, Toronto, Ontario. 1962. 41 pp. A definitive discussion of the fur brigade routes during the heyday of the Canadian Voyageurs. This intriguing treatise on the fur trade is, unfortunately, out of print at this writing. There are, however, copies still available in some libraries, and it is such a consummate study and delightful story about the Voyageurs that it is worth tracking down!

Cape Lookout National Seashore

Stick, David. *The Outer Banks of North Carolina 1584-1958.* University of North Carolina Press, Chapel Hill, North Carolina. 1958. 352 pp. The geography, history, and the political and economic forces at work on the Outer Banks from the days of early European explorers to the early years of the national seashore. Description of major communities from the Virginia border to Shakleford Banks.

Cumberland Island National Seashore

Andrews, Larry F. , H. Grant Rice, and Joanne C. Werwie. *Cumberland Island: A Treasure of Memories.* World-wide Publications, Tampa, Florida. 1986. 64 pp. A collection of beautiful color photographs illustrating the magnificent bounties of nature to be viewed on Cumberland Island.

Camden County Historical Commision. *Cumberland Island.* 1985. 16 pp. Short history of Cumberland Island with several photographs of structures and activities during the era of the Carnegie family's residency.

Swinburne, Stephen R. *Guide to Cumberland Island National Seashore.* Eastern Acorn Press, Eastern National Park and Monument Association, Philadelphia, Pennsylvania. 1984. 64 pp. A guided narrative of a walk across Cumberland Island from salt marsh to ocean with a discussion of the island's special complement of wildlife and vegetation. Many detailed drawings of the animals, birds, insects, fish, and shells found at the seashore.

Biscayne National Park

Voss, Gilbert L. *Coral Reefs of Florida.* Pineapple Press, Sarasota, Florida. 1988. 80 pp. The story of Florida's beautiful coral reefs and the efforts made to save them from destruction. Written by a professor of biological oceanography who has spent many years studying and enjoying the reefs. Many illustrations and color photographs.

The Six "P's"
Plan–Price–Phone–Pack–Passport–Pre-File

PLAN. When your dates are set, presumably well in advance, start planning your trip. First, where will you sleep? In a tent? Recreational vehicle? Motel, lodge, inn, or bed and breakfast establishment?

If you take children with you, consider camping. It's a great family adventure, and the cheapest way to travel. If you have never camped and you are uncertain about how your family will take to this type of vacation, borrow a tent, sleeping bags, and cooking, food storage, and other equipment from a friend who is an experienced camper, and camp for a weekend at a nearby state park. Ask questions of the campers you know and at camping supply stores. If you enjoy your try-out period, go to the library or bookstore and get a campground directory. Write to the tourist offices of every state you will be traveling through for information about state and other campgrounds, as well as for state maps.

If you own a recreational vehicle, you have already found traveling patterns that work best for you. Renting a recreational vehicle offers certain conveniences, but the cost of renting and additional cost of fuel adds considerably to your vacation expense. If you aren't familiar with driving and parking such vehicles, you will need some practice before you feel completely comfortable with this mode of travel. There are books and directories specifically relating to traveling in a recreational vehicle. If you decide this is the way to go, get one from the library or bookstore to guide preparations for your trip.

Information about campsites for tenting and recreational vehicles within or near the national parks discussed in this book is provided in each chapter.

If you want to stay in overnight lodgings on your way to the park and while you are there, send for information about lodgings right away. To know what your choices are en route, call the toll-free numbers of some of the motel chains, listed on page 218, and ask to have a directory of their motels sent to you. (Allow at least a week for delivery.) Don't count on a motel chain to have units near the parks in this book. Most of these parks are not close to highly-traveled, major highways. Park headquarters and visitor centers usually are in small communities that do not attract a significant number of out-of-towners year-round. For information about accommodations in the vicinity of the park you will visit, write or call the Chamber of Commerce, Tourist Bureau, or other source listed at the end of the appropriate chapter.

PRICE. When you have all the information you need, do some research. For overnight stops en route, study the maps and decide where you will stop each night. Then check your motel directories to see which motels are located in or near that place, and compare prices, kind of accommodations offered, and discounts for which you may be eligible. Ways to save money that may be offered include no charge for children sleeping in the room with parents, weekend or off-season rates, discounts for senior citizens (eligible age may vary), members of certain organizations, or the chain's own "clubs." Directories also list information about special circumstances that may be of interest to you, e.g. a non-smoking room, wheelchair accessibility, a small refrigerator or plug-in hot drink facility, on-site pool and playground, and on-site or nearby restaurants. By comparing all the circumstances that apply to you, you can choose the least expensive and most satisfactory accommodations.

(If you prefer to take a chance on finding overnight lodging while traveling, you may find locally-owned motels with cheaper rates than those at chain operated motels, but you may not. That's the kind of adventure only you can decide to seek!)

Try to make the same type of comparisons of accommodations at or near the parks. However, although some of the information you receive about lodgings near the parks may list price range and other information, most will only list the name, address, and phone number. You may then have to write or phone for more information. You probably will not find discounts at lodgings near the parks. They are often "Mom and Pop" enterprises operated only seasonally, and they must make their income in a short period of only a few months.

PHONE. When you have chosen the motel you'd like to stay in while traveling, call the chain's toll-free reservation number and make your reservation. *Always* ask about possible discounts. Some may not be listed in the directory and this kind of information is not volunteered. Before you finish your conversation, review all aspects of your reservation with the reservation clerk - dates, type of bed or beds, the floor your room is on, smoking or non-smoking, and price, including discount. Write this information, along with the *confirmation number,* on your directory in the event you have to cancel. By providing your card number for a major credit card, your reservation will be held for you, regardless of your time of arrival. Check the time of day by which you must notify the motel chain reservation clerk if you must cancel your reservation. Otherwise you will be charged for the room whether or not you use it. When cancelling, always write down the *cancellation number,* also on your directory, so that you have proof of cancellation in the event there is an error in billing.

A word about phone calls from your motel. Check the motel's charges for telephone calls made from your room. You may find it saves money to use a nearby public phone booth. On long distance calls, using a telephone credit card or calling collect will usually cost you less than charging calls to your room.

If you decide to fly and rent a car to drive to the park you visit, do some research to get the best possible discount—the earlier the better. The best airfares may require as much as a 30-day advance reservation; other discounts apply to 14-day advance reservations. Check several airlines for other discounts you may be eligible for—age, willingness to travel on certain days, membership in various organizations, including an airline's "frequent flyer," or other club. Check also for tie-ins the airline may have with particular car-rental agencies. If you rent a car, before you leave home don't forget to check your car insurance policy to see if you are covered for collision damage to rental cars. Certain credit cards include such coverage also. If you are already covered in one form or another, you can save money by declining collision damage insurance from the car rental agency.

To save your own time, work with a travel agent you know or one who has been recommended to you, and review with the agent all the discount possibilities you are aware of, and your preferences, and let him or her do the research.

PACKING. Think money-saving when you pack. First, food. Even if you plan to stay in motels or other overnight lodgings, you can save money on meal expenses by taking a cooler with you. Ice is available at convenience and grocery stores everywhere. Take breakfast juices, cold drinks, sandwich ingredients, and late night snacks with you. This enables you to reduce the cost of eat-out breakfasts and late night munching, and save lunch expense by having picnic lunches at highway rest areas, state "Welcome" centers, or in small town parks. (Don't forget to take paper plates, cups, and napkins, and a backpack to carry food and drink when hiking.) When you eat in restaurants, if you don't consume all the rolls and bread on your table, ask to have what's left put in a "doggie bag" and use them in sandwiches the next day.

Very few "fast food" chain outlets are located in the small communities in or near the parks. By carrying lunch with you, you have greater flexibility in following a sudden urge to hike on a trail or take a scenic drive to a remote area.

Next, clothing. Informality is the order of the day when choosing clothing for a park visit: jeans, slacks, shorts, knit shirts, sweaters, jackets, rain gear, walking shoes and/or hiking boots, and headgear suitable for the climate and season. Clothing should be "wash and wear." Every few days make a stop at a laundromat and catch up on some reading while all your clothing is getting clean and dry again.

PASSPORTS. Not all national parks have entrance fees, but many do, including two of the parks discussed in this book. However, park entrance fees may be eliminated or reduced by the use of one of the following "Golden Passports": Golden Eagle Passport, Golden Age Passport, and Golden Access Passport.

The Golden Eagle Passport is an annual entrance permit to all National Park Service parks, monuments, historic sites, and recreation areas, as well as to other federal recreation areas that charge entrance fees. The passport admits the permit holder and any accompanying passengers in a single, private, non-commercial vehicle. It costs $25 and is good for one *calendar* year. If you expect to go to a number of national parks during one year, this passport may save you money. A Golden Eagle Passport may be purchased in person at any Park System unit that charges entrance fees, from

National Park Service or Forest Service headquarters in Washington, D.C., or from their regional offices. It also may be obtained by mail from Park Service or Forest Service headquarters.

A Golden Age Passport is a free lifetime entrance permit to all the park units mentioned above. Any citizen or permanent U.S. resident who is 62 years or older may obtain one. It must be obtained in person by showing proof of age at National Park Service or Forest Service headquarters, their regional offices, or at a National Park Service or other federal recreation-related area where entrance fees are charged. The passport admits the permit holder and all the people in his private, non-commercial vehicle. It also provides a 50 percent discount on federal user fees, such as camping, boat launching, and parking, but not on facilities operated by park concessioners.

A Golden Access Passport is a free lifetime entrance permit to national parks and other federal recreation-related areas as mentioned above. It is issued to citizens or permanent U.S. residents "who have been medically determined to be blind or permanently disabled and as a result, are eligible for receiving benefits under federal law." It, too, provides a 50 percent discount on federal user fees, but not on concession-operated facilities. Free park admission of the permit holder includes the persons accompanying him in the car. A Golden Access Passport may also only be obtained in person and proof of eligibility as outlined above must be shown.

Other federal agencies with recreation facilities where the Golden Passports are accepted include the Bureau of Land Management, Bureau of Reclamation, Corps of Engineers, Fish and Wildlife Service, Forest Service, and the Tennessee Valley Authority.

PRE-FILE. Before you leave home, prepare a written itinerary for yourself, one for a family member or friend who will serve as "message central" for others while you are away, and one for your travel agent, if you use one. (Sometimes a flight is cancelled and your agent will need to reach you to discuss alternate arrangements.) On your copy of your itinerary, include dates and motels or other places you will stay each night, kind of accommodations reserved, and price, including type of discount and proof of eligibility, if required. Also note any deposits you may have made.

Record both the motel chain reservation number and the motel's local phone number.

On the itinerary sheet you give others, just note dates, name and location of motel, and local motel or lodging phone number. By doing this, both you and your family members will be reassured that you can be contacted should there be a need. You may or may not want to give this information to business contacts!

Motel Toll-Free Numbers

Below is a list of toll-free telephone numbers of a selection of moderate priced and "economy" motels.

Best Western: 1-800-528-1234
Comfort Inns: 1-800-228-5150
Days Inn: 1-800-325-2525
Econolodge: 1-800-446-6900
Friendship Inns: 1-800-453-4511
Holiday Inn: 1-800-HOLIDAY
Howard Johnson: 1-800-654-2000
La Quinta Inns: 1-800-531-5900
Ramada Inns: 1-800-228-2828
Red Carpet Inns: 1-800-251-1962
Red Roof Inns: 1-800-843-7663
Rodeway Inns: 1-800-228-2000
Super 8: 1-800-843-1991
Travelodge: 1-800-255-3050

Glossary

archipelago: a group of islands.

Banker: a native of one of the Outer Bank islands of North Carolina.

basalt: a fine-grained volcanic rock of high density and dark color.

basin: a broad area of the earth where the surface is shaped like a saucer and surface drainage flows to the central portion.

bedrock: the solid rock underlying the unconsolidated materials of the earth's surface—"down to bedrock."

bench: a terrace formed in rocks; also, elevated land along the bank of a river.

biota: the combined flora and fauna of a geographical area.

boreal forest: the northern forest of North America dominated by evergreen, coniferous trees, contrasted with the hardwood forests to the south, dominated by deciduous trees.

butte: an isolated hill or natural turret, especially one with steep sides and a flattened top.

Canadian shield: the massive, primordial, granitic layer of the earth's crust that surfaces under half of Canada and other areas of the northern hemisphere. It is the largest area in the world where surface and upper layers of rock are so old they contain little or no evidence of fossils.

canot du nord: a type of canoe (literally: north canoe) used on the Canadian fur trade routes west of the Great Lakes.

chanson: a song with a simple tune and, usually, robust lyrics sung by the Canadian voyageurs. Similar to a sea chanty.

climax forest: the last stage in the renewal of timber growth after deforestation. It concludes a succession of tree species vying to establish a forest. It is a final stage that is dominated by a species fully adapted to the environment.

col: a gap in a ridge serving as a pass from one valley to another.

copse: a thicket, grove, or growth of small trees.

cryptogamic: pertaining to plants that reproduce by spores and do not produce flowers or seeds (ferns, mosses, fungi, etc.).

ecology: the comprehensive pattern of relations between organisms and their environment.

ecosystem: an ecological unit that is bounded by environmental relations rather than by geography.

endangered species: a species of fish, wildlife, or plant that is so depleted in numbers and/or range that it is in danger of extinction. The federal and state governments issue lists of species considered "endangered" and regulations for their protection.

exotic: not native (as a plant or animal) to the place found.

escarpment: a steep slope or precipitous cliff face, usually resulting from erosion or faulting.

Fresnel lens: a lens system developed for lighthouses in 1820 by Augustin Jean Fresnel, French physicist and pioneer in optical theory. The Fresnel lens creates the intense light beam of a gigantic simple lens by the use of a system of smaller lens sections or units.

glacier: a field or body of ice formed in an area where snowfall exceeds melting. It moves slowly over a wide area.

glacial till: the unstratified mixture of sand, clay, gravel, and boulders deposited by glaciers.

glacial lobe: the projection of a glacier beyond its nearby face, like the projection of a peninsula beyond nearby shoreline.

hammock: a fertile area in the southern U.S. that is usually higher than its surroundings and that is characterized by hardwood vegetation and deep humus-rich soil.

interpretive program: the many-faceted efforts of the park rangers to communicate with park visitors: visitor center displays, slide, tape, and movie presentations, trail and roadside exhibits, demonstrations, campfire programs, guided walks and tours, and personal one-on-one conversation.

jetty: a structure extended into a sea, lake, or river to influence the current or tide or to protect a harbor.

key: one of the coral islands or reefs off the coast of Florida.

lightering: the practice of unloading cargo from large ships for subsequent transport in other boats through shallow waters.

loess: a pale yellow or buff clay or loam deposit found in Asia, Europe, and North America and believed to be chiefly deposited by the wind.

mesa: a high, relatively flat-topped, natural elevation with precipitous, usually rocky slopes descending to a surrounding plain.

metamorphic: pertaining to the changes in composition and texture of rocks caused by earth forces accompanied by heat, pressure, and moisture.

midden: a refuse heap.

"no-see-ums": tiny biting flies so small they are difficult to see. They attack their victims in swarms.

one hundred year flood plain: a flat area of land bordering a body of water that experience and/or evidence indicates will be flooded as frequently as once in a hundred years.

oxbow: a U-shaped bend in a river resembling the shape of a frame (oxbow) forming a collar about the neck of an ox.

pays d'en haut: literally, the "high country" of Canada west of the Great Lakes.

perched dune: a sand dune on top of, and frequently moving across, an elevation of land composed of different material—clay, silt, gravel, etc.

Petoskey stone: a stone-like fossil of an ancient, extinct coral found in the upper part of Lower Michigan. The finest specimens are of gem quality.

pictograph: an ancient or prehistoric drawing or painting on a rock wall.

primitive camping: camping in remote, natural areas to which all equipment and supplies have to be backpacked.

petroglyph: a carving or inscription on rock.

sedimentary: formed by or from deposits of sediment.

slough: a creek in a marsh or tidal flat.

tabby: building material made of lime, shells, and sand or gravel mixed with water.

tarn: a small, steep-banked mountain lake or pool.

trailhead: the point at which a trail begins.

vulcanism: volcanic power or action; also called volcanism

INDEX

Other Books Available From Mills & Sanderson

Touring Europe by Motorhome, by Helen Vander Male. A wonderful resource for the first time motorhome traveler in Europe. Answers your questions and tells you how to make the most of this special mode of travel. $9.95

The World Up Close: A Cyclist's Adventures on Five Continents, by Kameel B. Nasr. Discover the essence of humanity through various cultures by vicariously wandering the world by bicycle. $9.95

The Alaska Traveler: Year 'Round Vacation Adventures for Everyone, by Steven C. Levi. With maps and cartoons, this is a unique insider's guide to gold panning, stalking big game, windsurfing, dogsledding, etc. $9.95

The Portugal Traveler: Great Sights and Hidden Treasures, by Barbara Radcliffe Rogers and Stillman Rogers. A companion to fascinating places to eat and sleep, festivals and other events as well as insider tips to enrich your visit. Includes city maps. $9.95

Sicilian Walks: Exploring the History and Culture of the Two Sicilies, by William J. Bonville. Self-guided tours (with maps)of Sicily and the adjacent Italian mainland. $9.95

Childbirth Choices in Mothers' Words, by Kim Selbert, M.F.C.C.. Twenty-one mothers tell in their own words about their birth experiences—the highs and the lows—with the varied types of childbirth currently available in the U.S. $9.95.

Bedtime Teaching Tales for Kids: A Parent's Storybook, by Gary Ludvigson, Ph. D. Eighteen engrossing stories to help children 5-11 work through problems such as fear of failure, sibling rivalry, bullies, divorce, death, child abuse, handicaps,etc. $9.95

Your Food-Allergic Child: A Parent's Guide, by Janet E. Meizel. How to shop and cook for children with allergies, plus nutrient and chemical reference charts of common foods, medications, and grocery brands. $9.95

Winning Tactics for Women Over Forty: How to Take Charge of Your Life and Have Fun Doing It, by Anne De Sola Cardoza and Mavis B. Sutton. For women left alone through separation, divorce or death, "this title presents many positive, concrete options for change." — *The Midwest Book Review* $9.95

Fifty and Fired: How to Prepare for It - What to Do When It Happens, by Ed Brandt with Leonard Corwen. How to deal with getting forcefully "restructured" out of your job at the wrong time in your career. $9.95 / $16.95 (hardcover)

Aquacises: Restoring and Maintaining Mobility with Water Exercises, by Miriam Study Giles. Despite age, obesity or physical handicaps, anyone can improve their fitness with this instructive illustrated handbook. $9.95

60-Second Shiatzu: How to Energize, Erase Pain, and Conquer Tension in One Minute, by Eva Shaw. A helpfully illustrated, quick-results introduction to do-it-yourself acupressure. $7.95

Bachelor in the Kitchen: Beyond Bologna and Cheese, by Gordon Haskett with Wendy Haskett. Fast and easy ways to make delectable meals, snacks, drinks from easily obtainable ingredients. $7.95

Order Form

If you are unable to find our books in your local bookstore, you may order them directly from us. Please enclose check or money order for amount of purchase and add $1.00 per book handling charge.

( ) Bonville / *Sicilian Walks* $9.95 _____
( ) Levi / *The Alaska Traveler* $9.95 _____
( ) Nasr / *The World Up Close* $9.95 _____
( ) Rogers / *The Portugal Traveler* $9.95 _____
( ) Vander Male / *Toruing Europe by Motorhome $9.95* _____
( ) Wolverton / *Thirteen National Parks* $9.95 _____
( ) Ludvigson / *Bedtime Teaching Tales for Kids* $9.95 _____
( ) Meizel / *Your Food-Allergic Child* $9.95 _____
( ) Selbert / *Childbirth Choices in Mothers' Words* $9.95 _____
( ) Cardoza/Sutton / *Winning Tactics for Women* $9.95 _____
( ) Brandt/Corwen / *Fifty and Fired* $16.95 (cloth) _____
( ) Brandt/Corwen / *Fifty and Fired* $9.95 (paper) _____
( ) Giles / *Aquacises* $9.95 _____
( ) Shaw / *60-Second Shiatzu* $7.95 _____
( ) Haskett / *Bachelor in the Kitchen* $7.95 _____

$1.00 per book handling charge _____
5% sales tax for MA residents _____

Total amount enclosed _____

Name: _____

Address: _____

City: _____ State: _____ Zip code: _____

Mail to: **Mills & Sanderson, Publishers**
        442 Marrett Road, Suite 6
        Lexington, MA 02173
        617-861-0992

Our Toll-Free Order # is 1-800-441-6224